# SEXUAL EXPLOITATION

Volume 155, Sage Library of Social Research

# RECENT VOLUMES IN
# SAGE LIBRARY OF SOCIAL RESEARCH

# SEXUAL EXPLOITATION

## Rape, Child Sexual Abuse, and Workplace Harassment

## DIANA E.H. RUSSELL

Volume 155
SAGE LIBRARY OF
SOCIAL RESEARCH

 **SAGE** PUBLICATIONS  Beverly Hills  London  New  Delhi

*For information address:*

SAGE Publications, Inc.
275 South Beverly Drive
Beverly Hills, California 90212

SAGE Publications India Pvt. Ltd.
C-236 Defence Colony
New Delhi 110 024, India

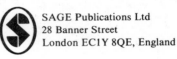

SAGE Publications Ltd
28 Banner Street
London EC1Y 8QE, England

Printed in the United States of America

**Library of Congress Cataloging in Publication Data**

Russell, Diana E. H.
    Sexual exploitation.

    (Sage library of social research ; v. 155)
    Bibliography: p.
    Includes index.
    1. Rape—California. 2. Child molesting—California.
3. Sexual harassment—California. I. Title. II. Series.
HV6565.C2R87    1984        364.1'532'09794        84-6950
ISBN 0-8039-2354-6
ISBN 0-8039-2355-4 (pbk.)


FIRST PRINTING

*To those working for the eradication
of the pain and suffering caused
by sexual exploitation*

# CONTENTS

## LIST OF TABLES

# LIST OF FIGURES

# ACKNOWLEDGMENTS

The data gathering phase, as well as some of the analysis of my research on rape and child sexual abuse, was funded by the National Institute of Mental Health (grant R01MH 28960). A more extensive analysis of the interviews on child sexual abuse was funded by the National Center on Child Abuse and Neglect (grant 90-CA-813/01). I am very grateful to both agencies for recognizing the merits of this research and for funding it. Without their support this project would have been an impossible undertaking.

The findings of this NIMH- and NCCAN-funded research are cited extensively throughout this book. I am therefore indebted to the hundreds of people who have contributed to this and prior research— and to my thinking—since I started work on the subject of rape in 1971. Over 150 people were individually acknowledged in my book *Rape in Marriage* for their participation in the survey research project for which I was the principal investigator. Although I cannot name each of them here, I would like to thank them again collectively, with special mention of those who have been particularly helpful in the process of writing this book.

First, I'd like to thank Brooke Allison for selecting me to be the expert consultant for the California Commission on Crime Control and Violence Prevention in August 1981. The final report that I wrote for that commission became the first draft of this book.

Many of the people who were helpful to me in the preparation of that report have thereby also contributed to the creation of this book. These people include Shela Brooks, Sandra Butler, Cheryl Colopy, Phyllis Crocker, David Finkelhor, Grace Hardgrove, Abigail Hemstreet, Pat Loomes, Catherine MacKinnon, Kee MacFarlane, and Richard Snowdon. In particular I'd like to thank Kee MacFarlane for her considerable help with the section on child sexual abuse, and for her general support and encouragement of my work on sexual abuse. I am also grateful to Catherine MacKinnon for many useful conversations, for informing me about a key study on sexual harassment, and for encouraging me to publish the report.

David Finkelhor, one of my most valued colleagues, has been of great assistance in a number of ways. First, I have organized my entire discussion of the causes of rape, child sexual abuse, and sexual harassment within a framework that his work provided. Second, after reading my final report he encouraged me to revise and publish it, and he played a key role in its publication by Sage. I would also like to thank Mildred Pagelow (who suggested the title of the book) and Ann Maney, Director of the Rape Center at NIMH, for their endorsement of the merits of my final report to Sage.

I am extremely grateful to Karen Trocki, the data analyst on this project, for her indispensable role in all phases and aspects of the quantitative analysis. She has been serving this vital function for four years now, and I truly don't know what I would do without her skill, as well as her thorough knowledge and understanding of my complex data base. Karen also plotted all the graphs included in this book, wrote the first draft of the section comparing the respondents in my survey with the 1980 Census data for San Francisco, and other segments on the methodology of my study.

I am also indebted to Nancy Howell for her assistance with the demographic analysis of the trends in rape and child sexual abuse over time, to Bill Wells for his contribution as the computer programmer, and to Eda Regan, the reference librarian at Mills College, for her willingness to try to find the answers to the many often difficult questions I have brought to her.

Many others have helped me in numerous ways with this research— sometimes by making useful suggestions on drafts of particular chapters, sometimes by discussing important theoretical issues with me, and sometimes by offering encouragement. These people include Constance Backhouse, Judith Herman, Jane Loebel, Michelle Morris, Patricia Mrazak, Pat Phelan, and Sue Saperstein.

I am intellectually indebted to many different people for their research, writing, or thinking on the subjects of rape or child sexual abuse. Some of these people will become obvious to the reader, because of the frequency with which I cite their work. In particular, I would like to acknowledge my indebtedness to Susan Brownmiller, Lucy Berliner, David Finkelhor, Judith Herman, Kee MacFarlane, Florence Rush, and Roland Summit. I also wish to thank Sedelle Katz and Mary Ann Mazur for their invaluable synthesis of research findings in their book *Understanding the Rape Victim*. Their thorough review of the research literature on many aspects of rape made my task significantly easier.

I am grateful to Marny Hall not only for her encouragement but also for introducing me to her editor, Meredith Maran Graham. Every writer should be so lucky as to find an editor like Meredith. Not only has she been very helpful in making my prose more accessible to a wider range of readers, but she has removed some of the burden of anxiety and isolation that results from being the sole parent of a book. The sense of responsibility and enthusiasm that she brought to the task made the birth process feel like a shared one.

I am also indebted to Pat Loomes, who has helped in whatever way was needed: puzzling over the meaning of confusing tables, discussing the implications of the findings, or just listening to me talk about whatever aspect of the project was on my mind at the time.

Finally I would like to thank Jan Dennie for the excellent job she did in keying the manuscript into the word processor, her careful and accurate editing of numerous redrafts, her persistence despite the enormous frustrations that appear to be endless and inevitable for users of the UC Berkeley computers, and her willingness to work long hours when deadlines loomed. I am also grateful to the Committee on Faculty Research Grants at Mills College for contributing to the cost of preparing this book for publication.

# INTRODUCTION

## THE ORIGINS OF THIS BOOK

In 1977, I received funding from the National Institute of Mental Health to research the prevalence of rape and other sexual abuse. The study was conducted by interviewing a random sample of women residents of San Francisco about their experiences with incest, extra-familial child sexual abuse, unwanted sex with authority figures, and rape by strangers, acquaintances, friends, dates, lovers, ex-lovers, husbands and ex-husbands. In 1980 I was funded by the National Center on Child Abuse and Neglect to further analyze the data on incest gathered in this survey.

In 1981, the California Commission on Crime Control and Violence Prevention asked me to be their expert consultant on sexual violence. The commission had undertaken an investigation into "the root causes of crime" to guide their formulation of recommendations aimed at preventing these crimes in California. As their expert consultant, my tasks were to review the literature on the causes of sexual violence and abuse; to provide basic information on their prevalence; and to propose solutions.

The commission originally intended to publish the 11 final reports for which they had contracted; later they decided that their funding was not sufficient to accomplish this. After summarizing what they considered to be the major findings and recommendations of these reports (including mine), they decided which ones they as a commission could accept and support, and then published their own summary report titled *Ounces of Prevention* (1982). A limited number of the original 11 final reports were distributed to those who requested them. Several readers of my report, believing the material in it to be both valuable and unique, urged me to get it published. This book is a revised version of that report.

## THE GOALS OF THIS BOOK

When reviewing the available material on sexual exploitation for the commission, I became acutely aware of a void in the literature:

Nowhere could I find a comprehensive review of the theories of causation of rape, child sexual abuse, or sexual harassment—either separately or together. This void is particularly gaping in the area of rape research, since its recent history now spans the length of a decade. Public awareness about child sexual abuse and sexual harassment is much more recent, so the void on those issues is less surprising.

The public awareness of sexual and nonsexual abuse of adults and children has steadily grown over the past few years. Nonsexual child abuse—particularly the physical beating or gross emotional neglect of children—was the first form of physical abuse to be generally acknowledged. Next to receive attention was rape, especially rape by strangers and other nonintimates. Then nonsexual wife abuse (often referred to as wife-battering) was recognized as a serious problem, followed by concern about the sexual abuse of children, particularly incest. Most recently, the public eye has been focused on the issues of sexual harassment of women on the job and in educational institutions; sexual abuse of women by mental health professionals; and rape of adult women by intimates, particularly their husbands.

In the literature I reviewed, I found the connections between these various forms of physical and sexual abuse to be largely absent. Each issue has been written about, spoken about, lobbied about, and intervened in by different people with different orientations. And each problem has its separate history, theories, and agencies (Finkelhor, 1983). This separation has resulted in the artificial compartmentalization of analysis and treatment of these problems. For example, research on rape and research on sexual abuse of children are rarely combined—although children are raped, and adults are sexually abused in ways other than rape.

The goal of this book is to break down this compartmentalization by addressing the issue of causation—a fundamental research question in the study of any crime. This book examines the common causes of different forms of sexual assault. The focus will be on three types of sexual exploitation: rape; child sexual abuse; and sexual harassment in the workplace. The major emphasis will be on rape and child sexual abuse, in part because the California Commission had no interest in sexual harassment.

Social structural and cultural theories of causation are particularly apt to relate to all kinds of sexual abuse. The sexual objectification of females that has been stressed so strongly in the literature on rape causation, for example, is clearly important to an understanding of sexual harassment. It likely plays a part in sexual abuse of female children as well.

By contributing to a better integration of these three subfields, I hope that this book will facilitate a deeper understanding of each. Our comprehension of these three forms of sexual exploitation can be enriched by such a view of their interrelatedness.


## THE STRUCTURE OF THIS BOOK

In their 1978 survey of the literature on rape, Duncan Chappell and Faith Fogarty noted that since 1974 there had been "a veritable explosion in the volume of publicity about rape. Almost certainly in the present decade, and possibly in those past," they maintain, "no single crime has received such sustained and widespread attention from so diverse a range of sources" (1978, p. 1). This attention has resulted in a great profusion of scholarly books, articles, and reports on rape.

Public interest and research about the sexual abuse of children has a more recent origin. But in the past few years, there has been a proliferation of research and publications on this subject as well. Less research has been done on sexual harassment, but this field, too, is developing.

Given the volume of research on sexual exploitation currently available, I have not undertaken a mere summary of the most important works. Rather, I have provided what I consider to be a useful framework within which I have organized the key existing theories. This framework is itself a multicausal theory. It discourages the idea that the existing theories of rape, child sexual abuse, and sexual harassment are competing. It shows that they are in fact contributing on different levels of explanation to different questions about the occurrence of all of these forms of sexual abuse.

The title of this book was chosen because I believe that the concept of sexual exploitation aptly describes the three different forms of sexual abuse focused on herein: Rape requires the use of force or threat of force to obtain sexual contact. Child sexual abuse, while often not violent, is extremely violating. When perpetrated by adults it involves the exploitation of adult authority and power for sexual ends. Child sexual abuse perpetrated by other children involves either the use or threat of force, or the exploitation of the abuser's power by virtue of age, sex, or status. Sexual harassment, also, is often not violent, but it usually entails the exploitation of economic power, often bolstered by male authority. Since violence often does not accompany child sexual abuse or sexual harassment, the term sexual exploitation seems more appropriate than sexual violence to the forms of abuse discussed.

In traditional Marxist analysis, exploitation is a fundamental concept. But by limiting their analyses to the economic sphere, Marxists fail to recognize the equally basic nature of sexual exploitation (which often occurs in combination with economic exploitation). The term sexual exploitation conveys the structural context of most sexual victimization. Such victimization most frequently occurs, after all, in contexts of male power over females, of adults over children, of the economically powerful over the economically dependent, and of the physically strong over the physically less strong.

### THE RUSSELL STUDY AND THIS BOOK

Some major findings of my own NIMH-funded study of sexual exploitation will also be presented in various sections of the book. This random sample survey was based on interviews with 930 adult women residents of San Francisco.

My study is unique in the literature on the prevalence of sexual exploitation because it combines the use of random sampling techniques with a deep knowledge of, and sensitivity to, the subject of sexual assault. The findings of other studies on the prevalence of rape and child sexual abuse will be reviewed, and it will become apparent that they are severely flawed in various ways. In most of these studies, respondents were self-selected and were therefore highly unrepresentative of the female population at large. Many of those surveyed belonged to a particular group, such as students, and were not representative of persons outside these groups. Finally, the interviewers in many studies were not educated about sexual exploitation; hence, their attitudes likely discouraged their respondents from disclosing experiences of sexual assault. The methodology of my study (described in more detail in Chapter 1) does not suffer from any of these particular shortcomings.

This book is in fact a review of the current literature on sexual exploitation. But, because of the uniquely valuable nature of my study's findings, these findings are given particular weight in relation to several subjects, including the following: the prevalence of rape; the social characteristics of rape victims and rapists; the comparison of reported and unreported cases of rape; and the prevalence of child sexual abuse.

Space limitations required the omission of the research literature and of my survey findings on the social characteristics of perpetrators of child sexual abuse and their victims. This information will be published in a book (currently in preparation) devoted entirely to the subject of child sexual abuse.

I have drawn substantially from two chapters of my book *The Politics of Rape: The Victim's Perspective* (1975): "Rape and the Masculine Mystique" and "Rape and the Feminine Mystique." Included also are rewrites of portions of four previously published articles:

"Pornography and violence: What does the new research say?" In Laura Lederer (Ed.), *Take Back the Night: Women on Pornography*, 1980.

"The incidence and prevalence of intrafamilial and extrafamilial sexual abuse of female children." *Child Abuse and Neglect: The International Journal*, 7, 2 (1983).

"The prevalence of rape in the United States revisited," coauthored with Nancy Howell. *Signs: Journal of Women in Culture and Society*, 8, 4 (1983).

"The prevalence and incidence of forcible rape and attempted rape of females." *Victimology: An International Journal*, 7, 1–4 (1983).

Chapter 11, "The Gender Gap Among Perpetrators of Child Sexual Abuse," was coauthored with David Finkelhor. It is published here for the first time, but will also be included in his forthcoming book under the title "Women as Perpetrators of Sexual Abuse: Review of the Evidence." The chapter has been edited by each of us, to be consistent with our own styles.

A 100-page bibliography was included in my final report on sexual assault for the commission. But because on-line computerized data base reference services are so widely available now, either through personal subscription or through libraries, it seemed unnecessary and uneconomical to publish an extensive bibliography here.

In the remainder of this book my research will be referred to as the Russell survey, or some other similar phrase. This method of referral is similar to that used for other researchers.

## SEXUAL EXPLOITATION: A CASE STUDY

Popular beliefs hold that a tiny percentage of American women have ever been victimized by child sexual abuse or by rape. To cast this myth aside—as this book does—is to make the inappropriateness of viewing rape, child sexual abuse, and sexual harassment as separate issues even more apparent. Indeed, many women experience all three of these forms of sexual exploitation at some time in their lives.

What follows is a selection of a few of the experiences of Rachel Goodner (not her real name). Ms. Goodner is one of the 930 women interviewed in my random sample survey. Her experiences illustrate how interconnected various types of sexual exploitation can be; they also remind us that the statistics and theories presented in this book are all based on the real-life experiences of real women who live with the aftershocks of these experiences.

Rachel Goodner was 27 years old at the time of the interview. She had had some college education, and had worked in various waitressing jobs since she was 14 years old. Ms. Goodner was separated from her husband; she was living with her 5-year-old child and a lover.

For the first 14 years of her life, Rachel lived in a city. Her biological mother was "in and out" during those years; Rachel lived more consistently with her stepfather from the ages of 5 to 17. Her mother worked outside the home during most of Rachel's childhood, usually as a cocktail waitress. After Rachel turned 14, she and her mother never lived together again.

Rachel was sexually abused when she was 10 years old by a 14-year-old babysitter who molested her and her brother, as well as her and a girlfriend. These incidents occurred from 6 to 10 times over a period of a year.

The interviewer's questions are paraphrased and placed in parentheses.

> He was our babysitter for a long time. When my girlfriend spent the night, he wanted us to undress and take our clothes off and do things to each other. We wouldn't do these things so he tied us up in the shower with my mom's nylons. He tied our wrists together, then tied our hands to the shower. We were there for about an hour.

> He showed my brother and me pornographic pictures. After we refused to do it [have sex] he would barricade us in the bathroom and make us watch him jerk off. He also made us touch him (Where?) On his genitals. He'd show us pictures and he'd demonstrate a hard-on for us so we'd know what it was. He made fun of my brother because he was so little.

> Sometimes he would dress up in my mom's clothes. He'd take us out and do other stuff we weren't supposed to do. (Did he attempt intercourse?) No, but one time he asked me to open my mouth wide so he could put his penis in. I refused. Then he'd lock us in the bathroom. He must have known we wouldn't do it, so maybe he was into punishing us. He was only 14. (Did he threaten you verbally?) Yes, he said, "If you don't do this, then I'll do something to you." If we said no, then he'd lock us up in the bathroom with him or he'd tie us up.

> (How did it end?) After the time my girlfriend and I were tied up, we went to her house and she told her mother, and her mother told mine. We got a new babysitter after that. (Was the experience reported?) I think so, but I don't know for sure. I think there was some confrontation my mom had with his mom. Then he moved and we also moved.

> (Upset?) Extremely upset. (Effect on your life?) It totally upset my life. My mom was so angry at finding the stockings. My girlfriend's mother

was sympathetic but my mom was angry at having to quit her job. And she was mad at me; she thought I'd provoked it.

That was my first real exposure to sex in a way that I couldn't ignore— sex as an impersonal act where not all the people are consenting. A sick feeling and a memory of the pornographic pictures stayed with me for a long time. (Other effects?) Because of being tied up, I don't like to wear bracelets. Also I guess his having that power and control over me might have made me more passive around men after that, because I was afraid of saying no and then being tied up—bonded. I get angry now at porn pictures of women being tied up and enjoying it.

(Has pornography had any effect on your ideas or feelings about sex?) Yes. This was my first exposure to it. The babysitter showed me 8 by 10 glossy photos of people fucking. I felt repulsed and that it was ugly and wrong. I didn't want to grow up and have to do it. I thought about becoming a nun and I became more religious. I didn't feel good about my body. It took me a long time to feel comfortable with sex and certain sexual positions.

The interviewer noted that Rachel did not tell her mother about the sexual abuse sooner because she feared that her mother would not believe her. Although her mother did believe her, she apparently blamed Rachel for provoking the experience. Hence Rachel's lack of trust in her mother appears to have been sadly appropriate.

Rachel was 11 years old when her brother started sexually molesting her. These incidents occurred from 2 to 5 times over a period of two months.

It wasn't exactly upsetting. It may have been more mutual than against my will. In the summer after sixth grade, I moved back home. My brother had started junior high, and he had changed a lot; we used to be really close. Because we had shared that experience with the babysitter, he knew that I knew as much about sex as he did. We were alone in the house a lot, and he would corner me and expose himself to me. A tension was always there when we were alone, like he'd say, "You know about it, so why don't we do it!" He made it impossible to forget the experiences [with the babysitter].

The most traumatic part was that any physical affection was taken by him as sexual. One time I was in shorts and a halter top. He started talking to me about sex, and then he lay on top of me and dry humped me saying, "It doesn't feel bad. It doesn't hurt." He tried to convince me to take off my clothes, but I wouldn't; I found it morally wrong. Then my sister walked in. He was contemptuous of me as a sexually permissive person. He must have believed my mother's attitude toward me—that I had brought it all on myself.

One time when my cousin was spending the night I went into their room in the morning to wake them up and they told me to shut the door. They both had erections and they wanted me to touch them. I left the room, but it was scary because my cousin was in on it too. Their attitudes were, "Don't play innocent. You've seen this before." But I didn't want to do it.

(Did anything else sexual ever happen with your brother?) I touched him on his genitals. (Did he touch you?) Yeah. (Where?) My genitals. (Else?) No. (How did it happen?) We were alone in the house a lot. (How did it end?) When my sister caught us.

(Upset?) Not very upset. (Effect on your life?) Some effect. It affected my relationship with my brother a lot. We never talk about it. I know he still has those attitudes toward me, because his relationship with my sister is different. I still feel his disrespect for me. It reinforced what Mom said, that I brought on the sexual things that happened to me. She called me a slut and I believed it. If my own brother wanted to have sex with me, she must be right. It made me uncomfortable with my first sexual feelings.

Not even being a fellow victim with her brother saved Rachel from her brother's typical double-standard response. Having been abused by the babysitter, she was seen to have lost her purity; therefore she had also lost her right to respect, and even her right to say no. The fact that a fellow victim, who was also a member of her immediate family, responded in this sexist fashion makes one wonder how often this double standard is applied to other victims in similar fashion. If it is quite common, this might help to explain the phenomenon of multiple victimization.

When Rachel was 21 years old she was raped by her husband. She said that he raped her more than 20 times over a period of 2 years. In addition, when Rachel was asked whether she had ever been upset by anyone trying to get her to do what they'd seen in pornographic pictures, movies or books, she mentioned her husband.

It was real hard for me to enjoy oral sex. I didn't want to do it with him but he made me. I would ask him, "Why are you making me do something I feel uncomfortable with?"

There were certain positions I didn't want to do. I'd tell him so and he'd get defensive. He would fuck me real fast and get it over with. I didn't like oral sex at all. I thought it was degrading and that he should respect my feelings but he'd force me to do it. He'd push my head down on top of him and hold it there. He made me do it because I was his wife. "It's your duty," he said.

He'd be drunk and not affectionate. When I didn't want to have sex, he'd do it anyway. Once he wanted to have anal intercourse. I didn't want to so he held me down and did it. He didn't care that it hurt. When I was in pain—when sex was painful—he didn't care. (How did it end?) I left him.

(Upset?) Extremely upset. (Effect on your life?) A great effect. I don't ever want to get married again. I was very untrusting of men for a long time, and very afraid of physical violence. For a long time I didn't want to have any sex with anyone. I went through a long period of celibacy after I left him. I feel like I want to be in control of my sexual experiences. I've become real self-centered about my sexuality, real protective of my sexual space, refusing to let myself be somebody else's sexual object!

(Other physical violence?) Yes, right before I left him. We had just come from seeing a marriage counselor whom I'd been seeing alone. He'd been making excuses for not going, but he finally went with me. I was bewildered at his anger, as *I* was the one who was angry. When we got home, he grabbed me and pushed me out of the car. We were on the sidewalk and he was sitting on my chest, punching me and beating my head on the sidewalk with my hair. I was screaming. Then he left and ran off.

We had many steps to the house and he finally came back to help me up them. He was sorry and gentle by then.

Rachel said the physical violence occurred from two to five times over a period of two and one-half years. After the one violent episode that Rachel described, her husband was very apologetic about his behavior; however, he was clearly not apologetic after the rapes. He appears to have felt that he was simply taking what he was owed when it came to sex; he seemed indifferent as to whether his satisfaction required force or not. At that time the law in California would have been in agreement with him since rape in marriage was legal in that state until January 1980.

In addition to her experience with the babysitter when she was 10 years old, Rachel reported three other unwanted sexual experiences with authority figures. She said that the first one occurred with a "higher up in the Church."

I was at an interview and I needed him to recommend me. He asked a lot of sexual questions which humiliated me. (Was there any physical contact?) No.

One of my employers kept making me interview over and over. He implied that if I was looser with him he would hire me, but I never gave in. I talked to other waitresses and learned that he did the same thing to them. (Was there any physical contact?) No, it was just innuendos.

Another time a bartender-employer gave me a hard time. He said if I would be friendlier he'd make it easier for me. (Was there any physical contact?) Nothing more than that.

While this amount of sexual abuse may strike many readers as almost beyond belief, the fact remains that many women in this survey reported as many and sometimes more experiences.

Victims of sexual abuse, including child victims, have commonly been blamed for their victimization, not just by their families but by clinicians, researchers, and others with whom they shared the information. Victims who have been abused more than once have been treated as even more suspect—the more experiences, the more suspect. Particularly tragic is the fact that victim blaming can itself actually lead to further victimization. First, it may bring forth the latent victimizer in a potential perpetrator, as was evident in Rachel's sexual abuse by her brother. Second, it can result in the internalization by the victim of the notion that she is responsible, and hence, must be provoking the behavior. Guilt therefore replaces anger in her response to sexual abuse, and undermines her capacity to protect herself effectively.

## CONCLUSION

Little did I realize in 1977, when I wrote my grant proposal to the National Institute of Mental Health, that I would spend more than the next decade of my life analyzing and writing about the results of this monumental study. But indeed this promises to be the case. My book *Rape in Marriage* (1982) was based on some of these survey results. I am currently working on another book, *The Incestuous Abuse of Females* (to be published by Basic Books), also based on these interviews. And I have plans for three more books: the sexual abuse of girls outside the family; the sexual abuse of females by authority figures (particularly doctors, employers, and teachers); and rape of adult women outside of marriage.

I am grateful for having such a rare research opportunity—one that few scholars have been fortunate enough to have. It is my fervent hope that these survey findings will contribute to a deeper understanding of the many and varied forms of sexual exploitation. Armed with this understanding, perhaps more of us can and will campaign for the resources necessary to implement policies that begin to alleviate the anguish that these acts are causing every day on such a massive scale.

# PART I

# RAPE: PREVALENCE, SOCIAL AND PSYCHOLOGICAL CHARACTERISTICS

## 1

## THE INCIDENCE AND PREVALENCE OF RAPE

Prior to 1981, the rate of forcible rape reported to the police had been increasing dramatically in the United States for many years. In 1980, 71 out of every 100,000 females in the United States reported being victims of rape or attempted rape (FBI, 1981). This represented a 6 percent increase over 1979, and a 38 percent increase over 1976.

In 1981, however, there was a slight decrease in the rape rate; in 1982, the rape rate was 6 percent lower than it was for 1981 (FBI, 1982, 1983). A similar decrease occurred for two other violent crimes: between 1981 and 1982 the rates for murder and robbery[1] declined by 7 percent.

Of the four most serious crimes of violence recognized by the police (rape, murder, robbery, and aggravated assault), only the rate of aggravated assault remained the same. This sudden decrease in three of the four crimes roughly corresponds to the decrease in young males in the most crime prone age groups, due to the aging of the so-called baby boomers.[2]

Interpreting trends in the official rape statistics is even more difficult than interpreting the trends in other crimes. This is a direct result of the "unfounding" process, which applies only to rape. According to the FBI, unfounding means "the police established that no forcible rape offense or attempt occurred" (FBI, 1973). What this euphemistic definition actually describes is the process by which rape cases are dismissed by the police as false reports. The basis for, and error rate in these judgements, is unknown and therefore unmeasurable.

The most recent volumes of the *Uniform Crime Reports* no longer report the percentage of cases that are unfounded. No reason for this change in practice is given, but unfortunately it is not because the police have eliminated the unfounding process. In 1976, the last year the unfounding rate was reported in the *Uniform Crime Reports,* the rate was 19 percent—the highest it had been for several years.

Jim Galvin and Kenneth Polk have attempted to prove that the attrition of rape cases as they move through the criminal justice system is "similar to that experienced with other major felonies" (1983, p. 126). However, these authors ignore the unfounding process unique to cases of rape.[3] In addition, the low percentage of reported rapes that result in arrests—as reported annually in the *Uniform Crime Reports*—indicates that enforcement of rape laws presents particular difficulties for law enforcement officers. Even when rape cases *do* survive the unfounding process, it is relatively rare for their perpetrators to be apprehended, let alone incarcerated. In 1982, 74 percent of all reported homicides resulted in arrests, as did 60 percent of aggravated assaults. But only 51 percent of reported forcible rapes resulted in arrests.

Forcible rape is a particularly acute problem in the United States. International statistics on reported incidents suggest that rape is considerably more prevalent in this country than in other Western nations. Researcher Arthur Schiff reported in a 1971 article that while the rate per 100,000 was 35 in the United States, it was only 1.9 in France, 1.2 in Holland and .8 in Belgium (1971, pp. 139–143).

Professor of Psychiatry John MacDonald agrees that "Available statistics, despite their deficiencies, suggest that the United States has an unusually high rape rate" (1971, p. 25). He contrasts his figure of 30 per 100,000 females in the United States (year unspecified) with less than 1 per 100,000 in Norway, 3 in England, and 7 in Poland (1971, pp. 25–26).

The high rate of reported rapes in the United States compared to rates in other countries is not likely due to a higher rate of reporting of rape in the United States. However, statistics in the United States and other countries that are limited to reported cases are highly unreliable because so many rapes never become known to the police.

The report rate for rape in the United States has been a matter of speculation for some time. Almost a quarter century ago, criminologist L. Radzinowicz argued that rape had a high degree of reportability because of the injury suffered by the victim and the importance to the culture of protecting women and defending their sexual morality (1957). J. F. Short and F. I. Nye concurrred with this view (1958). Ten years before that, W. Haines et al, had estimated that only 5 percent of rapes are reported (1948); K. M. Bowman and B. Engle, on the other hand, estimated 20 percent (1954), and the *Uniform Crime Reports* estimated 30 percent (1960). Most recently, the *National Crime Surveys* have claimed the extraordinarily high report rate of 56 percent (McDermott, 1979, p. 43).

Diana Russell's random sample survey found a report rate for rape of only 9.5 percent. In addition, a comparison of the kinds of cases that were reported to the police with those that were not shows that the reported cases were extremely unrepresentative of the majority of unreported cases. These findings are of great significance to the study of rape. Hence Chapter 3 will include a comparison of reported and unreported rapes. Suffice it to say here that the value of the official statistics on rape published annually by the FBI in the *Uniform Crime Reports* is seriously limited.

## National Surveys of Reported and Unreported Rape

Incidence is usually defined as the number of new cases or events that occur within a specified period of time. Prevalence is a measure of the number of cases that exist at a specific point in time. For purposes of this analysis, the *incidence* measure of rape will include *rape cases that occurred within the previous year,* and the *prevalence* measure of rape will refer to *any rape event that occurred over a woman's lifetime.*

A national survey of the prevalence of reported and unreported rape has never been attempted. But some national surveys of the incidence of rape and attempted rape have been undertaken. These were based on sophisticated random sampling techniques and rape was included as one of many crimes (Ennis, 1967; *National Crime Panel Surveys,* 1974, 1975, etc.). Unfortunately, methods were used in these surveys that, although appropriate for other crimes, would likely discourage reporting of rape. Nevertheless, these surveys—and their limitations—are of interest to those involved in the study of rape.

### NATIONAL OPINION RESEARCH CENTER (NORC) SURVEY

In the 1967 NORC study of 10,000 households, one adult per household was given a 20-minute screening interview "to see if anyone in the household had been a victim of any crime within the previous twelve months" (Ennis, 1967, p. 1). It is known that many rape victims tell no one, particularly no one in their households, about their rape experiences (Kanin, 1957; Kirkpatrick and Kanin, 1957; Burgess and Holmstrom, 1974; Russell, 1975). So, it is much less likely that the adult interviewed would know of another family member's rape, compared to, for example, a robbery or nonsexual assault. This is true today, and was even truer when the NORC survey was undertaken. At that time, discussion of rape was even less socially acceptable than it is at present.

Even with its limitations, the NORC survey found that the estimated number of rapes per 100,000 population in 1965 was almost four times higher than the rate reported in the *Uniform Crime Reports*. This indicates that for every rape reported to the police—and not dismissed by them as unfounded—approximately four others had occurred.[4]

This discrepancy is particularly remarkable in light of the NORC study requirement that any report included as a crime "had to be graded as 'confirmed' or 'probable' on seven criteria. If the case was 'unfounded' on any one of the seven, it was excluded" (Ennis, 1967, p. 4). These criteria included "that the interviewer gave the case a certain likelihood of having occurred" and "that it really took place in the judgment of the research staff." Using this procedure, one-third of the cases were disqualified (Ennis, 1967, p. 91).

Despite increased study and analysis of rape and its causes, the classic myths about rape persist (for example: Most rapists are strangers to their victims; well-educated white men rarely rape; reports from sexually active females who claim to have been raped are unreliable). These stereotypes may render unbelievable accounts of rape that contradict them. Interviewers, such as those who conducted the NORC study, are not immune to the biases rampant in the general population. All of these factors provide reasons to believe that the true incidence of rape was seriously underestimated in NORC's national survey.

### NATIONAL CRIME SURVEYS

In the early 1970s, the National Crime Surveys were instituted by the federal government. The goal of the surveys was to obtain more accurate incidence rates by taking into account the large number of crimes never reported to the police. These victimization surveys were designed and carried out for the Law Enforcement Assistance Administration (LEAA), and more recently for the Bureau of Justice Statistics, by the U.S. Bureau of the Census. They are based on representative samples of households and commercial establishments in various cities as well as nationally.

The method by which these surveys obtained information about rape victimization is likely to result in a considerable underestimation of the prevalence of rape. As pointed out in one of the early National Crime Surveys,

> [R]ape is not only a traumatic experience for the victim, but also the only crime for which the victim can be socially stigmatized. More so than for any other crime, there are strong pressures on the victim not to report the incident to a complete stranger. (Law Enforcement Assistance Administration, 1974, p. 12)

While researchers for the National Crime Surveys recognized this problem, their survey techniques did not (and still do not) enable them to surmount it. The particular study from which this quotation is drawn involved personal interviews with 5,500 household members and at 1,000 business locations in San Jose, California, and its suburbs. The study uncovered not a single case of completed rape in this region with its population of one million for the entire year of 1970. The 600 incidents that were reported were all cases of attempted rape. As the researchers acknowledge, "It is unreasonable to assume that no rapes were successfully committed in San Jose in 1970." They concluded that rape "is less well reported than any other crime in the survey" (Law Enforcement Assistance Administration, 1974, p. 12).

Subsequent National Crime Surveys have been more successful in finding rape victims who are willing to admit their victimization. The large majority of cases disclosed to the survey interviewers in every city continue to be *attempted* rapes. Examples include the following: Boston, 78 percent; Buffalo, 83 percent; Cincinnati, 80 percent; Houston, 70 percent; Miami, 66 percent; Milwaukee, 66 percent; Minneapolis, 66 percent; New Orleans, 73 percent; San Francisco, 75 percent; (National Crime Panel Surveys, June 1975). These findings are exactly the opposite of those reported by the *Uniform Crime Reports* according to which "74 percent of all forcible rape offenses were actual rapes by force. The remainder were attempts or assaults to commit forcible rape" (for example, see FBI, 1974, p. 225). However they are consistent with the Russell survey findings that 68 percent of all rapes were attempted. It appears that women are much more likely to report a completed rape to the police.

The National Crime Surveys state repeatedly that "rape is clearly an infrequent crime." It seems reasonable, however, to suspect that underreporting to their interviewers, rather than rare occurrence, accounts for their findings (Law Enforcement Assistance Administration, 1974, p. 12). Misleading statements such as this one add credence to the commonly held myth that rape seldom occurs.

The failure of the National Crime Surveys to produce a single case of completed rape in San Jose in 1970 clearly indicated the need to reevaluate the questionnaire design and the training of interviewers. However, revisions are not evident in later surveys (for example, see Bureau of Justice Statistics, 1980). Only four questions were (and are still being) asked that might possibly elicit information on rape victimization:

> Did anyone beat you up, attack you or hit you with something, such as a rock or bottle?
>
> Were you knifed, shot at, or attacked with some other weapon by anyone at all?
>
> Did anyone THREATEN to beat you up or THREATEN you with a knife, gun, or some other weapon, NOT including telephone threats?
>
> Did anyone TRY to attack you in some other way?

The last question is presumably the one most specifically designed to elicit a revelation of this apparently unmentionable crime. But even this question is indirect and insufficient. The fact that it is phrased with the emphasis on the word "try" may account for the low reporting of completed acts in all published National Crime Surveys.

If no information on rape victimization was elicited by the four questions quoted above, the interviewer did no further probing. In light of the tremendous reluctance of most rape victims to reveal their experience to strangers, it is not surprising that little information has been gathered from these four questions.

## The Russell San Francisco Survey

The Russell survey was conducted in San Francisco. Its major goal was to obtain a more accurate estimate of the incidence and prevalence of rape and other forms of sexual assault, including the sexual abuse of children, among the general population of females.

In-person interviews with 930 randomly selected adult female residents of San Francisco were conducted throughout the summer of 1978. A probability sample of households were drawn by Field Research Associates, a well-respected public opinion polling organization in San Francisco. Carefully trained female interviewers went to each address drawn in the random sample to determine whether a woman of 18 years or older resided there. If there was more than one eligible woman in a given household, a procedure was applied to randomly select the one to be interviewed. A detailed interview followed, the average length of which was one hour and 20 minutes.

San Francisco was selected as the locale for this survey rather than Oakland, Berkeley, or other nearby communities because it is the largest and most prominent of these cities. Results obtained in San Francisco were most likely to be taken with the seriousness they deserve. While San Francisco is known to have a large population of gay people, this fact would likely have no impact on the prevalence of heterosexual rape or the sexual abuse of female children.

Comparisons of rape rates for different cities are made problematic by different definitions of rape and by different reporting practices by the police. Nevertheless, the rape rate per 100,000 people in 1978 was very similar in the following cities: San Francisco, 86; Los Angeles, 83; Boston, 84; Cleveland, 88; and Dallas, 91 (FBI, 1979).[5] The relationship (if any) between these figures and the true incidence of rape, including unreported cases, is unknown. But by finding out the prevalence rates in San Francisco, the Russell study hoped to be able to draw conclusions relevant to other cities as well.

Because prior surveys suffered from underdisclosure, particular effort was made to minimize this problem in the Russell study. The interview schedule was carefully designed to encourage good rapport with the respondent. Interviewers were selected for their sensitivity to the issue of sexual assault, as well as for their interviewing skills. They received an intensive two-week training that included education about rape and incestuous abuse, as well as desensitization to sexual words and rigorous training in administering the interview schedule. Interviews were held in private; whenever possible, race and ethnicity of interviewer and respondent were matched. Each respondent was paid $10 for her participation.

## PREVALENCE RATES FOR RAPE AND ATTEMPED

These interview methods enabled respondents to disclose experiences often not shared with anyone, let alone an unknown interviewer. The study used the legal definition of rape in California and most other states at that time: *forced intercourse (i.e., penile-vaginal penetration), or intercourse obtained by threat of force, or intercourse completed when the woman was drugged, unconscious, asleep, or otherwise totally helpless and hence unable to consent.*

Of the 930 women 223 (24 percent) reported at least one completed rape, and 291 (31 percent) at least one attempted rape. When the categories of rape and attempted rape are combined, as is customary in the official statistics, 407 (44 percent) reported at least one completed or attempted rape. Only 66 (8 percent)—or less than 1 in 12—

**TABLE 1.1**

**Number of Women Victimized
by Rape/Attempted Rape
Once or More by Different Assailants**

| Number of Rapes with Different Assailants | Number of Women Raped | Number of Incidents (Number Attacks x Number Women Attacked) |
|---|---|---|
| 1 | 205 | 205 |
| 2 | 112 | 224 |
| 3 | 47 | 141 |
| 4 | 27 | 108 |
| 5 | 7 | 35 |
| 6 | 2 | 12 |
| 7 | 3 | 21 |
| 8 | 2 | 16 |
| 9 | 2 | 18 |
| Total | 407 | 780 |

of the total number of rape and attempted rape incidents (780) were ever reported to the police.

When the rapes by husbands are excluded, to bring the statistics in line with the exclusion of marital rape from rape laws in California and most other states in 1978, the prevalence rates are as follows: 175 of the 930 women (19 percent) reported at least one completed nonmarital rape, and 284 (31 percent) reported at least one attempted nonmarital rape. When the categories of rape and attempted rape are combined, 379 (41 percent) reported at least one completed or attempted nonmarital rape.

Since no cases of wife rape were reported to the police, the 66 rapes and attempted rapes that were reported constitute 9.5 percent of the total number of nonmarital rape and attempted rape incidents (693). This means that only about 1 in 10 nonmarital rapes in the Russell sample were ever reported to the police.

These figures focus on the numbers and percentages of women who have ever been victims of rape or attempted rape. It is significant that 50 percent of the 407 women who had ever experienced either kind of attack had been raped more than once. The frequency distribution for the numbers of women who were victimized from one to nine different times by different assailants (a pair or group rape is counted as one attack) is presented in Table 1.1

Of those women who were attacked, the average number of incidents with different rapists is almost two (1.92). This remarkably high prevalence rate raises the question of whether some respondents fabricated the rape experiences they disclosed.

Such fabrication was unlikely for a number of reasons. First, the interviewers were instructed to convey to respondents that contributions of respondents with no sexual abuse experience was every bit as valuable as those who had been sexually victimized. Second, few women are likely to believe that being a rape victim would enhance their status and worth in the eyes of others. As an additional precaution, interviewers, interview supervisors, and coders were asked to try to assess the honesty and reliability of respondents' answers. The consensus among these people was that underdisclosure, not fabrication, was a significant problem in the case of some respondents. A few respondents even admitted on a self-administered questionnaire completed at the end of the interview that they were unwilling to disclose or talk about some of their experiences. Not one admitted to fabricating or embellishing an experience.

The 44 percent prevalence rate of rape uncovered in the Russell survey was due in part to the number of questions asked, and the manner in which they were presented. Only 1 of the 38 questions on sexual assault and abuse actually used the word rape. This question was: "At any time in your life, have you ever been the victim of a rape or attempted rape?" Of those interviewed, 22 percent answered in the affirmative, and offered descriptions that met the study's definition of rape or attempted rape.

In a few cases, it was clear that a respondent's definition of rape was broader than that used in the study. For example, some respondents reported *feeling* forced rather than *being* forced, or having intercourse because of a threat that was not a threat of physical force or bodily harm. These cases were not counted as instances of rape or attempted rape.

Many additional questions were designed to elicit other experiences of rape or attempted rape. For example, the three questions that follow were each asked three times, the first time about strangers, the second time about acquaintances or friends, the third time about dates, lovers, or ex-lovers. This was to allow the respondent enough time to consider thoughtfully these different categories of potential rapists.

(1) Did a stranger (etc.) ever physically force you, or try to force you, to have any kind of sexual intercourse (besides anyone you've already mentioned)?

(2) Have you ever had any unwanted sexual experience, including kissing, petting, or intercourse with a stranger (etc.) because you felt
physically threatened (besides anyone you've already mentioned)? IF
YES: Did he (any of them) either try or succeed in having any kind
of sexual intercourse with you?

(3) Have you ever had any kind of unwanted sexual experience with a
stranger (etc.) because you were asleep, unconscious, drugged or in
some other way helpless (besides anyone you've already mentioned)?
IF YES: Did he (any of them) either try or succeed in having any
kind of sexual intercourse with you?

The pronoun "he" was used in these questions because a prior
question had already been asked about any unwanted sexual experiences with females.

For every episode of rape or attempted rape elicited, a separate
questionnaire was administered. This included a description of the
assault sufficiently detailed to ensure that the definition of rape or
attempted rape had been met.

## REFUSAL RATE AND REPRESENTATIVENESS OF SAMPLE

There are several ways to calculate a refusal rate. The proportion
of respondents who, knowing that the study was about rape, refused
to participate was 19 percent. Including the men as well as women
who declined even to give a listing of those in the household in the
refusal rate, it increases to 36 percent. The final category of refusals
includes the following: households in which no one was ever at home;
households made inaccessible to the interviewer by locked gates or
other physical deterrents; women who had agreed to be interviewed
but were unavailable because of logistics, or because their husbands
or some other person would not give the interviewer access to them.
If this final category is included, the refusal rate rises to 50 percent.

Many of the households that were inaccessible or where no one
was at home might have been households in which no eligible woman
lived (for example, there are a large number of all male households in
San Francisco). Therefore, the 36 percent refusal rate seems to be the
most valid of the three presented.

One major factor affecting the refusal rate stemmed from the concern of the staff of the Rape Center at the National Institute of Mental Health (which funded the research) for the protection of human
subjects. Because of this concern, they forbade any attempts to
change refusers' minds by sending back to that household a second
interviewer who was particularly adept at this task or who was better
matched in age and social class to the person who refused.

One method of assessing the bias introduced by refusals is to compare the characteristics of those who refuse (where this information is available) with the characteristics of those who do not. Such a comparison reveals few, if any differences between the race or ethnicity of these two groups, the number of persons living in each household, and the employment status of those who refused (i.e., the percentage who were working full-time, part-time, were laid off or looking for work, or were retired.)

There is, however, a significant difference in age and marital status. Women who refused to participate in the study were more likely to be older than those who agreed to be interviewed (an average age of 50 years versus 43 years) and married (60 percent versus 39 percent. To assess the effect of this potential bias on the sample, weights were established so that married women and older women would count for more. In particular, the impact of these weights on the prevalence of rape was assessed.

This weighting procedure resulted in a small difference in the rates of rape and attempted rape; for instance, the prevalence of completed rape (including wife rape) declined from 24 percent to 21 percent, and the prevalence of attempted rape declined from 31 percent to 30 percent. Combined rates of rape and attempted rape declined from 44 percent to 41 percent. Since the discrepancy between these prevalence figures is so small, the Russell project decided to continue using the unweighted figures.

Another method of assessing the adequacy of a sample is to compare the characteristics of those who were interviewed with the characteristics of the population from which the sample was drawn—in this case, women residents of San Francisco. The 1980 census provides data two years after the Russell survey interviews had been conducted. Clearly these data are more comparable with the 1978 Russell sample than are those obtained in the 1970 census.

Three demographic characteristics were chosen from the 1980 census to check for biases in Russell's San Francisco sample: age, ethnicity, and marital status.[6]

Comparison of the marital status of Russell's 1978 sample of women with the 1980 census data for San Francisco reveals a remarkably similar distribution (see Table 1.2).

On race and ethnic distribution, as may be seen in Table 1.3, Russell's sample had proportionally the same number of Black women and those of "Other" ethnicities. However, there were proportionally more white women and fewer Asian and Hispanic women.

Two factors make the underrepresentation of Asians in Russell's sample less serious than the 7 percent difference suggests. First, there

**TABLE 1.2**

**Comparison of Marital Status of Respondents
in Russell's Sample and 1980 Census
Data for San Francisco**

|           | *Russell Sample* | *1980 Census* |
|-----------|------------------|---------------|
| Single    | 31.0             | 33.0          |
| Married   | 39.0             | 38.0          |
| Separated | 4.0              | 3.0           |
| Widowed   | 12.0             | 15.0          |
| Divorced  | 14.0             | 11.0          |

has been a tremendous influx of Asians into San Francisco in the past few years, so that the 1980 figures are probably less comparable to 1978 for Asians than is the case for the other comparisons being made. More specifically, since the 1970 census was undertaken, the percentage of Asian people has risen from 13 percent in 1970 to 20 percent in 1980.

Second, the Russell survey was limited to English- or Spanish-speaking people. A significant number of Asians living in San Francisco do not speak English, and hence were not eligible for Russell's survey. Thus, Russell's sample of Asians was not as unrepresentative of the number of English speaking Asians in the San Francisco population in 1978 as Table 1.3 indicates.

Comparison of the age distribution shows that Russell's 1978 sample of women was somewhat younger on the whole than women in San Francisco in 1980. As may be seen in Table 1.4, in the three age groupings between 20 and 34, there were 2 percent more in Russell's sample in the group between 20 and 24, 4 percent more in the middle group, and 3 percent more in the 30 to 34 age group. Russell's sample had proportionally fewer women over 40 in several age groups. However, the figures rarely varied by more than one percentage point.

A significant relationship exists between age and the number of rape and attempted rape experiences reported by women in the Russell sample (with the younger women reporting more experiences). Hence, the small overrepresentation of younger women in this sample has slightly raised the prevalence rates found in her study from what they would have been had her age distributions been identical to those reported in the 1980 census. The difference is small, however, and the 1980 census data only became available very recently (after

**TABLE 1.3**

**Comparison of Race/Ethnicity of
Respondents in Russell's Sample
and 1980 Census Data for San Francisco**

|        | Russell Sample | 1980 Census |
|--------|:--------------:|:-----------:|
| White  | 67.4           | 57.2        |
| Latina | 7.1            | 10.8        |
| Black  | 9.6            | 10.8        |
| Asian  | 13.1           | 20.1        |
| Other  | 2.7            | 1.1         |

many of the analyses reported in this book had already been completed). So, use of a weighting procedure to correct for the small overrepresentation of younger women in Russell's sample will not be employed at this time.

The refusal rate in the Russell survey was higher than had been hoped. However, given the immense difficulties of tackling a random sample survey on this subject, the data obtained are quite remarkable. Previous researchers such as Alfred Kinsey and his colleagues (1948, 1953), William Masters and Virginia Johnson (1966), as well as Shere Hite (1976, 1981), all based their studies on volunteers, presumably because they considered a random sample too difficult to accomplish.

Because the samples of these researchers were all self-selected, it is not scientifically valid to generalize their findings beyond their specific respondents. The fact that so many researchers, as well as nonresearchers, ignore this limitation, does not make it any less true. If a researcher wishes to generalize her or his findings to a population larger than the one studied, some kind of random sampling process is necessary. It is this process that makes even an imperfect random sample such as Russell's both extremely valuable, and unprecedented for research in the area of sex or sexual abuse.

## Rape Incidence Rates Compared

### THE RUSSELL SURVEY AND THE UNIFORM CRIME REPORTS DATA

The official statistics (i.e., those published annually in the *Uniform Crime Reports*) and the National Crime Surveys report on the incidence of rape and attempted rape, but not on the prevalence of these

**TABLE 1.4**

**Comparison of Age of Respondents
in Russell's Sample and
1980 Census Data for San Francisco**

| Age | Russell Sample | 1980 Census |
|-----|----------------|-------------|
| 18–19 | 3.0 | 3.0 |
| 20–24 | 13.0 | 11.0 |
| 25–29 | 17.0 | 13.0 |
| 30–34 | 14.0 | 12.0 |
| 35–39 | 8.0 | 7.0 |
| 40–44 | 4.0 | 6.0 |
| 45–49 | 6.0 | 6.0 |
| 50–54 | 5.0 | 7.0 |
| 55–59 | 6.0 | 7.0 |
| 60–64 | 6.0 | 6.0 |
| 65–69 | 6.0 | 6.0 |
| 70–74 | 6.0 | 6.0 |
| 75–79 | 3.0 | 4.0 |
| 80–84 | 2.0 | 3.0 |
| 85+ | 1.0 | 2.0 |

crimes. In order to compare the Russell statistics with these sources, interviewers asked each victim of rape or attempted rape if the assault had occurred in the 12 months prior to the interview. For purposes of these comparisons, all cases of wife rape will be excluded.

According to the 1979 edition of the *Uniform Crime Reports,* 583 rapes and attempted rapes of females of all ages were reported in San Francisco in 1978, the year of the Russell survey. Based on the population in July 1978 of 340,060 females in San Francisco (California Department of Finance estimate, 1979), this yields a rape rate of 1.71 per 1,000 (or 171 per 100,000) females of all ages in this city in 1978.

Thirty-three out of the 930 women interviewed by the Russell survey reported nonmarital rapes and attempted rapes during the 12 months prior to the interview (i.e., from mid-1977 to mid-1978). Since women had to be 18 years old to be eligible for the survey, these 33 rape victims were all at least 17 years old at the time of the rape. This age limit does not apply to the *Uniform Crime Reports* data. One way to compensate for this difference is to calculate the rape rate for the Russell survey on the basis of the female population who were 17 years and older, rather than the total female population in San Francisco. The estimated population of females 17 and older in San Francisco in 1978 is approximately 283,575 (California Department of Employment Development, 1977).[7]

Of the rapes or attempted rapes reported by Russell's respondents, 8 occurred outside of San Francisco. Since the statistics from the *Uniform Crime Reports* for San Francisco are limited to rapes occurring in that city, these 8 cases are also excluded from the Russell estimate. This leaves 25 nonmarital rapes and attempted rapes occurring in San Francisco in the 12 months prior to the interviews.

Extrapolating from this figure (25 rapes out of 930 women), the total number of nonmarital rapes and attempted rapes of women 17 years and older in San Francisco in 1972 is estimated to be 7,685.[8] *This figure is 13 times higher than the total incidence (583) reported by the Uniform Crime Reports for females of all ages.*

The Russell survey estimates then, that the incidence rate of rape in San Francisco is approximately 3 percent of all female residents 17 years and older (or 2,688 per 100,000 females. This figure is obtained as follows: $25/930 \times 100,000 = 2,688$).

There are some important differences between the Russell survey and the *Uniform Crime Reports* statistics. First, as already mentioned, the Russell statistics are limited to women 17 years and older, whereas the *Uniform Crime Reports* do not give information on the ages of victims of rape and attempted rape. In the Russell data, one-quarter (25 percent) of the total number of rape and attempted rape victims were females 16 years old or under. Hence, the estimate of the incidence of rape and attempted rape obtained from the Russell survey would likely be higher were it not limited to women 17 years and older.

Second, the Russell survey was limited to *residents* of San Francisco, not tourists or those of no fixed abode. The *Uniform Crime Reports* include rape reports by nonresidents of San Francisco.

And third, the Russell study was based on a sample of *households*. Hence, women residing in institutions such as mental hospitals, prisons, shelters, nursing homes, and halfway houses were excluded.

The *Uniform Crime Reports* figures are more broadly based than Russell's for all these reasons. They include females of all ages, who are not necessarily residents of San Francisco. Nonresidents are likely to be a particularly vulnerable group because, for example, they may not know which parts of the city are especially dangerous. Also, those with no fixed address are frequently very unprotected. Finally, those most traumatized by rape experiences may be more likely to be institutionalized. Women residing in institutions could be included in the

*Uniform Crime Reports* statistics if the rape was reported to the police.

Another relevant factor is that the figures reported by the *Uniform Crime Reports* do not actually include *all* reported cases, since unfounded cases are excluded. In 1976, the last year in which the percentage of unfounded cases was reported in the *Uniform Crime Reports*, 19 percent of the reported rapes were unfounded. So, almost one-fifth (or 10,779 cases) of the total number of founded rapes and attempted rapes (56,730) were dismissed as false reports. This represents an increase of 2,269 discounted reports—or 4 percent—over the previous year (FBI,1975).

Prior to 1975, the unfounding rate was about 18 percent for most years. If 18 percent is added to the total number of rapes and attempted rapes reported to the police in San Francisco, then the *Uniform Crime Report* figure of 583 would be increased to 688. However, the disparity between this figure and Russell's (7,625) is still enormous; Russell's rate is 11 times higher.

A missing element in this attempt to explain the discrepancy is compensation for the fact that the Russell figure includes unreported as well as reported rapes.

Only 4 out of the 25 (16 percent) nonmarital rapes and attempted rapes that occurred in San Francisco in the 12 months prior to the interview had been reported to the police, according to the Russell survey. This is approximately 1 in every 6 rape incidents. Four cases of rape is too small a number from which to safely project an overall report rate. Hence, the percentage of *all* rapes that were reported to the police in the Russell survey will be examined instead, not just the percentage of those that had occurred in the last 12 months.

As already mentioned, 66 (or 9.5 percent) of the total number (693) of nonmarital rapes and attempted rapes were reported to the police in the Russell survey. This is only 1 in every 10.5 rape or attempted rape incidents. If we assume this to be an accurate assessment of the percentage of unreported cases in general and if we were therefore to multiply the corrected *Uniform Crime Reports* figure of 688 rapes by 10.5, we would obtain a total of 7,224 reported and unreported incidents. This figure is remarkably close to Russell's estimate of 7,625 cases of rape or attempted rape (a difference of only 401 cases).

As was stated earlier, the estimate based on the Russell survey data, unlike the *Uniform Crime Reports* figures, does not include nonresidents of San Francisco who were raped in that city in 1978, nor women who were subsequently institutionalized, nor women under the age of 17 years. Given these differences, the similarity between the Russell figure and the corrected *Uniform Crime Reports* figure is indeed perplexing. The Russell figure, after all, has not been corrected to make it more comparable to that or the *Uniform Crime Reports*; it was therefore expected that the *Uniform Crime Reports* figure would be considerably higher than Russell's. A recent study undertaken in Philadelphia provides an explanation.

Of a sample of 1,401 rape cases studied by Thomas McCahill, Linda Meyer, and Arthur Fischman (1979)—all of which had been reported to the police—information about the police response was available in 1,397 cases (99.7 percent). These researchers found many more than 18 percent of the reported cases to have been discounted or lost in one way or another. For example,

> The police reported no record in their files of 199 of these 1,397 cases (14.2 percent).... [A] portion of these missing cases may be attributed to deliberate nonrecording. Of the remaining 1,198 cases, police marked unfounded 218 complaints (18.2 percent).... *Of 1,401 women who were seen at Philadelphia General Hospital in connection with an alleged sexual assault the police reported 747 "rapes" (53.8 percent) to the FBI.* (McCahill et al., 1979, p. 98, emphasis added)

As if the unfounding and/or loss of 46 percent of the reported rape and attempted rape cases was not sufficient cause for alarm, McCahill et al. concluded their analysis as follows:

> [A]mong cases marked as founded, about ten percent are given a lesser sexual offense charge. Although these cases may come to trial, the worst possible sentence is typically less than would be possible if the charge was rape, and *these cases do not contribute to the number of cases reported as complaints of rape by the police.* (1979, p. 102, emphasis added)

And so we see that in Philadelphia in 1973–1974, approximately 56 percent of reported cases were not recorded as rapes in the *Uniform Crime Reports* statistics for that city.

Given the enormous variation in the methods used for recording rape statistics by police departments in different locations, it would not be legitimate to assume that 56 percent of the rapes reported in San Francisco in 1978 were lost in a similar fashion.[9] Nevertheless, the Philadelphia study indicates that an 18 percent unfounding rate is a gross underestimate of the actual percentage of reported rapes that are excluded from the official statistics that are offered to the public as statistics on all reported rapes. Hence it is not surprising that despite the correction made for some of the differences in the figures reported by the Russell survey and by the *Uniform Crime Reports*, it is not possible to completely reconcile them.

### THE RUSSELL SURVEY AND THE NATIONAL CRIME SURVEY DATA

Incidence rates found by the Russell survey may readily be compared to the 1974 National Crime Survey, since San Francisco was one of 13 cities studied. Census Bureau interviewers obtained information for the National Crime Survey from 18,410 San Francisco residents aged 12 years and over (Law Enforcement Assistance Administration, 1977, p. iii). Respondents were asked about criminal acts that had occurred within the prior 12 months (i.e., in 1973). One thousand and six-hundred rapes and attempted rapes were reported to the interviewers. Roughly three-quarters of these attacks were attempted rapes. The rape rate was 5 per 1,000 females.

The National Crime Survey in San Francisco was not limited to crimes occurring in that city. Therefore, the 8 cases reported to Russell's interviewers as having occurred outside of San Francisco in the prior 12 months will be included in Russell's statistics for purposes of this comparison. Extrapolating from these 33 cases of rape and attempted rape in the same fashion as was done previously, the Russell estimate of the total incidence of rape and attempted rape is 10,062.

When including the cases that occurred outside of San Francisco, the Russell estimate of the incidence rate of rape is approximately 3.5 percent—or 3,548 per 100,000 females. This compares to figures from the National Crime Survey of .5 percent, or 500 per 100,000 females, respectively. Hence, *the Russell rate is just over seven times higher than that reported by the National Crime Survey.*

### NATIONAL ESTIMATE OF THE INCIDENCE OF RAPE OF ADULT WOMEN

There is no question that generalizing from the Russell San Francisco sample to the population of the United States at large is highly speculative. Still, it is tempting to use the Russell survey data as a basis for estimating what the incidence of rape and attempted rape of women 17 years and older might have been in 1978 when the survey was undertaken.

The incidence figure for rape in the Russell survey cited above was 35 per 1,000 females. (This includes cases of rape and attempted rape that occurred to residents of San Francisco, both inside and outside of that city.) This is *24 times higher* than the 1.71 per 1,000 females reported by the *Uniform Crime Reports.*

The *Uniform Crime Reports* estimated a total of 67,131 forcible rapes (including attempts) for 1978 in the entire United States. Since the incidence rate for the Russell study was 24 times higher than the incidence rate reported in the *Uniform Crime Reports,* 67,131 forcible rapes multiplied by 24 comes to a total of over one and a half million (1,611,144) rapes and attempted rapes, reported and unreported, having occurred in that year. This figure indicates a rape problem of far greater magnitude than is conveyed by the *Uniform Crime Reports* figures.

## SUMMARY AND CONCLUSION

Russell's random sample revealed that of 930 women 18 years and older interviewed in San Francisco in 1978, 41 percent reported at least one experience that met the legal definition of rape or attempted rape common in most states at that time. When wife rape is included, the percentage of women with at least one experience of rape or attempted rape rises to 44 percent.

There is no reason to believe that the percentage of raped women would be higher in San Francisco than in other cities of comparable size.

While this prevalence figure for rape is very high, the unwillingness of some respondents to disclose their experiences provides reason to believe it is still an underestimation of the problem.

When focusing on the incidence rather than the prevalence of rape and attempted rape (i.e., the number of rapes and attempted rapes in the prior 12-month period), Russell found that the number of rapes reported to interviewers by adult women in San Francisco 12 months prior to the survey was 13 times higher than the total incidence reported by the *Uniform Crime Reports* for females of all ages in that city. (Based on the Russell survey data, it is estimated that the incidence rate of rape and attempted rape is approximately 3 percent, or 2,688 per 100,000 females.) A similar comparison with statistics gathered by the National Crime Survey in San Francisco (whose data include cases not reported to the police) reveals that the Russell incidence figure is 7 times higher.

Assuming that the Russell survey has implications for cities other than San Francisco, its findings on the incidence of rape and attempted rape provide concrete evidence of the inadequacy of current methods used to measure the magnitude of these crimes. More specifically, they suggest that the questionnaire and interviewing process employed by the National Crime Surveys need to be radically overhauled. For example, if respondents are expected to disclose their experiences of rape and attempted rape, the interview questions concerning rape must be changed. Interviewers should also be sensitized to the issue of rape, particularly the myths surrounding it.

The *Uniform Crime Reports* are not to blame for the fact that only a small minority of women report their experiences of rape and attempted rape to the police. However, the handling of rape reports, including the unfounding process, reveals gross insensitivity, sexist bias, and disdain for the right of women to seek redress through the criminal justice system.

## The Probability of Rape

In the autumn 1980 issue of *Signs,* Allan Griswold Johnson applied life-table analysis (a technique commonly used by demographers) to statistics on rape. On the basis of his analysis, Johnson constructed estimates of the probability that a woman will be the victim of sexual violence during her lifetime. Johnson concluded that "nationally, a *conservative* estimate is that, under current conditions, 20–30 percent of girls now twelve years old will suffer a violent sexual attack during the remainder of their lives" (1980, p. 145). Johnson went on to comment,

> It is difficult to believe that such widespread violence is the responsibility of a small lunatic fringe of psychopathic men. That sexual violence is so pervasive supports the view that the locus of violence against women rests squarely in the middle of what our culture defines as "normal" interaction between men and women. (1980, p. 146)

Albert Gollin took issue with Johnson's analysis on a number of counts. He was especially critical of what he perceived to be Johnson's "deeply committed personal stance," which Gollin inferred from Johnson's use of terminology such as "oppression of women" and "patriarchal society" (1980, p. 346). Gollin also expressed great skepticism about Johnson's conclusion that 20–30 percent of girls who are now 12 years old will suffer a violent sexual attack in their lifetimes. Gollin described this statement as "sensational news indeed, and if taken up and broadcast by the media or feminist groups, will return to haunt him" (1980, p. 348).

The objective of this chapter section is to evaluate the conclusions of both Johnson and Gollin. To this end, the life-table analysis methodology used by Johnson will be applied to the age-specific rape rates found in the Russell survey, so that Russell's results can be compared with Johnson's. Such an analysis rejects the simple assumption that

**TABLE 1.5**

**Lifetime Probability of Being a Victim of
Completed Rape for Females in San Francisco**

| Age* | Women Raped (N) | Women at Risk (N) | Age-Specific Probability of Completed Rape | Women Raped (in percentages) |
|------|-----|-----|-----|-----|
| 0–11 | 8 | 926** | .0086 | .86 |
| 12–15 | 24 | 918 | .0261 | 2.59 |
| 16–19 | 48 | 894 | .0537 | 5.18 |
| 20–24 | 76 | 824 | .0922 | 8.42 |
| 25–34 | 53 | 663 | .0799 | 6.63 |
| 35–49 | 9 | 423 | .0213 | 1.63 |
| 50–64 | 1 | 285 | .0035 | .26 |
| 65 and over | 0 | 156 | .0000 | — |
| Total | 219 | — | — | 25.57 |

*These age categories were chosen to match those in Johnson (1980, pp. 136–46).

**Since information on age is missing for four victims of completed rape, these cases were omitted from this analysis.

because 44 percent of Russell's random sample of women reported an experience of rape or attempted rape, the same percentage of women is likely to be raped in the future. Life-table analysis recognizes that the probabilities of being raped vary with age. Estimates based on age-specific rates of rape and attempted rape provide the basis for a more accurate prediction.

Johnson obtained his age-specific rape rates from data gathered by the National Crime Surveys in 1972 on 250,000 people in 13 cities. In contrast, Russell's survey data were gathered on 930 women in San Francisco in 1978; its age-specific rates were calculated from these data. The National Crime Surveys data are limited to individuals who were 12 years of age and older at the time of the interview, and to attacks that had occurred in the prior 12 months (Johnson, 1980, p.139). Russell's statistics are based on attacks that occurred at any time in the woman's life; hence the under-12 age group is included.

Despite these differences, Russell's statistics are comparable with Johnson's because both studies assume that women are at risk of attack over all ages, and that those risks cumulate throughout life.

Based on the assumption that the rape rate will remain the same in the future, the Russell survey data predict a 26 percent probability that a woman will be the victim of a completed rape at some time in her life (see Table 1.5).

TABLE 1.6

Lifetime Probability of Being a Victim of
Attempted or Completed Rape for Females in San Francisco

| Age | Women Who Experienced Attempted or Completed Rape (N) | Women at Risk (N) | Age-Specific Probability of Attempted or Completed Rape | Women Who Experienced Attempted or Completed Rape (in percentages) |
|---|---|---|---|---|
| 0–11 | 18 | 922* | .0195 | 1.95 |
| 12–15 | 68 | 904 | .0752 | 7.38 |
| 16–19 | 112 | 836 | .1340 | 12.15 |
| 20–24 | 114 | 708 | .1610 | 12.64 |
| 25–34 | 67 | 531 | .1262 | 8.31 |
| 35–49 | 17 | 340 | .0500 | 2.88 |
| 50–64 | 3 | 233 | .0188 | 1.03 |
| 65 and older | 0 | 122 | .0000 | — |
| Total | 399 | — | — | 46.34 |

*Since information on age is missing for eight victims of attempted and
completed rape, these cases were omitted from this analysis.

Both the statistics gathered by the FBI published annually in the
*Uniform Crime Reports,* and those collected by the LEAA-sponsored
National Crime Surveys on which Johnson based his analysis, combine incidents of rape and attempted rape. When Russell does the
same (making the same assumption of stability in the rape rate), there
is a 46 percent probability that a woman will be a victim of completed
or attempted rape at some time in her life (see Table 1.6).

Tables 1.5 and 1.6 also provide information on the rape rates for
women in different age groups (in the right-hand columns). For
example, Table 1.6 reveals the following:

The rate of attempted/completed rape for females 0–11 years of age was
approximately 2.0 percent;
the rate of attempted/completed rape for females 12–15 was 7.4 percent;
the rate of attempted/completed rape for females 16–19 was 12.2 percent;
the rate of attempted/completed rape for women 20–24 was 12.6 percent;
the rate of attempted/completed rape for women 25–34 was 8.3 percent;
the rate of attempted/completed rape for women 35–49 was 2.9 percent;
and the rate of attempted/completed rape for women 50–64 was 1.0
percent.

These figures reveal that women in the 16–19 and 20–24 age groups
are the most vulnerable to attempted or completed rape. This is par-

ticularly true since the later age groups cover periods of 10–15 years rather than only 4 or 5. Usually in life-table analyses equal-interval age groups are used; for purposes of comparison, Russell used the same age groups as Johnson did.

It is indeed shocking that 46 percent of American women are likely to be victims of attempted or completed rape at some time in their lives. It is even more shocking to realize that half of these women, according to the Russell data, will be raped again by a different assailant. As already mentioned, fully 50 percent of the 407 women who disclosed a rape or attempted rape experience reported having been raped more than once. To put it another way: Of those women who were attacked at least once, the average number of rape/attempted rape incidents with different assailants was close to two (1.92).

Russell's 46 percent probability figure may seem extraordinarily high compared to Johnson's figure of 8 percent (1980, p. 143). But Johnson raised his estimate to 20–30 percent from 8 percent on the assumption that only 30–40 percent of rapes and attempted rapes were reported to the Census Bureau interviewers on whose data he based his analysis (1980, p. 144). However, the main objective of the National Crime Surveys was in fact to obtain data on incidents that were not reported to the police, as well as on those that were reported. Hence, it is not legitimate for Johnson to assume that estimates of the percentage of rapes never reported to the police are also applicable to the National Crime Surveys.[10] How, then, can the large discrepancy between Johnson's results and Russell's be explained?

Quite simply: Johnson based his analysis upon the National Crime Surveys—the goal of which was to uncover information about unreported crimes. Johnson himself pointed out that the total rate of rape reported in the National Crime Surveys of 13 American cities was only slightly higher than the FBI's urban rates for the same year (1980, p. 139). Johnson's observation is further evidence of the National Crime Surveys' failure to obtain more accurate reports of rape than do the police. The point he makes seriously undercuts his own description of these National Crime Surveys as offering "high-quality survey data" (1980, pp. 137–138). Yet, he chose to draw his conclusions from this admittedly faulty data base.

## SUMMARY AND CONCLUSION

Data from Russell's random sample of 930 women in San Francisco provide a basis for estimating that there is at least a 26 percent probability that a woman in that city will become the victim of completed rape at some time in her life. And there is at least a 46 percent probability that she will become a victim of rape *or* attempted rape.

(The words "at least" are used because the incidence of rape appears to be increasing—a topic to be discussed at length in the next section.)

Johnson's analysis, and most particularly the data on which he based it, is certainly seriously flawed. But Russell's findings do indeed justify his conclusion (which so exercised Albert Gollin) about the normativeness of rape in this culture. Johnson is correct in his assertion that "sexual violence against women is part of the everyday fabric of American life" (1980, p. 146). This is a fact that feminists have been pointing out for the past 10 years (for example, Griffin, 1971; Brownmiller, 1975; Medea & Thompson, 1974; Russell, 1975).

## Is the Rape Rate Increasing
## in the United States?

As stated in the Introduction, up until 1980 the rape rate had been increasing steadily—often dramatically—for about 20 years (FBI, 1930-1982). Many experts speculated that the increase was due to more rapes being reported by victims and not a genuine increase in the number of rapes occurring. Since the *Uniform Crime Reports* are limited to cases reported to the police, this question cannot be answered by studying its findings.

Russell's survey was conducted once only. Yet, for the following reasons, its data offer a unique opportunity to evaluate whether or not the frequency of rape and other types of sexual assault is increasing.

Russell's data allow a comparison of the experiences of different groups of women of different ages. The respondents range in age from 18 to over 80, so rape experiences that occurred before 1900 may be compared to those that occurred through 1978 (when the survey was undertaken). Of particular interest is the ability to compare different cohorts of women (subgroups of women who were born around the same period of time and who are currently about the same age).

### COHORT RATES OF RAPE AND ATTEMPTED RAPE

Figure 1.1 shows the cumulative proportion of women who disclosed one or more experiences of rape or attempted rape at some time in their lives, for five cohorts of women:

Cohort 1: those born in 1918 and earlier, who were 60 and older at the time of the interviews;

Cohort 2: those born 1919–1928 who were in their 50s;
Cohort 3: those born 1929–1938 who were in their 40s;
Cohort 4: those born 1939–1948 who were in their 30s;
Cohort 5: those born 1949–1960 who were from 18 to 29 years of age.

When women disclosed more than one experience of rape or attempted rape, only their first experiences are tabulated here.

Figure 1.1 reveals that the percentage of women who reported a first experience of rape or attempted rape accelerates for all age groups during the late teenage years. There is also an acceleration in the women's early 20s, which slows during their late 20s. Although the acceleration drops greatly by age 30, increases in the percentage ever raped continue for some cohorts up to age 40, and even age 50.

Even more striking than the increases that occur for all cohorts is the strong linear relationship that exists between the current age of the cohort and the percentage of the cohort who reported being a victim of rape or attempted rape at any age. Rates of rape and attempted rape have steadily and substantially increased at each age for the women reporting.

While the oldest women reported a cumulative incidence of 21.5 percent, the comparable figure for the women between 50 and 59 is 33.9 percent, for women between 40 and 49 it is 46.2 percent, for women between 30 and 39 it is 58.7 percent, and for women between 18 and 29 it is already 53.2 percent.

These data predict that the rates for women currently in their teens and 20s will eventually be still higher. By age 20 the percentage reporting one or more completed or attempted rape has increased steadily from 11 percent of women 60 and older to almost 30 percent of the youngest group.

The enormous increase in rape rates for the younger age groups raises a question: Were the younger women in the sample simply more willing than the older women to admit having had such experiences? In order to ascertain whether this possibility accounts for the findings reported in Figure 1.1, it is useful to know whether the younger women are also reporting more experiences of child sexual abuse.

Figures 10.2 and 10.3 in Chapter 10 indicate no comparable linear relationship between the youthfulness of the cohort and high rates of child sexual abuse. Hence, it is unlikely that the higher rates of rape and attempted rape reported by the younger age groups is a result of their greater willingness to admit to such experiences.

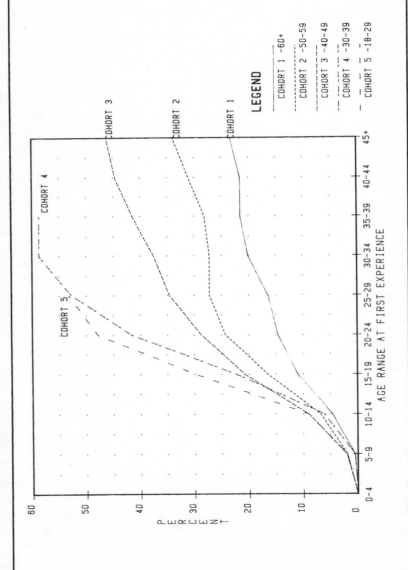

**Figure 1.1   Cumulative Proportion Reporting a First Experience of Rape/Attempted Rape for Five Cohorts of San Francisco Women**

### PERIOD RATES OF RAPE AND ATTEMPTED RAPE BY SPECIFIED AGES

Next to be analyzed are the fluctuations in the incidence of rape and attempted rape over time, specifically from 1931 to 1976. Figure 1.2 presents data on what are known as *period rates*. The same data plotted in Figure 1.1 are here reorganized by combining first experiences of rape or attempted rape reported by different groups of women, then focusing on the years in which the assault occurred. For example, these period rates combine the experiences of the women who were aged 5–9 years in 1949–1953, with those of women who were 10–14 in 1949–1953, and so on.

Figure 1.2 shows that the rates for rape and attempted rape have increased dramatically since 1931 for women between 15 and 20 years of age, as well as for those who are older than 20. This increase is not apparent for girls in the two youngest age groups. More specifically, the rape rate of girls who are younger than 10, or younger than 15, has not increased significantly.

It is important to be aware that this analysis is limited to forcible rape; it does not include statutory rape. Only cases of forced vaginal intercourse, or vaginal intercourse because of threat of physical force, or vaginal intercourse when the child was unable to consent because she was drugged, unconscious, or in some other way physically helpless, met the definition of rape used in this study. Considerable data were also obtained on sexual abuse of children not involving forcible rape. The second half of this book focuses on findings on a broader-based notion of child sexual abuse, including the trends over time.

The rape rates of women in all the other age groups have more than trebled in most instances. For example,

for women under 20, the rape rate increased from 11 percent in 1931 to 36 percent in 1976;

for women under 25, the rape rate increased from 14.6 percent in 1931 to 51 percent in 1976;

for women under 30, the rape rate increased from 16.4 percent in 1931 to 56 percent in 1976;

for women under 35, the rape rate increased from 20.1 percent in 1931 to 63.5 percent in 1976;

and for women under 40, the rape rate increased from 21.5 percent in 1931 to 63.5 percent in 1976.

The increases in the rape rates for women in the two older age groups were almost the same as for women under 40.

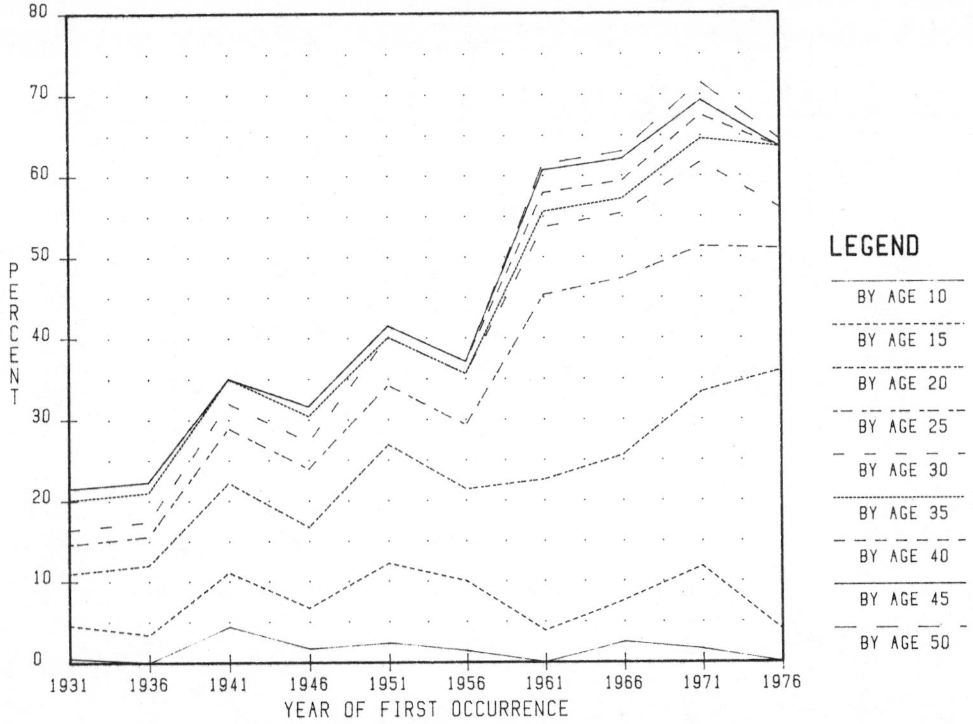

**Figure 1.2  Period Rates for Forcible Rape/Attempted Rape for Five Cohorts of San Francisco Women**

Peaks in the rape rates occurred in 1941, 1951, 1961, and 1971; dips occurred in the years that follow these peaks (1946, 1956, and 1976). All the dips prior to 1976 appear to have been temporary.

Similar period rates for incestuous and extrafamilial child sexual abuse will be presented in Chapter 10. Suffice it to say here that the peaks and dips for incestuous abuse appear to be exactly the opposite of those evident for rape and attempted rape. The peaks for incest occurred in 1936, 1946, and 1956, and the dips in 1941, 1951, and 1961. Hopefully other researchers will discover plausible explanations for these trends in the rates of sexual assault over time.

### SUMMARY

The Russell survey offers the first solid basis for determining whether or not the increase in reported rape over the years reflects a real increase in the rape rates. The tragic finding of this survey is an alarming increase in the true rape rate over the years. When tracing the rape rates for five different cohorts of women, it is evident that the rates become significantly higher for every younger cohort. By age 20, the percentage reporting one or more completed or attempted rape has increased steadily from 11 percent of the women who were 60 and older, to almost 30 percent of the youngest group.

The cumulative incidence of rape for women between 30 and 39 is 58.7 percent and for women between 18 and 29, it is already 53.2 percent.

These increases are also evident when tracing the rates of rape and attempted rape between 1931 and 1976, except for a slight decline between 1971 and 1976.

The different analyses offered in this chapter all show in various ways that rape in the United States has truly reached epidemic proportions.

## The Prevalence of Rape
## by Different Types of Perpetrators

The authors of the influential National Commission on the Causes and Prevention of Violence argued that "the kind of personal relationship between victim and offender is probably more important in forcible rape than in any of the other major violent acts" (Mulvihill et al., vol. 11, 1969, p. 219). The basis for their conclusion was that the more intimate the relationship, the more likely the victim is to be held responsible for the rape. Support for this conclusion is provided by the fact that only in the latter half of the 1970s did a few states acknowledge that rape can and does occur in the most intimate of all relationships—marriage (Russell, 1982).

It is surprising, then, that the authors of the federal government Commission Report were so credulous about the validity of their finding that as many as 53 percent of the reported rapes were by strangers (Mulvihill et al., vol 11, 1969, p. 217). They argued that "considerable justification does appear to exist for the fear that the offender will be a stranger" (1969, p. 217). A more realistic approach would anticipate that many victims of rape by nonstrangers do not report being attacked, and that the reports of those who do are more often unfounded by the police.

The percentages of different kinds of victim-offender relationships reported by the federal government commission were as follows: 53 percent of the victims reported being raped by a stranger, 29 percent by an acquaintance, 7 percent by a family member (other than a husband), 3 percent by a neighbor, 3 percent by a close friend or lover, and the remaining 5 percent by some other category of person or where the relationship was unknown (1969, p. 217). The federal Commission also reported that these results "differed little between blacks and whites" (1969, p. 220).

Sedelle Katz and Mary Ann Mazur report the percentages of stranger rape in 18 different studies. These percentages range from 27 percent to 91 percent (1979, p. 110–111). This wide range may be explained by the extent of underdisclosure of less "acceptable" rapes that studies reporting very high percentages of stranger rape suffer from. Victims are less likely to disclose, for example, rapes perpetrated by husbands, lovers, dates, friends, and other relatives. (This observation will be substantiated in Chapter 3.)

Of the few people who have actually written about wife rape, several have speculated that rape by husbands occurs more frequently than rape by other kinds of assailants (Gelles, 1977; Hunt, 1979; Groth, 1979, 1980; Barry, 1980; Frieze, 1983). Richard Gelles wrote in 1977, "[W]e believe that a woman is most likely to be physically forced into having sexual intercourse by her husband" (1977, p. 345). Morton Hunt was less tentative. "Incredible as it may seem, *more women are raped by their husbands each year than by strangers, acquaintances or other persons*" (1979, p.24, emphasis in original).

The correctness of these speculations depends on the way the comparison is made. Since the Russell study of rape is the only one (aside from the National Crime Surveys) based on a random sample, it offers the best available information on the prevalence of rape by different kinds of perpetrators. According to the Russell survey, rapes by strangers, acquaintances, friends, dates, lovers and ex-lovers, authority figures, and relatives (aside from husbands), when combined into one category, reveal that many more women have been raped by men in these categories combined than have been raped by husbands. Of the 930 women interviewed 44 percent had been subjected to at least one rape or attempted rape in the course of their lives, but only 8 percent of the entire sample, which includes women who had never been married, had been raped by a husband.[11]

However, it is more meaningful to divide nonmarital rape into several categories than to combine all the rapists who are not strangers into one category. For this reason, the rates for completed rape (excluding attempted rape) have been broken out by 10 different types of rapists. Table 1.7 indicates that 8 percent of the women in the sample were raped by a husband or ex-husband[12]—more than any of the other nine types of perpetrators. Of the 930 women 5 percent were raped by an acquaintance and 5 percent by a lover or ex-lover; 3 percent were raped by a stranger; 3 percent by a date; and 3 percent by a friend of the respondent. Two percent were raped by boyfriends and 2 percent by authority figures; 1 percent by a friend of the family; and 1 percent by relatives other than husbands or ex-husbands.

When cases of completed and attempted rape are taken together, as is done in the official statistics, the picture changes considerably. Table 1.8 shows that the more intimate the relationship, the more likely it is that attempts at rape will succeed. The number of *attempted* rapes by husbands, lovers and boyfriends are all low in comparison to the number of attempted rapes by nonintimates. So, when rape and attempted rape are combined, acquaintances become the most prevalent type of rapist: 14 percent of the 930 women were victims of rape or attempted rape by acquaintances, 12 percent by dates, 11 percent by strangers, 8 percent by husbands or ex-husbands, 6 percent by lovers or ex-lovers, 6 percent by authority figures, 6 percent by friends of the respondents, 3 percent by boyfriends, 3 percent by relatives other than husbands, 2 percent by friends of the family.

When the category of acquaintance rape/attempted rape is expanded to include rape by the respondents' friends, friends of their families, dates, boyfriends, lovers, ex-lovers, and authority figures, as well as acquaintances, then 35 percent of Russell's sample of respondents were raped at least once by an acquaintance. This compares with 11 percent by strangers, and 3 percent by relatives (other than husbands or ex-husbands).

### TABLE 1.7

**Prevalence of Completed Rape by Relationship Between Victim and Perpetrator**

| Relationship with Victim at Time of First Rape | Number of Women | Percentage of Women in Sample | Number of Incidents with Different Perpetrators[1] | Percentage of Incidents[1] |
|---|---|---|---|---|
| Stranger | 31 | 3 | 38 | 12 |
| Acquaintance | 47 | 5 | 55 | 17 |
| Friend of family | 8 | 1 | 8 | 2 |
| Friend of respondent | 25 | 3 | 26 | 8 |
| Date | 26 | 3 | 27 | 8 |
| Boyfriend | 15 | 2 | 15 | 5 |
| Lover or ex-lover[2] | 43 | 5 | 47 | 15 |
| Authority figure[3] | 20 | 2 | 21 | 7 |
| Husband or ex-husband[4] | 71 | 8 | 73 | 23 |
| Other relative | 13 | 1 | 13 | 4 |
| Total | | | 323 | 101 |

1. Many women were the victims of rape more than once by different perpetrators. A group or pair rape is counted as one incident. Multiple attacks by the same person are counted as one incident.
2. Lover was defined as a friend, date, or boyfriend with whom voluntary sexual intercourse had occurred prior to the first rape experience.
3. Examples of authority figures are doctors, teachers, employers, ministers, therapists, policemen, and—for children—much older persons.
4. Rape by husbands and ex-husbands is presented here as a percentage of the entire sample, not only of the women who have been married.

**TABLE 1.8**

**Prevalence of Rape and Attempted Rape (Combined) by Relationship Between Victim and Perpetrator**

| | A | B | C | D |
|---|---|---|---|---|
| Relationship with Victim at Time of First Rape | Number of Women | Percentage of Women in Sample | Number of Incidents with Different Perpetrators[1] | Percentage of Incidents[1] |
| Stranger | 100 | 11 | 122 | 16 |
| Acquaintance | 134 | 14 | 178 | 23 |
| Friend of family | 15 | 2 | 17 | 2 |
| Friend of respondent | 54 | 6 | 64 | 7 |
| Date | 112 | 12 | 128 | 16 |
| Boyfriend | 27 | 3 | 29 | 4 |
| Lover or ex-lover[2] | 54 | 6 | 61 | 8 |
| Authority figure[3] | 57 | 6 | 65 | 8 |
| Husband or ex-husband[4] | 78 | 8 | 80 | 10 |
| Other relative | 29 | 3 | 32 | 4 |
| Total | 776 | | | 98 |

1. Many women were the victims of rape more than once by different perpetrators. A group or pair rape is counted as one incident. Multiple attacks by the same person are counted as one incident.
2. Lover was defined as a friend, date, or boyfriend with whom voluntary sexual intercourse had occurred prior to the first rape experience.
3. Examples of authority figures are doctors, teachers, employers, ministers, therapists, policemen, and—for children—much older persons.
4. Rape by husbands and ex-husbands is here presented as a percentage of the entire sample, not only women who have been married.

It could be argued that this is not an entirely reasonable comparison. It is possible for *any* woman to be raped by any or all of the following: a stranger, an acquaintance, a friend, an authority figure, a relative other than a husband, and, assuming the woman had ever had a date, a boyfriend, and a lover, she could be raped by any of these categories of people too. But only women who have ever been married can be raped by a husband. If rape and attempted rape by husbands and ex-husbands were calculated as a percentage of women who had ever been married (rather than as a percentage of the whole sample), then the prevalence of wife rape increases from 8 percent to 12 percent. This percentage places rape and attempted rape by husbands second only to rape and attempted rape by acquaintances.

Other ways of analyzing the prevalence of rape by different kinds of perpetrators are discussed in *Rape in Marriage* (Russell, 1982, pp. 65–68). For example, the analysis just undertaken ignores the fact that rape by intimates frequently occurs more than once, in contrast to rape by strangers or acquaintances.

## Conclusion: Rape as an Epidemic

The magnitude of the rape problem revealed by the Russell survey is supported by a growing body of research. For example, Eugene Kanin's studies of male sexual aggression and the victimization of females over the past two decades reveal the widespread nature of forced sex in the high school and college-age populations (Kanin, 1957, 1970, 1971; Kirkpatrick & Kanin, 1957).

Approximately 62 percent of a group of female first-year university students reported "experiencing offensive male sexual aggression during the year prior to university entrance" (Kanin, 1957, p. 197). Forceful attempts at intercourse were reported by 21 percent, and 9 percent reported "more violent attempts at sexual intercourse accompanied by 'menacing threats or coercive infliction of physical pain'" (1957, p. 198). Similar figures were obtained for a more varied group of college students (Kirkpatrick & Kanin, 1957, p. 53).

These studies cannot be regarded as representative samples from a defined student universe—as the authors point out (Kirkpatrick & Kanin, 1957, p. 53). But if comparable questions were asked of a randomly drawn sample of women, the studies indicate that a much higher incidence and prevalence of rape victimization than expected would likely be found in the female population.

More recently, Neil Malamuth, Scott Haber, and Seymour Feshbach asked a sample of 53 male students to read a "rape story"

(1980). As is customary in much psychological research, the students were not drawn in any random sampling process; they volunteered to participate in the research as part of their work in introductory psychology courses. After the male students had read the rape story, they were asked whether they personally would be likely to act as the rapist did in the same circumstances. The identical question was then repeated, this time with an assurance that they would not be punished. The results:

> On a response scale ranging from 1 to 5 (with 1 denoting "none at all" and 5 "very likely"), 17 percent of the men specified 2 or above when asked if they would emulate such behavior "under the same circumstances"; but a total of 51 percent responded that they might do it if they were assured that they would not be caught. (Feshbach & Malamuth, 1978, pp. 116–117)

Feshbach and Malamuth point out that the men who reported some likelihood of rape "also found the rape story more sexually arousing, believed that the victim enjoyed it, and were more likely to try to justify the act" (1978, p. 117). In interpreting these results, it is helpful to know the content of the rape story:

> An approximately 500 word passage was written depicting a male student raping a female student:

> "Bill soon caught up with Susan and offered to escort her to her car. Susan politely refused him. Bill was enraged by the rejection. 'Who the hell does this bitch think she is, turning me down,' Bill thought to himself as he reached into his pocket and took out a Swiss army knife. With his left hand he placed the knife at her throat. 'If you try to get away, I'll cut you,' said Bill. Susan nodded her head, her eyes wild with terror."

> The story then depicted the rape. There was a description of sexual acts with the victim continuously portrayed as clearly opposing the assault. (Malamuth et al., 1980, p. 124)

This study has since been replicated, mostly on college students in areas such as Los Angeles and Stanford in California, and Winnipeg in Canada. Malamuth comments on these different studies as follows:

> While, as might be expected, there was some variability in the distribution of responses across studies, in general there was a great deal of consistency in that a sizable percentage of the respondents indicated some likelihood of raping. Across these varied studies, *an average of about 35% of males indicated any likelihood at all of raping* (i.e., a 2 or above on the scale) and an average of about 20% indicated higher likelihoods (i.e., a 3 or above). (1981b, p. 140, emphasis added)

Of these male college students 35 percent admit that there is some likelihood that they would commit a violent rape of a strange woman who had merely rebuffed a mild advance if they were assured of getting away with it. One wonders how much the percentage might increase if the story were about a man who forced intercourse on his wife after she had declined his sexual advances for over a month.

Or consider the likely response to another story: A man invites a woman he perceives as very attractive, and whom he believes to be "promiscuous," out for a date. He wines and dines her in anticipation of sexual intercourse. When he initiates physical contact with her at his home later in the evening, she turns him down in a rude and abrupt fashion. What percentage of men might rape a woman in such a situation if assured of no punishment? A precise answer awaits the conducting of such an experiment. However, it's safe to predict that the percentage would be very much higher than the 35 percent of college students who indicated some willingness to rape a stranger at knife point—if they could get away with it.

Another noteworthy feature of the methodology of these studies is that the word "rape" was specifically used in questioning these men. How much higher than 35 percent might the percentage have been if this word had been avoided? How much higher might it be, for example, if the students had been asked whether they might be willing to force or threaten use of force to obtain intercourse with an acquaintance or a date?

Recent research by John Briere and his associates (to be reported in Chapter 5) reveals that, when asked if they would force a female to do something sexual she really did not want to do, as well as the same question concerning rape, 60 percent of a sample of college men indicated some likelihood of either rape or force or both "given the right circumstances" (1981).

Although male college students are clearly not representative of the male population at large, many researchers in this field would argue that college students are less inclined to rape than non-college students (e.g., Brownmiller, 1975).

In a study of high school students, Roseann Giarusso and her colleagues report that more than 50 percent of the high school males they interviewed believed it was acceptable "for a guy to hold a girl down and force her to have sexual intercourse in instances such as when 'she gets him sexually excited' or 'she says she's going to have sex with him and then changes her mind'" (1979).

Neil Malamuth, John Briere, Joe Ceniti, James Check, and other co-researchers argue that their findings "reinforce the contention of feminist writers that there exists within the general population many males with a propensity towards sexual violence" (Briere et al., 1981, p. 2).

This finding is consistent with the very high prevalence of rape found in Russell's survey. The considerable percentage of men who acknowledge some likelihood that they might rape if they could get away with it, plus the widespread prevalence of actual rape victims revealed by Russell's random sample survey in San Francisco, suggest that continued efforts to explain rape as a psychopathological phenomenon are inappropriate. How could it be that all of these rapes are being perpetrated by a tiny segment of the male population? Clearly, rape must be seen as primarily a social disease.

Rape and attempted rape of females in the United States is a particularly traumatic form of sexist violence. Research now shows that both rape and attempted rape occur in epidemic proportions and in a pattern that is escalating over time. Knowledge of the prevalence of these crimes should stimulate strenuous efforts to find a truly effective means of preventing rape and other sexual assaults.

## Notes

1. By the *Uniform Crime Reports'* definition, robbery involves force, threat of force, violence, or "putting the victim in fear."

2. See Landon Jones' *Great Expectations: America and the Baby Boom Generation* for a discussion of the correlation between the baby boom and the crime boom (1980, pp. 142-150).

3. Galvin and Polk also appear to be unaware of a key study that shows that 56 percent of reported rapes in Philadelphia were never recorded as rapes in the police statistics (1979). The findings of this study—to be elaborated on later in this chapter—provide even stronger evidence that these researchers are seriously mistaken in their conclusion that "Rape has no unique pattern of attrition, clearly distinguished from that experienced in other serious felony cases" (1983, p. 152).

4. The exact ratio was 42.5 per 100,000 population (estimated rate) compared to 11.6 per 100,000 population (reported rape rate; Ennis, 1967, p. 8).

5. The rape rate per 100,000 people in San Francisco in 1978 was higher than some major cities, for example: New York, 55; Washington D.C., 70; Chicago, 45; but lower than others, for example: Detroit, 107; Atlanta, 139; Memphis, 103 (FBI, 1979).

6. Comparison of a fourth variable, household composition, was problematic since the 1980 census changed its previous methods of gathering data on this factor. Hence, the Russell survey lacked the information necessary to make household composition exactly comparable with the census.

As closely as could be determined, Russell's sample tends to live in slightly less populated households (i.e., 2.10 per household as opposed to 2.19 in the 1980 census). However the census data do not show the proportion who live in various size households, other than one member versus two or more member households. There were slightly fewer single-person households in Russell's sample (42.6 versus 35.0 in the census) and there were somewhat more married couple households (39.4 in the sample versus 35.1). In addition, 16.2 percent of the households in Russell's sample were headed by females as opposed to 10.3 percent in the census data. The large gay male population in San Francisco makes it difficult to adjust Russell's figures since her sample is all female. The census data on household composition is not broken out separately for each sex.

7. Females of 16 and 17 years of age were placed in the same category. So, to obtain an approximation of the number of females who were 17, the total for this category (8,250) was divided by two.

8. This figure is obtained by dividing the total population of females 17 years and over in San Francisco in 1978 (283,575) by Russell's total sample size (930 women), then multiplying by the number of nonmarital rapes reported by the surveyed women as occurring in San Francisco in the prior 12 months (25).

9. For example, Chappell, Geis, Schafer, and Siegel set out to explain the considerable difference in rape rates between Boston and Los Angeles (7.7 and 35.4 per 100,000 population in 1972, respectively). They found that cases of bottom-pinching were counted as forcible rape in Los Angeles but not in Boston. However, the Boston police included a number of incidents in which girls of eight and nine years were molested by equally young boys as cases of forcible rape although sexual intercourse did not occur. In Los Angeles, such cases were "handled by the juvenile division and classified under the more amorphous rubric of 'delinquency'" (1977).

10. Johnson specifically refers to Brownmiller's estimate that "only one in five incidents are actually reported" to the police (1980).

11. In contrast to the definition of wife rape used in *Rape in Marriage* (Russell, 1982) which includes forced oral or anal intercourse, the narrower, more traditional legal definition is here applied to make it comparable with rape by other kinds of perpetrators.

12. Three ex-husbands are included in all the analyses of wife rape, since the dynamics of rape by them appeared so similar to rape by the 86 husbands.

2

# MALE RAPE AND FEMALE RAPISTS

All of the information presented so far has focused on female rape victims. Until recently, the notion that only females could be raped was embedded in the laws of most states. Rape was traditionally defined as penile-vaginal penetration by force or threat of force. Penetration of a woman not married to the perpetrator who was unable to consent due to unconsciousness or some other form of physical helplessness was also defined as rape. Only in recent years have many states recognized the existence of male rape victims.

## *Male Rape by Females*

Even before the laws in some states recognized the possibility of male rape, a few women were convicted of rape each year in the United States. Approximately .8 percent of those arrested for forcible rape each year are females (FBI, *Uniform Crime Reports*).

No explanation of these cases is offered in the *Uniform Crime Reports,* but it is most likely that they involved women cooperating with, or assisting men in, the raping of another woman. Judging from the few cases of this kind that get reported in the newspapers, these women are rarely (if ever) the instigators of the rape. Frequently, they are obeying men's orders—or they are in a subserviant relationship to one or more male rapist. A recent shocking example of this phenomenon involved murder as well as rape. Susanne Perrin of Oakland helped her husband, who repeatedly raped and strangled her (although never fatally), to hunt down other potential victims (Russell, 1982, pp. 280–282).

In order to ascertain the number of female rapists in the Russell survey, the definition of rape was broadened to include forced oral or anal sex, or oral or anal sex because of a physical threat, or when the victim was unable to consent because she was unconscious, drugged, or in some other way totally physically helpless. Five respondents reported being raped by another female—as defined here—which constitutes only .7 percent of the total number of rapes.

It must be remembered that the Russell survey did not define similar experiences of forced oral or anal sex as rape for men. Had these experiences been included for males, the percentage of female rapists would have been even lower than .7 percent.

In three out of five of the cases of female rape, the women participated in the attack with one or more male rapists. These cases will be described briefly here because it is so rare to find rape by women described in the literature.

In one case two of the rapists were male and one was female. The woman participated by pulling the victim's hair when she was struggling to resist being raped by one of the men. The victim bit her as well as the penis of one of the men. However, this victim was not attacked sexually by the other woman.

In the second case the woman participated in the actual sexual attack along with two men. The victim, who was drugged, said, "I was out most of the time but I would wake up periodically and they were all using me. I know they were raping me. I woke up once and the woman was on top of me."

In the third case, the respondent was attacked by her employer and a female acquaintance of his. They drugged her and she passed out. "All I know is I was on the bed and she went down on me," the respondent explained. This, then, was a case of being raped by virtue of an inability to consent.

The remaining two cases of rape by women did not involve men. In one case both victim and perpetrator, who were friends, were drunk. The victim described the following situation: "I was practically out of it, till I realized I was in my bedroom nude and she was on top of me. She made an attempt at oral sex."

In the fifth case, the respondent was asleep when a woman houseguest got in bed with her and "grabbed at my crotch with her mouth." Both these cases were rape due to inability to consent rather than rape by force or threat of force.

In 1982, William Masters and Philip Sarrel described as a sexual myth the widespread belief that "it would be almost impossible for a man to achieve or maintain sexual arousal if he were assaulted by a woman." These researchers presented clinical documentation on only four men who had been raped by one or more women who threatened them with physical violence or death. They acknowledged that "female rapes of males are rare." Still, they argued that because of the myth of impossibility "men who have been sexually assaulted by women have been extremely loath to admit this experience to anyone" (1982). Masters and Sarrel concluded that cases of males raped by females are even more underreported than are cases of females raped by males.

Case histories of men raped by women have not previously appeared in the scientific literature. Masters stated that acknowledgment of such assaults is long overdue. He and Sarrel reported that "the raped males reacted emotionally and physically to their experiences in the same way as female victims. Each male developed immediate impotence and loss of self-esteem and confidence, and each rejected intimacy" (1982).

Reporter Alan Petrucelli misquoted one of the most noted experts in the field of sexual assault (who prefers to be nameless) as saying that "one out of every four male rape cases reported involves a woman as the rapist" (Petrucelli, 1982, p. 68). The quote continues: "And if we include marital rape, incestuous relationships and the sexual abuse of younger boys by older women ('the baby-sitter syndrome'), the numbers increase." Petrucelli proceeds to argue that "because female-male rape is a relatively new phenomenon, the effects are usually more devastating" (1982, p. 69).

It is distressing that such reputable experts on rape are being used, and in the last case even misquoted, to bolster such an extreme exaggeration of the problem of rape of males by females. (See Rosenfeld's article, "When Women Rape Men," *Omni,* December 1981, for another example of this phenomenon.) Hopefully, the problem of rape of males by other males as well as by females can be acknowledged, studied and treated without being exaggerated and/or used to blunt recognition of the far more extensive problem of rape of females by males.

## Male Rape in Prison

One of the first books in recent years to focus on rape of prison inmates was Anthony Scacco's *Rape in Prison* (1975). Scacco repeatedly emphasized that rape in prison "is not the act of homosexual perverts" but rather that "heterosexually-oriented males are partaking in this kind of conduct" (1975, p. 4). He argued that rape in prison "is an act whereby one male (or group of males) seeks testimony to what he considers is an outward validation of his masculinity" (1975, p. 3).

How does an act usually regarded as homosexual become one that actually validates heterosexuality *if* it is actively sought and imposed on a member of the same sex? The rules of patriarchal culture explain this apparent paradox. Even homosexual rape is seen as manly behavior, because it is a violent act of conquest. The victim of sexual assault, by being used and controlled and forced to submit against his will, is thereby transformed into a member of one of the lower castes—a punk, a queer, a female. "We're going to take your manhood" is how it's often put (1975, p. 52); and further: "A male who fucks a male is a double male" (1975, p. 86).

In the past few years, feminist researchers on the rape of females outside of prison have drawn a connection between the traditional male sex role and rape (although no feminists are given credit for this by Scacco[1]). (These theories will be presented in Chapter 5.) Scacco's theory about rape in male prisons applies this sex role analysis. For example, he argues that sex role analysis is crucial to understanding the relationship between "the keepers and those who are kept." Both groups, he maintains, "are attempting to prove their masculinity to one another while simultaneously seeking not to be emasculated in the eyes of one another" (1975, p.77).

Daniel Lockwood, author of *Prison Sexual Violence*, considers a report on male sexual aggression in the Philadelphia prison system to be the most significant investigation of rape in prison to date (1980, p. 5). The study was carried out by the Police Department and the District Attorney's office, and received widespread coverage by the media (Davis, 1968). According to this report, of the 60,000 inmates who went through Philadelphia's prison system in a 26-month period, an estimated 2,000 men (3.33 percent) were subjected to sexual assaults (Lockwood, 1980, p. 7).

Commenting on this situation, A. J. Davis maintained that "virtually every slightly built young man committed by the courts is sexually approached within hours after his admission to prison" (1968, p. 3). C. Weiss and D. J. Friar believe that the rape rate found in the Philadelphia study applies to other prisons in the United States (1975). However, Lockwood argues that data fail to support this claim (1980, p. 8). He concludes that "no estimates exist for the percentages of prisoners who have been targets of aggressors" (p. 8).

Despite Lockwood's words of caution, in the most recently published collection of articles on prison rape, Scacco maintains the following:

> In today's world the judge who sentences a young person to reform school or prison passes male rape on him as surely as the sentence.

Every inmate has a very short time, once inside, to pick a "wolf" (a tough protector) or face gang rape, becoming the "girl" of the institution, or death. (1982, p. vii)

More and better research is needed to determine the true prevalence of prison rape. Where significant variations in prevalence are found in different institutions, an effort should be made to discover the factors related to high or low rates. Policies designed to control and prevent prison rape must then be implemented.

### Male Rape of Males Outside Prison

Anthony Scacco argues that the phenomenon of male rape in prison could not exist "if it did not first exist on the streets. Where kids in school had once paid off the local bully with their lunch money, by 1975 they were using their bodies. The sexual domination of other males had become a fashionable street means to show off one's *machismo"* (1982, p. vii).

Scacco may be correct in his contention that rape by males of other males is quite commonplace outside of as well as inside prison. But there is remarkably little data to substantiate his claim. None is offered even in his own book (mistakingly titled *Male Rape,* 1982, as if it will deal with the rape of males outside of prison).

Sedelle Katz and Mary Ann Mazur summarized the research findings about rape, providing the following information on male rape outside of prison:

> In the general population, only a small percentage of male rapes are reported. Two rape studies (Hursch & Selkin, 1974; Massey et al., 1971) each reported that 4% of victims were male, while Hayman et al. (1972) reported 5%.
>
> However, rape may be even more unreported among males than among females. One study (Schultz & DeSavage, 1975, p. 80) found that among college men aged 19–24, 30% (6 of 20) admitted anonymously in a confidential questionnaire that they had been victims of "at least one act of criminally forced sodomy" (20%) or violent attempted sodomy (10%) "while on campus or the surrounding community." None were ever reported to the authorities. Even though the number of subjects in this study was small, and, therefore, limited, the data revealed that adult male college students were vulnerable to rape (30%), but not as frequently as were females in this study (50%). (1979, pp. 33–34)

A sample size of only 20 males, as was the case for this study by Schultz and DeSavage, is far too small to warrent much confidence.

Because of the scarcity of data on male victims, as well as for other reasons, Nicholas Groth and Ann Burgess conclude their article on male rape as follows: "As a result, then, of a combination of cultural, social, legal, and psychological issues, male rape remains one of the most unaddressed issues in our society" (1980, p. 810). Groth, currently editing a manuscript on the sexual abuse of males, observes that "The assumption appears to be that the adult male does not get raped unless he has the misfortune to wind up in prison, and that once he has reached adulthood, a male is safe from sexual assault" (1979, p. 119).

Groth points out that police statistics appear to support this assumption. He reports that out of 355 rapes reported in Boston in 1976, only 4 (1 percent) were males of 17 years or older (1979, p. 119). Groth raises the possibility that "even more than women, the stigma of being sexually assaulted discourages men from reporting such events" (1979, p. 119).

Drawing on his population of incarcerated rapists, Groth analyzed data in his own small sample of 20 males who had sexually assaulted other males. He also studied 7 nonincarcerated men who had been raped by other men, none of whom had been convicted for this offense (1979, p. 119). Of these rapists 16 had assaulted men in the community, and 4 in prison. Six of the raped men had been assaulted in the community, and one in prison.

Groth reported that "one-third (9 or 33%) of the men who sexually assaulted other men were heterosexually oriented. One-quarter (7 or 26%) of them could be described as bisexual, and a small minority (2 or 7%) appeared to be homosexually oriented" (1979, p. 124). The sexual orientations of the remaining 33% were presumably unknown.

Unfortunately, Groth's analysis of these data is fraught with problems. First, he combines information gathered about the offenders from the victims as well as from the offenders themselves. This is acceptable for variables such as sex, race, or estimated age, but sexual orientation is another matter, particularly when "the majority of offenders (15 or 56%) were total strangers to their victims" (1979, p. 120). Second, Groth fails to explain how he defined bisexual, or how the offender's sexual preference was ascertained. Identifying as bisexual is more acceptable in a homophobic society than identifying as homosexual. These problems combined with his small and highly unrepresentative sample raise serious doubts about the validity of his conclusions about the sexual orientation of men who rape other men.

Groth concluded that the reasons men rape men are similar to the reasons men rape women (1979, p. 126). None of these men had to rape to obtain sexual gratification. All were sexually active and had access to consenting relationships at the time of their offenses. "Sexual desire, then, did not seem to be the paramount force prompting their assaults," Groth inferred. "Instead, rape could be understood as the sexual expression of aggressive issues and motives" (1979, p. 126).

Groth's analysis raises a question: Why is it overwhelmingly women who are the victims of rape in the community? If the sex of the victim were immaterial, and exactly the same needs could be met by raping males as by raping females—as Groth infers—then there would not be such a skewed distribution of rape victimization. In focusing on male rape, one must not lose sight of the fact that the vast majority of heterosexual rapists outside of prison choose women as victims.

Groth points out an interesting difference between the impact of rape on male and female victims. "Women victims do not report that they feel less of a woman for having been raped, but men victims do often state that they feel that the offender took their manhood" (1979, p. 139). Consequently, Groth maintains, "a male victim may show increased need for sexual activity with a woman to reestablish and reaffirm his manhood" (1979, p. 139).

If no willing woman is available to these men, are they more likely to rape a woman, or are they less likely because of their victimization experience? No answer to this question is available at this time, since the appropriate studies have not been conducted.

## Rape of Men by Homosexual Men

In a 923-page book on *Sex Offenders: An Analysis of Types,* Paul Gebhard and his colleagues at the Institute for Sex Research in Indiana reported on their investigation of inmates convicted of sex offenses. Their research excluded the category of homosexual aggressors on the grounds that "the use of force is rare in homosexual activity" (1965, p. 11).

A more recent work, *Homosexualities: A Study of Diversity Among Men and Women* by Alan Bell and Martin Weinberg, is described as an official publication of the Institute for Sex Research. Its authors maintain that

> rape and sexual violence more frequently occur in a heterosexual than a homosexual context. Rape (outside of prisons) generally involves sexual attacks made by men upon women, while the relatively rare violence occurring in a homosexual context is usually the result of male youths "hunting queers" or a man's guilt and disgust over a sexual episode just concluded. (1978, p. 230)

It seems unlikely that rape and other forms of violence do not pose even a small problem in the gay male community. Bell and Weinberg themselves present ample evidence that lesbians are more like heterosexual women in their sexuality and in their relationships than they are like homosexual men, and that homosexual men are similarly more like heterosexual men (1978). It is strange indeed that these researchers are so offhanded about the finding that relatively little violence occurs in male homosexual relationships. If the finding is true, it certainly deserves an attempt at explanation.

Even if it is true that rape and other sexual violence occur much more frequently in a heterosexual than a homosexual context—as Bell and Weinberg maintain—given the magnitude of the heterosexual rape problem, this still leaves room for a significant amount of rape by homosexual men. The politically controversial nature of this issue appears to have resulted in a nearly universal unwillingness to discuss it. It is ironic indeed that the relatively insignificant problem of female rape of men has received more attention in the literature than rape of men by homosexual men.

The frequency of rape by gay men is an important question both theoretically, as well as because of the distress it causes. Ignoring the issue is destructive.

Let us consider why there may be proportionately much less rape by gay men than heterosexual men.

(1) Because there is easy access to consensual sex of all kinds through bath houses, gay bars (including leather and SM bars), and so-called adult bookstores and movie houses that cater to gay males.
(2) Because men are more difficult to overpower than women, due to their greater strength, better trained fighting skills, and greater willingness to use them.
(3) Because rape is a misogynist act of hatred toward women. Hatred of men by other men is not deeply imbedded in the culture, and therefore not acted out by rape of men by other men.

It may be true that in sizable gay male communities, such as the Castro district in San Francisco, that there is easy access to consensual sex of all kinds. However, many gay men do not live in or near such communities. Furthermore, rape is not motivated by sexual desire alone, but by the desire to dominate, control, humiliate, and so on. Why would gay men be immune to the factors responsible for the development in heterosexual men of such desires? Bell and Weinberg show that the sexuality of gay and heterosexual men has much in common (1978). Why would it be so totally different in this one regard?

The fact that men are more difficult to victimize than women seems a more plausible explanation for why gay men may rape less than heterosexual men. However, there are obviously marked disparities in strength and fighting skills among men that could be exploited. Men in vulnerable situations can also be taken advantage of, such as when they are drunk, drugged, asleep, or ill. This factor could also lead to more rape of men being done by pairs or groups of other men.

Furthermore, Groth and Burgess may be right to dismiss the significance of this factor in explaining the lower incidence of male rape. They maintain that

> Although it is commonly believed that a male is powerful enough to defend himself from a sexual assault, he is in fact susceptible to the same techniques by which assailants gain control over their female victims. In many cases a combination of entrapment, intimidation, and brute strength were employed in the commission of the assault. (1980, p. 809)

Rape of a woman by a man is frequently a misogynist act. But studies of rape in prison show that this is not the only cause of rape. Many men appear to have no problem victimizing men rather than women when they lose access to women (see earlier section of this chapter). And the occurrence of rape of men by other men outside prison shows that male victims are not only used as substitutes for women.

The literature on rape in prison poses another theoretical problem of relevance here. Experts seem to be agreed that the rapists in prison are all heterosexual. For example, Anthony Scacco writes: "The issue, categorically, is not homosexuality but heterosexual brutality" (1982, p. vii). It is usually presumed that gay men in prison are always forced into the victim role. But what about very big, strong, tough gay men who are not perceived as gay, and who are able to successfully avoid the victim role? Do these men never rape, while the big, strong, tough heterosexual men do? Or do researchers as well as fellow prisoners assume that every big, strong man who does not fit the stereotype of a gay man must be heterosexual? The latter would seem to be the case. This assumption is made more credible by the likelihood that those gay men who can pass as heterosexual in prison do so.

At the very least, no rationale exists for believing that gay men in prison are not subject to the same forces that drive heterosexual men. The fact that gay men prefer sex with men, whereas heterosexual men prefer it with women, hardly provides convincing support for the notion that only heterosexual men rape other men in prison.

## Homophobic Violence Against Gays

In the past few years, several highly publicized incidents have occurred involving attacks on gay men by blatantly homophobic men. No research is yet available on this topic, but these cases, as well as sex role theory (to be explained) suggest that violence against gay men is one of the many serious consequences of homophobia. Lesbians and/or women perceived to be lesbians are also vulnerable to attack, sexual or otherwise, by men who feel threatened by, and/or hostile toward, their sexual preference.

Rigid definitions of "appropriate" male and female behavior force many men to repress aspects of themselves that do not fit into the male stereotype. Some of these men deal with their fears about their own masculinity by attacking others: those they perceive as unmasculine, or those who appear to defy the norms of appropriate sex role behavior and choices. Often, these attacks are suffered by gay men or lesbians.

Groth and Burgess describe as follows the motivation to rape of four men who "led bisexual lives but were conflicted about their sexual involvement with other males":

> The selection of a male as the target of their sexual assault can be seen in part as an expression of this unresolved aspect of their lives. The victim may symbolize what they want to control, punish, and/or destroy, something they want to conquer and defeat. The assault is an act of retaliation, an expression of power, and an assertion of their strength or manhood. (1980, p. 809)

This theory suggests that rigid sex role stereotyping may be a key factor in violence against gay men and women. Its role in the etiology of rape will be discussed in Chapter 5.

## Rape of Women by Lesbians

In the foreword to an anthology titled *Male Rape*, Stuart Miller writes that the book shatters the myth "that sexual violence consists of men raping women. The reality is," he maintains, "that young rape old, blacks rape whites, whites rape blacks, juveniles rape juveniles, men rape men and boys, and *women rape women and girls"* (in Scacco, 1982, p. ix, emphasis added).

Despite this implicit suggestion that we will learn about women raping women and girls, an entire article on "Homosexuality in Female Institutions" never mentions rape (Buffum, 1982, pp. 165–168). The only further mention of this subject in the entire book occurs in a first-person account by a woman prisoner who was severely attacked and set on fire by eight women inmates. In the course of the brutal attack she says, "I was raped" (West, 1982, p. 171). That is all we learn about the subject in the entire book!

Undoubtedly, there are cases of women raping other women and girls; indeed, some examples from Russell's research were cited at the beginning of this chapter. It is difficult to find documentation of such attacks, and lack of relevant research makes it impossible at this time to determine the sexual orientations of those women who rape other women.

## Note

1. Aside from Kate Millett, not one of these feminist scholars is even listed in Scacco's 106-item bibliography (1975).

3

# SOCIAL CHARACTERISTICS OF RAPE VICTIMS AND RAPISTS

## The Victims of Rape

It has been established that females of all ages, social classes, and racial or ethnic groups are vulnerable to rape. What is less widely recognized is that women from all social classes and racial or ethnic groups are not equally at risk of being raped.

A brief summary of the findings reported in the literature will be followed by data from the Russell random sample survey for the victims' age, race or ethnicity, social class, and marital status. Since wife rape was rarely included in prior studies, the data to be presented from the Russell survey will exclude all cases of wife rape. Excluding them will eliminate the necessity to continually examine whether or not any differences that emerge between the findings of the Russell survey and other studies are due to these cases of rape in marriage.

### AGE OF RAPE VICTIMS

Sedelle Katz and Mary Ann Mazur have undertaken a comprehensive review of the literature on rape victimization (1979). Although there are discrepancies in the ages of victims in different studies, Katz and Mazur conclude that based on reported cases "the high-risk ages are adolescents (ages 13–17) through young adulthood (ages 18–24)" (1979, p. 38). The risk appears to decline steadily as women get older.

Donald Mulvihill and Melvin Tumin, co-directors of the federal government commission report on *Crimes of Violence,* organized the first national survey on victims and offenders involved in criminal homicide, aggravated assault, forcible rape, and robbery. They collected a 10 percent random sample of offense and arrest reports from 17 large U.S. cities in 1967 (1969, vol. 11, p. 207). The victims in this large-scale city survey were somewhat younger than those reported by Katz and Mazur: Almost half (47 percent) of the victims were 17 years and younger, 29 percent were between 18 and 25 years, and 24 percent were 26 years and older.

**TABLE 3.1**

**Age When Victimized by Rape or Attempted Rape**
**(or first rape in multiple assaults)**
**in Five-Year Categories**

| Age | Number | Percentage |
|-----|--------|------------|
| 0–5 | 3 | 0.4 |
| 6–10 | 16 | 2.1 |
| 11–15 | 109 | 14.5 |
| 16–20 | 267 | 35.6 |
| 21–25 | 195 | 26.0 |
| 26–30 | 83 | 11.1 |
| 31–35 | 39 | 5.2 |
| 36–40 | 19 | 2.5 |
| 41–45 | 12 | 1.6 |
| 46–50 | 5 | 0.7 |
| 51–55 | 2 | 0.3 |
| 55+ | 1 | 0.1 |
| Total | 751 | 100.1 |

NOTES: Missing observations: 29. Mean age: 21 years.

Several researchers report that the peak age for rape is 14 years (Schiff, 1969; Hursch & Selkin, 1974; Hayman et al., 1968; Katz & Mazur, 1979, p. 38). Peters et al., found 15 to be the peak age (1976). However, Katz and Mazur point out that "it is difficult to say for certain what the high-risk age group actually is, because so many cases are not reported" (1979, p. 38). The same degree of caution is warranted in reviewing all the demographic factors analyzed in this section of the book.

*Rape of the Elderly*

Paul Gebhard et al. found that only 3 percent of the victims of the convicted rapists they studied were more than 50 years old (1965, p. 194). The comparable figure in Menachem Amir's study was 3.6 percent (1971, p. 52), in John MacDonald's study it was 7 percent (1971, p. 77) and in Nicholas Groth's study it was 12 percent (1979, pp. 164–165).

Focusing on the age disparity between victim and offender rather than the age of the victim, Groth reported that "of the 170 referred offenders who sexually assaulted adult victims, 30 (18 percent) selected women who were significantly older than themselves; that is, the victim was at least twice the age of her assailant" (1979, p. 165).

**TABLE 3.2**

**Exact Age When Victimized by Rape or Attempted
Rape (or first rape in multiple assaults)
for Most Vulnerable Years**

| Age | Number | Percentage of Total Known Cases | |
|-----|--------|-------------------------------|---|
| 13 | 39 | 5 | |
| 14 | 21 | 3 | |
| 15 | 34 | 5 | |
| 16 | 57 | 8 | |
| 17 | 47 | 6 | |
| 18 | 56 | 7 | N = 267 = 36% |
| 19 | 53 | 7 | |
| 20 | 54 | 7 | |
| 21 | 44 | 6 | |
| 22 | 43 | 6 | |
| 23 | 40 | 5 | |
| 24 | 27 | 4 | |
| 25 | 41 | 5 | |
| 26 | 33 | 4 | |
| Subtotal | 589 | 78 | |

## The Russell Survey Findings on Age

Table 3.1 provides a frequency distribution of the age of victims of rape and attempted rape at the time they were attacked. These data are based on the total number of rape incidents, not the number of women raped. It should be remembered that approximately 50 percent of the victims were raped more than once.

Table 3.1 shows that the vast majority of rapes (87 percent) occurred to victims between the ages of 11 and 30. An examination of the age of the victim on a yearly basis shows the most vulnerable years to be from 13 to 26. As indicated by Table 3.2, over one-third (36 percent) of the incidents of rape and attempted rape occurred to victims between the ages of 16 and 20 years. These high-risk age groups are consistent with those reported by Katz and Mazur above (1979). However, the mean age of 21 found by Russell is considerably older than the peak ages of 14 or 15 years reported by many other researchers. No particular peak age for rape emerged in the Russell study.

As may be seen in Table 3.2, only 1 percent of the rape victims in the Russell sample of 930 were over 46 years of age. Hence, the survey indicates that rape of the elderly occurs proportionately even less frequently than has been reported in other studies. Since most other studies are based on cases reported to the police, this suggests that elderly women may be more willing than their younger sisters to report their rapes to the police.

### RACE AND ETHNICITY OF RAPE VICTIMS

Sedelle Katz and Mary Ann Mazur report that "all researchers who presented data on the race of the rape victim agreed that black women were far more vulnerable to rape than white women" (1979, p. 39). These authors cite the following studies as documentation for this conclusion: Ennis, 1967; Eisenhower, 1969; Hayman et al., 1969, 1972; Schiff, 1969, 1973; Amir, 1971; Massey et al., 1971; Peters, 1975; Hursch and Selkin, 1974; Meier, 1948; Darwin, 1953; National Crime Panel Surveys, 1975; National Advisory Commission on Civil Disorders, 1968 (1979, p. 39).

According to the 17-city survey undertaken for the federal government commission in 1967, 69.5 percent of the rape victims were black (Mulvihill et al., vol. 11, 1969, p. 210). In the *Final Report* of the National Commission on the Causes and Prevention of Violence, Milton Eisenhower reported that nationally, black women—who accounted for only 10 percent of the female population—accounted for 60 percent of the rapes reported to the police in 1967 (1969).[1]

Data on female members of other minority groups are sparse. One study in Denver found that Spanish-American rape victims were "four times their numbers in the general population of the city" (Katz & Mazur, 1979, p. 39).

Katz and Mazur point out that the high percentage of black rape victims reported in these studies is consistent with the high percentage of black victims of other violent crimes. Thus these authors conclude that "the racial factor is no more a specific characteristic of rape than it is of any other violent crime" (1979, p. 40).

### The Russell Survey Findings on Race and Ethnicity

Given the considerable agreement in the literature about the overrepresentation of black women among rape victims, it seems surprising that Russell's survey data did not support this finding. Because of the controversial nature, as well as the uniqueness, of Russell's data on the race and ethnicity of victims, an explanation of how this factor was determined is warranted.

Near the end of each interview respondents in the Russell survey were shown a card and asked, "What racial or ethnic group do you belong to?" The choices on the card were Black, Latina/Latin American, Other White/Caucasian, Chinese/Chinese-American, Japanese/Japanese-American, Filipina/Filipina-American, Korean/Korean-American, Native American Indian, and Other. Respondents who reported "Other" were asked to specify their race or ethnic group.

Respondents were next asked: "Do you consider yourself as belonging to any other particular ethnic or national group?" If they answered affirmatively, they were asked to specify which group. Since the vast majority of Jews belong to the White/Caucasian category, the criteria for determining Jewishness depended on respondents' answers to the latter question. In addition, those women who described their religious upbringing or their current religious preference as Jewish were also so classified.

Table 3.3 shows that three race/ethnic groups were more frequently victimized by rape than black women. Although there were only 11 Native American women in the sample of 930 women, their victimization rate was 55 percent, the highest of all the groups identified in the Russell survey. However, because of the small number of Native Americans in the sample, this finding must be regarded as tentative.

It should be remembered when reading Table 3.3 tht 41 percent of the 930 women interviewed were victimized by an experience of non-marital rape or attempted rape at some time in their lives. Hence, when fewer than 41 percent of a particular group were raped, the prevalence of rape for that group is below the norm for the Russell sample; when more than 41 percent were raped, the prevalence is above the norm.

One of the most unexpected findings to emerge from this analysis is that Jewish women were the second most victimized group, at 50 percent. Sociologist Pauline Bart reported that Jewish women in her study appeared more likely to be victims of completed rape than attempted rape—a finding she is still endeavoring to explain (personal communication). She refers to the latter group of women as rape avoiders. However, the definition of rape in the Russell survey includes attempted rapes, or the avoiders, by Bart's definition (1981).

**TABLE 3.3**

**Race/Ethnicity of Women Who Were Ever
Victimized by Rape or Attempted Rape**

| Race/Ethnicity | Number of Women Raped | Total Number of Women in Sample by Race/Ethnicity | Percentage Raped |
|---|---|---|---|
| White (Non-Jewish) | 255 | 563 | 45 |
| Jewish | 32 | 64 | 50 |
| Black | 40 | 90 | 44 |
| Latina | 20 | 66 | 30 |
| Asian | 12 | 70 | 17 |
| Filipina | 7 | 41 | 17 |
| Native American | 6 | 11 | 55 |
| Other | 7 | 25 | 28 |
| Total | 379* | 930 | |

*This is the total number of *women* victimized by rape or attempted rape, not the total number of *incidents* of rape.

Aside from Bart's analysis, no published research before Russell's suggests that Jewish women might be overrepresented among rape victims.

White non-Jewish women were the next most frequently victimized by rape (45 percent), followed by black women (44 percent). Both of these groups of women were over two and one-half times more frequently victimized by rape than Filipinas (17 percent) or Asian women (17 percent). Latinas fell somewhere between these groups; 30 percent of them had been raped at some time in their lives.

Russell's findings on the prevalence of rape among black and white women are quite different from the rates reported in the literature. This is undoubtedly due to the restriction of prior studies to stranger or acquaintance rape, in contrast to the Russell survey which uncovered a great deal of rape by intimates as well.

## SOCIAL CLASS OF RAPE VICTIMS

Katz and Mazur conclude their literature review on this issue by saying that "most researchers agreed that rape victims come predominantly from the lower socioeconomic classes," but that few presented systematic data to substantiate this (1979, p. 41). Katz and Mazur cite the following studies as examples: Goldberg and Goldberg, 1940; Lipton and Roth, 1969; Hayman et al., 1972; Svalastoga, 1962; Amir, 1971; Eisenhower, 1969; Ennis, 1967; National Crime Panel Surveys, 1975.

Many of these studies are based on police reports; police departments and the FBI do not use standard classifications of socioeconomic status or occupations. This is one reason for the lack of systematic data available on this factor (Katz & Mazur, 1979, pp. 41–42).

The National Commission on the Causes and Prevention of Violence *did* provide some specific data on socioeconomic status. They found that females with family incomes under $6,000 reported being raped from three to five times more frequently than did females with family incomes over $6,000 (1969).

Some researchers have speculated that rape victims from the middle and upper social classes may be more likely to report to private physicians, who are not required by law to report the incident to the police (Katz & Mazur, 1979, pp. 42–43). Countering this interpretation is a study of private physicians which indicates that the majority of rape victims treated by them (57 percent) *did* report the rape to the police (McGuire & Stern, 1976). In another 15 percent of these cases, the physicians did not know whether or not the victim reported (Katz & Mazur, 1979, p. 43).

In conclusion, the available literature suggests that both men and women from the lower classes are more vulnerable to all forms of violent crimes, including rape (Katz & Mazur, 1979, p. 42).

## The Russell Survey Findings on Social Class

Sociologists are firmly convinced that social class is a key variable, and that almost everything—from life expectancy to mental illness to attitudes about war and peace or chewing gum—is significantly affected by a person's social class. Since there is no consensus on how to measure this variable, the Russell survey used many different indicators.

A great advantage of Russell's survey data is the comparison it allows of women who were victims of rape or attempted rape to those who had never been raped. This serves as a built-in control group. Each measure of social class will be examined separately.

*Father's occupation.* Nearly one half (47 percent) of the women whose fathers had upper middle class occupations (professional, technical, managerial) were victims of rape or attempted rape at some time in their lives. This compares with just over a third of the women whose fathers had middle class occupations (sales, clerical, crafts) and those who had lower class occupations (operatives, laborers, service and transportation workers), 35 percent and 36 percent, respectively (significant at <.01 level). By this criterion, contrary to prior studies, women from upper middle class backgrounds are more likely to become rape victims.

*Father's education.* Just over half (51 percent) of the women whose fathers went to college were raped, compared to 40 percent of those whose fathers had only completed high school, and only 38 percent of those whose fathers had an eighth-grade education or less (significant at <.01 level).

*Mother's occupation and education.* There was no relationship whatsoever between the women's mother's occupation and rape victimization. However, the association between their mother's education and rape was very similar to what was found for father's education. Just over half (51 percent) of the women whose mothers had some college education were raped, compared to 46 percent of those whose mothers had graduated from high school, and 30 percent of those whose mothers had an eighth-grade education or less (significant at <.001 level).

*Respondent's occupation and education.* There was no statistically significant relationship between the respondent's own occupational status and rape victimization. There was, however, a trend consistent with what was found for fathers—that is, the higher the class status, the higher the prevalence of rape victimization.

The relationship between the respondent's educational level and rape victimization, on the other hand, was highly significant (at <.001 level). Close to half (46 percent) of the respondents who had attended college, and over a third (37 percent) of those who had graduated from high school, had been victimized by rape or attempted rape at some time in their lives. But only 19 percent of those who had an eighth-grade education or less reported being so victimized.

*Husband's occupation and education.* Of the married respondents whose husbands had upper middle class occupation, 40 percent had been victimized by rape. This compares to 30 percent of those whose husbands had middle class occupations, and 25 percent of those whose husbands had lower class occupations (significant at .05 level).

While the relationship between the respondent's husband's education and her prior rape victimization did not reach statistical significance, there was a definite trend in the same direction. Only 18 percent of the respondents whose husbands had an eighth-grade education or less had been victimized by rape—compared with 35 percent for both of the other groups of respondents whose husbands had received more education.

*Respondent's total household income.* In contrast to all these measures of social class, women's total household income one year prior to the interview seems to have no bearing at all on the rate of rape.

For example, when comparing the total household income in 1977 of women who had never been a victim of rape or attempted rape with those who had been so victimized at least once in their lives, there was remarkably little difference between them; 33 percent of those with incomes of $7,499 or less had never been raped compared with 34 percent who had been; 32 percent of those with incomes between $7,500 and $14,999 had never been raped compared with 35 percent who had been; and 35 percent of those with incomes of $15,000 or more had never been raped compared with 31 percent who had been.

## Summary of Data on Victim's Social Class

The striking discrepancies between Russell's findings on social class and those of other researchers is a result of the overrepresentation in most other studies of stranger rape. For example, when all the rapes that occurred in Russell's survey are divided into stranger and nonstranger rapes, over twice as many women who were raped by strangers as those who were raped by nonstrangers had a household income of less than $3,000 at the time of the rape (26 percent and 11 percent, respectively; all income data were adjusted to 1978 dollar values).

Another way of reporting this finding is to say that over a quarter (26 percent) of all stranger rapes happened to women with an income of less than $3,000 at the time, compared to only 11 percent of all nonstranger rapes. This suggests that very poor women are significantly more vulnerable to rape by strangers than by nonstrangers.

### MARITAL STATUS OF RAPE VICTIMS

Several studies show that women who report rape to the police are more often single than married (Katz & Mazur, 1979, p. 41). Percentages of victims who were single at the time of the rape range from 85 percent (Svalastoga, 1962), 80 percent (Schiff, 1969), 75 percent (MacDonald, 1971), and 74 percent (Amir, 1971; Katz & Mazur, 1979, p. 41).

The high percentage of single women is partly due to the high incidence of rape of young females. According to Katz and Mazur, singleness also appears to be a factor when age is held constant (1979, p. 41). However, these statistics obviously do not reflect the experiences of wives who are raped by their husbands.

### The Russell Survey Findings on Marital Status

On the issue of marital status Russell's survey data are consistent with the findings in the literature. Eighty-five percent (85 percent) of the victims of rape or attempted rape were single at the time of the assault, and only 15 percent were married. Once again, rape by husbands is excluded from this analysis.

### Conclusion

The comparison undertaken in this section suggests that the more biased studies are toward stranger rape, the more overrepresented lower class victims will be among rape victims. The more comprehensive and realistic view of rape permitted by Russell's random sample survey suggests that by several measures, rape is actually overrepresented in the upper middle class. This finding illustrates how exceedingly distorted current knowledge of rape is because of the tremendous biases in the samples in which prior studies have been based.

## The Rapists

The National Commission on the Causes and Prevention of Violence concluded that arrest rates for all major crimes of violence (murder, forcible rape, aggravated assault, and robbery) are much higher for males than for females, for blacks than for whites, for low-income persons than for those of higher socioeconomic status, and for the young than for the old (Mulvihill et al., 1969, vol. 11, p. 208; see also Ennis, 1967, pp. 31, 33, 34–35).

Arrest data have been criticized as working to the detriment of minority groups, because of the presumed prevalence of racist and classist attitudes among the police. Nevertheless, the authors of the government commission report argued that arrest data are "the most reliable source of information about the personal characteristics of offenders" (Mulvihill et al., 1969, vol. 11, p. 81).

### AGE OF RAPISTS

Like rape victims, rapists are also primarily from the younger age groups, specifically between 15–24 years of age (Amir, 1971; Mac-Donald, 1971; Katzenbach, 1967; Eisenhower, 1969; Svalastoga, 1962; Katz & Mazur, 1979, p. 101). In most states, males below the age of 15 are protected from being criminally charged and prosecuted for rape (Katz & Mazur, 1979, p. 101).

The National Commission reported that 21 percent of the males arrested for rape were 17 years and younger, 48 percent were between 18 and 25 years of age, and 31 percent were 26 years and older (Mulvihill et al., 1969, vol. 11, p. 212). These figures indicate that rapists, although young, are significantly older than their victims (1969, p. 212).

Menachem Amir's Philadelphia study found a median age for rapists of 23 years; for victims, the median age was 19.6 years (1971, pp. 51–56). In 18.6 percent of the rapes the victim was at least 10 years younger than the rapist. However, Amir also reported that in 17.6 percent of the rapes, the victim was more than 10 years older than the rapist.

### The Russell Survey Findings on Age

Women who did not know the exact age of their rapists in the Russell survey were asked for their "best guess." The age categories used in Table 3.4 were those offered to the respondents by the interviewers. As may be seen in Table 3.4, just over one-quarter (26 percent) of the rapists fell into the 21–25 year age group. Exactly two-thirds of them (66 percent) were 16 to 30 years of age. Hence the finding reported in the literature that rapists are primarily from the younger age groups is confirmed.

**TABLE 3.4**

**Age of Rapists (at time of first rape in multiple assaults)**

| Age | Number | Percentage |
|---|---|---|
| Under 15 | 21 | 3 |
| 16–20 | 146 | 20 |
| 21–25 | 193 | 26 |
| 26–30 | 151 | 20 |
| 31–40 | 163 | 22 |
| 41–50 | 48 | 7 |
| 51–60 | 18 | 2 |
| Over 60 | 1 | 0 |
| Total | 741 | 100 |

Husbands who rape their wives tend to be somewhat older than other rapists. At the time they committed rape, 49 percent of the nonmarital rapists were 25 years or younger, compared to 37 percent of the men who raped their wives (Russell, 1982, p. 130).

As reported in other studies, rapists as a group are older than rape victims. Forty-nine percent (49 percent) of the nonmarital rapists were 25 years or younger; 79 percent of the victims were under 26 years of age.

Note that 21 rapists (3 percent) in the Russell survey were under 15 years of age, and therefore could not have been prosecuted for their crimes in most states.

**RACE AND ETHNICITY OF RAPISTS**

Menachem Amir reported that 82.5 percent of the rapists in his Philadelphia study were black, as compared with 80.5 percent of the victims (1971, p. 44). John MacDonald reported that black rapists were over five times more prevalent than expected in his Denver study, and that Hispanic men were also overrepresented (1971, p. 51).

The government commission concluded that most rapists came from urban areas and were "disproportionately from the ghetto slum where most Negroes live" (Mulvihill et al., vol. 11, 1969). Specifically, the commission reported that 70 percent of the men arrested for rape were black, and 30 percent were white.

This ratio of black to white arrests for rape is considerably higher than the ratio reported annually by the *Uniform Crime Reports* (FBI) in which the most frequently cited ratio is 48 percent black, 51 percent white, and 1 percent "Other." Presumably this discrepancy results from the commission's focus on large cities with high percentages of black inhabitants, and harsh conditions in the black ghettoes. However, the National Commission hastened to emphasize that

> Racial fears underlie much of the public concern over violence, so one of our most striking and relevant general conclusions is that serious "assaultive" violence—criminal homicide, aggravated assault and forcible rape—is predominately *intra*-racial in nature. (Mulvihill et al., vol. 11, 1969, p. 208)

More specifically, the government commission reported that 60 percent of rapes in their study involved black offenders and black victims, 30 percent involved white offenders and white victims, 11 percent involved black offenders and white victims, and .3 percent involved white offenders and black victims (1969, p. 210).

### The Russell Survey Findings on Race and Ethnicity

As previously mentioned, only 66 of the cases of nonmarital rape or attempted rape in the Russell survey (or 9.5 percent) were ever reported to the police. Of these 66 cases, only 13 (or 20 percent) were known to result in arrests. Consequently Russell's data base is very different from those described in the literature.

The information available from the Russell survey on the race or ethnicity of rapists is not as rich as are corresponding facts about the victims; victims could not be expected to correctly identify Filipinos, Native Americans, or Jews, for example, particularly when their rapists were strangers or acquaintances.

Since over two-thirds of the Russell sample of 930 women were white, one would expect there to be a majority of white rapists. This indeed was the case. As shown in Table 3.5, 64 percent of the rapists were white, 22 percent were black, 8 percent were Latin, 3 percent were Asian, and 3 percent were identified as belonging to some "other" race/ethnic group.

With rape victims it was a simple matter to calculate rape victimization rates for each race or ethnic group differentiated by the Russell survey. But one can not do a comparable calculation of rape perpe-

**TABLE 3.5**

**Race/Ethnicity of Rapists as a Ratio of
the Race/Ethnicity of Rape Victims**

| Race/
Ethnicity
of Rapist | Number of
Rapists | Percentage | Victims/
Rapists | Ratio of
Victims to
Rapists |
|---|---|---|---|---|
| White | 475 | 64 | 287/475 | 1:1.7 |
| Black | 160 | 22 | 40/160 | 1:4.0 |
| Latin | 63 | 8 | 20/63 | 1:3.2 |
| Asian | 23 | 3 | 19/23 | 1:1.2 |
| Other | 22 | 3 | 13/22 | 1:1.6 |
| Total | 743 | 100 | 379/743 | |

NOTES: Mean victim/rapist ratio: 1:2. Missing observations: 37. Significant at <.001 level.

tration rates. Since approximately 50 percent of the 930 women reported being raped more than once by different perpetrators, one would expect there to be more rapists in each race or ethnic group than there were victims in each group. So it is possible to compare the rape perpetration rates for different race or ethnic groups by calculating the number of rapists there were for every rape victim in each group identified. Table 3.5 reveals the following ratios:

> For every Asian rape victim there was approximately 1 Asian rapist;
> for every white rape victim, there were approximately 2 white rapists;
> for every Latina rape victim, there were approximately 3 Latin rapists;
> for every black rape victim, there were approximately 4 black rapists.

However, these ratios change significantly when a distinction is made between rape/attempted rape by strangers and nonstrangers. (The term nonstrangers here includes acquaintances, friends, authority figures, relatives—other than husbands—dates, boyfriends, lovers, and ex-lovers.) This is because black rapists are particularly overrepresented among stranger rapists, presumably because of the significant relationship between social class and stranger rape (to be discussed more thoroughly in the next section). Table 3.6 shows the ratio of victims to rapists for the different race or ethnic groups in cases of nonstranger rape, from the highest to the lowest ratio:

> For every black victim, there were 2.7 black nonstranger rapists;
> for every Latin rape victim, there were 2.5 Latin nonstranger rapists;
> for every white rape victim, there were 1.3 white nonstranger rapists;
> for every Asian rape victim, there was less than one Asian nonstranger rapist.

## TABLE 3.6

### Race/Ethnicity of Nonstranger Rapists
### as a Ratio of the Race/Ethnicity of Rape Victims

| Race/Ethnicity of Rapist | Nonstranger Rapes: Number | Nonstranger Rapes: Percentage | Victims/ Nonstranger Rapists | Ratio of Victims to Nonstranger Rapists |
|---|---|---|---|---|
| White | 374 | 48 | 287/374 | 1:1.3 |
| Black | 107 | 39 | 40/107 | 1:2.7 |
| Latin | 50 | 6 | 20/50 | 1:2.5 |
| Asian | 16 | 4 | 19/16 | 1:0.8 |
| Other | 15 | 4 | 13/15 | 1:1.2 |
| Total | 562 | 101 | 379/562 | |

NOTES: Mean victim/nonstranger rapist ratio: 1:1.5. Missing observations: 28. Significant at $<.001$

This analysis shows that black and Latin rapists are almost equally overrepresented among nonstranger rapists in comparison to white nonstranger rapists. But this overrepresentation is less significant than was evident when stranger rape was included. Asian rapists are even more greatly underrepresented among nonstranger rapists.

Hence, Russell's data confirm the finding reported in the literature that there are a disproportionate number of black and Latin rapists. But the disproportion is not as great as some other studies have suggested. The finding that Asian men are underrepresented among rapists is unique to Russell's study. Asians have not been mentioned before in this context, except as a presumed constituent of the category "Other" in the *Uniform Crime Reports*.

## SOCIAL CLASS OF RAPISTS

Two federal government commissions have reported that rapists are disproportionally from the poorest and most economically deteriorated areas (Katzenbach, 1967; Eisenhower, 1969; Katz & Mazur, 1979, p. 102). Other researchers concur with this conclusion, for example, Menachem Amir (1971) and Susan Brownmiller (1975).

As already pointed out, most studies report a significant relationship between minority status and rape; since there is considerable overlap between race and socioeconomic status, with black people being disproportionally poor, the finding that rapists are also disproportionately poor is as expected. As Brownmiller pointed out: "because of their historic oppression the majority of black people are contained within the lower socioeconomic classes and contribute to crimes of violence in numbers disproportionate to their population ratio in the census figures *but not disproportionate* to their position on the economic ladder" (1975, p. 181, emphasis in original).

The overrepresentation of poor men among rapists is pivotal in Julia Schwendinger and Herman Schwendinger's analysis of rape (1983). They emphasize that rape is consistent with other violent crimes in its greater prevalence among the poor. More specifically, the Schwendingers maintain that the socioeconomic status of rapists is likely to be "fairly similar to the status of most apprehended offenders" of other violent crimes (1983, p. 213). The Schwendingers conclude that

> The impoverishment of the working class and the widening of the gap between rich and poor, which is the bottom line of current federal policies, will lead to worse living conditions for the poor and a continued high incident of sexual violence. (1983, p. 220)

The Schwendingers' point is well taken when applied to stranger and acquaintance rape. It is less relevant for rape among intimates, since economic factors are probably less significantly related to this form of rape.

### The Russell Survey Findings on Social Class

The social class of rapists in a random sample survey is a question of considerable interest both sociologically and politically. But the difficulty of obtaining accurate racial and ethnic identifications of rapists from their victims is greatly compounded when asking victims to try to identify the social class of their assailants. Nevertheless the interviewers in Russell's survey asked respondents to say what they could about the occupation and educational level of their assailants *if* the rapists were over the age of 25.

This age distinction was made because many people are still in the process of obtaining an education prior to the age of 25. The Russell survey wanted to differentiate, for instance, between rapists who may have obtained only a high school education because they were young, and those whose formal education had ended at that point. Failure to make this distinction would exaggerate the number of rapists at the lower educational levels. The same rule was applied to information about the occupations of the rapists. When they were less than 25 years old, the Russell survey sought information on the occupation of the rapist's primary economic provider.

While the reasoning for establishing these criteria was sound, it resulted in a lot of missing data, since many rapists are in their late teens and early twenties. And, as might be expected, many respondents had no idea what the education and occupations of their rapists were—let alone that of their rapist's main provider! This is particularly true for stranger and acquaintance rape. Therefore, despite Russell's efforts, the data in this survey on the social class of nonmarital rapists are weak and must be regarded as tentative and incomplete.

Regarding men who rape their wives, for whom much better information was available on education and occupation, there was no significant relationship between social class and wife rape. (For a fuller discussion of these findings, see Russell, 1982, pp. 128–131.)

Because of all the missing information, the only distinction that will be made for nonmarital rapists is between stranger rapists and nonstranger rapists. Russell's survey data suggest that more stranger rapists than nonstranger rapists were from the lower social class. Stranger rapists had significantly lower job prestige than nonstranger rapists (significant at < .05 level). Of stranger rapists for whom information was available, 53 percent had lower class occupations, compared to 37 percent of nonstranger rapists.

These findings on the relationship between stranger rape and social class, although marred by the methodological problems described above, are consistent with the findings of other studies cited in the previous section.

## MARITAL STATUS OF RAPISTS

Since a large percentage of rapists are young men, one would anticipate that the large majority would be single. Menachem Amir, for example, reported that 66 percent of the offenders in his Philadelphia study were single. However, a few studies of convicted rapists show a higher percentage of married than single men (Katz & Mazur, 1979, p. 102). For example, a survey of the Colorado State Penitentiary found only 43 percent of the rapists to be single, while another researcher, R. J. McCaldon, reported only 36 percent (Katz & Mazur, 1979, p. 102).

Rape victims in the Russell survey were not aked about the marital status of their rapists, since it was presumed that they usually would not know it.

## Reported and Unreported Rape Compared

Some of the social characteristics of both rape victims and rapists that emerged from the Russell random sample survey have been presented. This chapter will address the question, How do cases of rape or attempted rape that are reported to the police differ from those that are never reported?

This question is critical to an understanding of the issue of rape, particularly because most knowledge about rape is based on reported cases. Since only a small minority of rapes are ever reported to the police, the similarities and differences between reported and unreported cases have enormous implications. To show that they are very different is to show that studies based on reported cases have little relevance to the rape issue in general.

The National Crime Surveys and the Russell study provide two of the major sources for comparison between reported and unreported cases of rape. The methodological problems with the National Crime Surveys are so severe that its findings on rape are to be regarded with great skepticism. (See Chapter 1 for a detailed discussion of these problems.) The Russell survey is probably the most accurate source of data available on this subject. What, then, do these data indicate?

As stated earlier, only 9.5 percent of all rape and attempted rapes in the Russell survey were reported to the police. Table 3.7 shows that close to one-third (30 percent) of all the rapes or attempted rapes by strangers were reported to the police. This percentage is far higher than reports of rape by any other type of perpetrator. Rape by authority figures was reported to the police next most frequently (13 percent), followed by rape by boyfriends (10 percent), acquaintances (7 percent), relatives and friends of the family (each 6 percent), lovers or ex-lovers (3 percent), friends of the victim (2 percent), and the lowest report of all was for date rape (1 percent).

Table 3.7 shows that the picture of rape that emerges from reported cases is tremendously distorted. Although *55 percent* of all rapes that were reported to the police involved strangers, stranger rapists were only *17 percent* of the total number of rapes, including unreported cases. Another significant disparity was found in rapes by acquaintances; they constituted 19 percent of the reported cases but 26 percent of the total number of cases. Only 2 percent of the reported cases were date rapists, compared to 18 percent of reported *and* unreported cases. Only the percentages of rape by boyfriends were the same for reported and unreported cases: 5 percent in both instances.

**TABLE 3.7**

**Perpetrator of Rape and Attempted Rape
and Reporting to Police***

| Perpetrator/Victim Relationship | Report Rates (in percentages) | Percentage of Reported Cases for Different Rapists (N) | | Percentage of Reported and Unreported Cases Combined, for Different Rapists (N) | |
|---|---|---|---|---|---|
| Stranger | 30 | 55 | (35) | 17 | (115) |
| Acquaintance | 7 | 19 | (12) | 26 | (173) |
| Friend of family | 6 | 2 | (1) | 3 | (17) |
| Friend of victim | 2 | 2 | (1) | 9 | (62) |
| Date | 1 | 2 | (1) | 18 | (124) |
| Boyfriend | 10 | 5 | (3) | 5 | (31) |
| Lover or ex-lover | 3 | 3 | (2) | 9 | (63) |
| Relative (not husband) | 6 | 3 | (2) | 5 | (31) |
| Authority figure (not relative) | 13 | 11 | (7) | 8 | (56) |
| Total | | 102** | (64) | 100 | (672) |

NOTES: Missing observations: 33. Significant at $< .001$ level.

*In cases of pair or group rape, the primary perpetrator only is included here.

**This column adds to 102 rather than 100 because of rounding to the nearest whole number.

The comparisons that follow separate reported and unreported cases, to illuminate the differences between them.

(1) More completed than attempted rapes were reported to the police—13 percent and 8 percent, respectively (significant at $<.05$ level).

(2) Just over one-fifth of the reported rapes (22 percent) involved more than one perpetrator, compared to only 7 percent of the unreported cases (significant at $<.001$ level).

(3) The only two cases involving female perpetrators were not reported.

(4) Victims who were raped on more than one occasion by the same perpetrator were less likely to report any of the rapes to the police than victims who were raped only once (significant at .07 level).

(5) Only 3 percent of the victims younger than 14 years old reported the rape to the police, compared with 10 percent who were 14 to 17 years old, and 10 percent who were over 18 (not statistically significant).

(6) Victims who were physically threatened in connection with being raped were more likely to report the rape to the police than those who were not threatened—24 percent and 7 percent, respectively (significant at <.01 level).

(7) When the rapist was armed with some kind of weapon, whether or not he actually used it, the victim was much more likely to report the rape to the police (33 percent and 7 percent, respectively; significant at <.001 level).

(8) The greater the degree of physical violence used, the more likely the rape was to be reported. Thirty-eight percent (38 percent) of the victims who were beaten or slugged, 18 percent of those who were hit or slapped, and only 5 percent of those who were pushed or pinned reported to the police (significant at <.001 level).

Some factors that proved unrelated to the reporting of rape victimization included the following: (1) whether or not the victim was married at the time of the attack; (2) the victim's household income at the time of the rape; (3) the age difference between the victim and the rapist; (4) the victim's religious upbringing or religious preference at the time of the interview; and (5) whether or not the rape or attempted rapes involved more than one female victim.

## PERPETRATOR CHARACTERISTICS AND REPORTING

Whether or not a victim reports rape is highly related to the rapist's race or ethnicity. Almost a quarter of the black rapists (24 percent) were reported to the police. This compares with only 7 percent of the Latin rapists and 5 percent of the white rapists. Not one out of 20 Asian rapists was reported to the police (significant at <.001 level).

Why are rape victims more than three times more likely to report a black rapist than a Latin rapist? And why were *no* Asian rapists reported?

One factor is the overrepresentation of black rapists among stranger rapists. Of the black rapists 30 percent assaulted strangers, compared to 20 percent of Asian rapists, 13 percent of white rapists, and 13 percent of Latin rapists (significant at <.001 level). In addition, black rapists were significantly more likely than rapists from the other three race or ethnic groups to complete the rape (in contrast to only attempting it), to have raped with one or more other rapists, and to use verbal threats, weapons, and other physical violence in the course of the rape. Rapes by black men were also associated with higher levels of reported upset and long-term effects. Since all these factors are known to be related to the reporting of rape, they help explain why rapes by black men are more likely to be reported to the police.

Some of these differences between black rapists and rapists from other race or ethnic groups, including their overrepresentation among stranger rapists, are likely to be related to social class. Crimes of violence that are reported to the police are disproportionately committed by lower class men. Because of the severe and long-lasting history of racism in this country, black people are disproportionately represented in the lower classes. Unfortunately, as discussed earlier, available data on the social class of rapists are scanty because so many victims have no knowledge of their rapists' education, occupation, or income.

Bearing in mind that there is therefore a great deal of missing data on these variables for rapists, the information that was available is nevertheless of interest: Only 8 percent of black rapists had a college education, compared to 19 percent of Latin rapists, 30 percent of Asian rapists, and 39 percent of white rapists (significant at $<.001$ level). In addition, the job prestige of black rapists was also slightly lower than that of other minority rapists, and substantially lower than that of white rapists.

In summary: Differences between rapists that might appear to be based on race may in fact be based on class. Because the Russell data on the race and ethnicities of perpetrators are unavoidably better than the data on their social class, there is a danger of conveying the erroneous impression that race and ethnicity are more important determinants of some aspects of rape than is social class. This incorrect notion is dispelled by awareness of the significant correlation between race and social class in this society.

A highly significant relationship was also found between reporting to the police and the interracial or intraracial (or interethnic or intraethnic) aspect of the rape (at $<.001$ level). For purposes of this analysis, blacks, Latins, and Asians were combined into one category described as "minority." Exactly one-fifth (20 percent) of the rapes of minority women by minority men were reported to the police. The next highest percentage of reported rapes involved minority rapists and nonminority victims (14 percent), followed by nonminority rapists and minority victims (7 percent). The least frequently reported combination involved nonminority rapists and nonminority victims (5 percent; significant at $<.001$ level). The overrepresentation of black men among stranger rapists is also an influential factor in these findings.

## VICTIM CHARACTERISTICS AND REPORTING

An examination of reporting behavior by the race and ethnicity of the victims, independently of the race or ethnicity of the rapists, provides a different view of the picture. It may be remembered that half the women in Russell's sample were raped more than once. Since these women were often inconsistent in their reporting behavior, the focus of this analysis will be on the rapes rather than on the women. Twenty percent (20 percent) of the rapes were reported to the police—the highest rate for all the groups studied. Of the rapes of black women 17 percent were reported, 9 percent of the rapes of Jewish women, 8 percent of the rapes of Asian and Filipina women, 7 percent of the rapes of white non-Jewish women, and—although there were 19 cases—0 percent of the rapes of native American women (significant at <.01 level).

There was no relationship between the occupational status or the total household income of the victim at the time of the interview, nor her educational level, and whether or not she reported the rape. Hence, the racial and ethnic differences in the report rates for rape victims can not be explained by social class (at least, not as they are measured by these three criteria).

Victims who were living with their parents at the time of the rape were less likely to report the rape to the police: Only 7 percent compared with 12 percent (significant at <.05 level).

There was a highly significant relationship between the degree of upset described by the victim, and whether or not she reported the rape to the police: 15 percent of those who described being extremely upset reported the rape, compared with 8 percent of those who were very upset, 5 percent of those who were somewhat upset and none of those who were less upset (significant at <.001 level).

Similarly, 16 percent of those who described having suffered great long-term effects reported the rape to the police. This compares to 10 percent of those describing some long-term effects, and only 4 percent of those describing little or no effect (significant at <.001 level). Despite this correlation between degree of upset and effects and the victim's decision to report, the large majority of very traumatic rapes, as well as the less traumatic rapes, were never reported to the police. It is unknown whether or not the relationship found between the trauma and decision to report was in fact due to stress surrounding the reporting process itself.

**TABLE 3.8**

**Rapist-Victim Relationship and Reporting,
Arrests, and Conviction**

| Rapist-Victim Relationship | Percentage Not Reported (N) | | Percentage Reported/ No Known Arrest (N) | | Percentage Arrest No Known Conviction (N) | | Percentage Arrest and Conviction (N) | | Total Ns |
|---|---|---|---|---|---|---|---|---|---|
| Stranger | 70 | (80) | 29 | (34) | 1 | (1) | 0 | (0) | 115 |
| Acquaintance | 93 | (161) | 3 | (6) | 2 | (3) | 2 | (3) | 173 |
| Friend of family | 94 | (16) | 0 | (0) | 0 | (0) | 6 | (1) | 17 |
| Friend of respondent | 98 | (61) | 2 | (1) | 0 | (0) | 0 | (0) | 62 |
| Date | 99 | (123) | 1 | (1) | 0 | (0) | 0 | (0) | 124 |
| Boyfriend | 89 | (25) | 7 | (2) | 4 | (1) | 0 | (0) | 28 |
| Lover or ex-lover | 97 | (59) | 2 | (1) | 2 | (1) | 0 | (0) | 61 |
| Other relative | 94 | (29) | 0 | (0) | 3 | (1) | 3 | (1) | 31 |
| Authority figure | 88 | (52) | 10 | (6) | 0 | (0) | 2 | (1) | 59 |
| Total | 90 | (606) | 8 | (51) | 1 | (7) | 1 | (6) | 670 |

NOTES: Don't knows and missing observations: 42. Significant at $< .001$ level.

## THE OUTCOME OF REPORTED CASES

The 66 rape victims in Russell's survey who reported being raped to the police had no way of knowing whether their cases were eventually unfounded or not. Most people are totally unaware that close to one-fifth of the rapes reported to the police every year are discounted in this way. Of the 670 cases of rape and attempted rape in the Russell survey where information on both the perpetrator and the outcome of the report were available, only 2 percent (13 cases) resulted in arrests, and only 1 percent (6 cases) led to convictions.

Table 3.8 provides a breakdown of the outcome of the report by the type of perpetrator reported. Although stranger rape was by far the most likely form of rape to be reported, not one of the 35 reported cases of stranger rape ended with a conviction. However, there was also only one arrest for stranger rape, whereas there were three arrests of acquaintance rapists. Presumably, stranger rapists are the most difficult of all to catch and identify, despite the fact that they are also the most likely to be believed by the police.

It is as clear as it is tragic that rapes perpetrated by the rapists who are least difficult to apprehend and identify—those who are known to the victim—are the cases that are least likely to be taken seriously and prosecuted vigorously. The rapes committed by men who are most difficult to apprehend and identify—strangers—are the cases that are most likely to be taken seriously. This seeming contradiction helps to explain the shockingly low 1 percent conviction rate found in the Russell survey.

*Note*

1. Why there is a 9.5 percent discrepancy between this figure and the one cited in the 17-city survey is not clear.

# 4

# PSYCHOLOGICAL CHARACTERISTICS OF RAPISTS

As Nicholas Groth points out, "one of the most basic observations one can make regarding men who rape is that not all such offenders are alike" (1979, p. 12). Many theorists (for example, Nicholas Groth, and Diana Scully and Joseph Marolla) have developed typologies of rapists, some suggesting as few as two or three basic types. Others, such as Paul Gebhard et al. and Richard Rada,[1] suggest five or six. Every one of these typologies (to be described in the following pages) is flawed by its failure to acknowledge the possibility that men who rape strangers, for example, may be very different from husbands who rape their wives or men who rape their dates.

## *Paul Gebhard et al.'s Typology*

Paul Gebhard, John Gagnon, Wardell Pomeroy, and Cornelia Christenson of the Institute for Sex Research in Indiana, described the majority of men who had raped an adult woman in their sample of incarcerated rapists as

> criminally inclined men who take what they want, whether money, material, or women, and their sex offenses are by-products of their general criminality. Aside from their early involvement in crime, there are not outstandingly ominous signs in their presex-offense histories; indeed, their heterosexual adjustment is quantitatively well above average. (1965, p. 205)

This last statement provoked Susan Brownmiller's caustic statement that it "says as much about Gebhard and his colleagues' standards of heterosexual adjustment as it does about rapists" (1975, p. 180). Indeed, their description of the majority of rapists makes little sense in light of both the widespread prevalence of rape and the widespread occurrence of men's proclivity to rape women (see Chapters 1 and 5). To define 35 percent of male students (the percentage who admitted some likelihood that they would rape a woman if they could get away with it) as "criminally inclined" is to stretch beyond recognition the usual meaning of that term.

Gebhard et al. argue that, unlike *most* rapists, a minority of these men are not involved in criminal activities but are "seemingly rather ordinary citizens leading conventional or even restrained lives" (1965, p. 206). Finally, a few rapists are described as "statistically normal individuals who simply misjudged the situation" (1965, p. 206). Whether this lack of judgment refers to the rapists' getting apprehended or their act of rape is not clear.

More specifically, Gebhard et al. suggested six categories of what they refer to as "heterosexual aggressors against adults": assaultive, amoral delinquent, drunken, explosive, double-standard, and other.

*(1) Assaultive rapists* are the most common type according to Gebhard et al. They have strong sadistic and hostile feelings toward women. They usually have a history of violence, and tend to select strangers as victims. This type of rapist more often suffers from erectile impotence than do the others. The explanation offered by Gebhard et al. is that "in some instances the violence seems to substitute for coitus or at least render the need for it less" (1965, p. 198).

*(2) Amoral delinquents.* This term is used by Gebhard et al. to label the second most common type of rapist. These men are described as "not sadistic—they simply want to have coitus and the females' wishes are of no particular consequence" (1965, p. 200). Gebhard et al. maintain that men of this type "are not hostile toward females, but look upon them as sexual objects whose role in life is to provide sexual pleasure" (1965, p. 200). Amoral delinquents rape women they have previously known as well as strangers.

*(3) The drunken variety* of rapist is about as common as the amoral delinquent, according to Gebhard et al. The aggression of this type of man "ranges from uncoordinated grapplings and pawings, which he construes as efforts at seduction, to hostile and truly vicious behavior released by intoxication" (1965, p. 201). This description suggests that aside from their common tendency to rape women while intoxicated, these men vary a great deal.

*(4) The explosive variety* (constituting from 10 to 15 percent of all rapists) are described as men "whose prior lives offer no surface indications of what is to come. Sometimes they are average, law-abiding citizens, sometimes they are criminals, but their aggression appears suddenly and, at the time, inexplicably" (1965, p. 203). According to Gebhard et al., there are often psychotic elements in the behavior of these rapists.

*(5) The double-standard variety.* This type divides females into the good ones, who should be treated with respect, and the bad ones, who are not entitled to consideration (1965, p. 204). These rapists are similar in attitude to the amoral delinquents, but are less criminal and more asocial. They resort to force "only after persuasion fails" (1965, p. 204).

*(6) "Other"* types of rapists (about one-third of the rapists studied by Gebhard et al.) include mixtures of the first five varieties, as well as mental defectives and psychotics.

The classification of one-third of the rapists as "other" itself indicates a weakly constructed typology. The greatest weakness, however, is shared with all the other typologies to be presented: It has been developed solely on the basis of interviews with *incarcerated* rapists. Rapists who are arrested, convicted, and then incarcerated are a highly unique group. They *cannot* be considered representative of the majority of rapists, who are never imprisoned for their offenses.

## Richard Rada's Typology

Richard Rada distinguishes between five kinds of rapists:

*(1) The psychotic rapist* who "often is only aware of an overwhelming rage and anger at the time of the rape and can give no other motivation for the crime" (1978, p. 122).

*(2) The situational stress rapist* who "rarely has a history of sadistic or violent masturbatory fantasies or sexual deviations. Prior to the situational stress, there may be no history of obvious emotional abnormality" (1978, p. 123). This type of rapist is rarely very violent and is unlikely to be as dangerous as the rapist who is psychotic. He is also more likely to feel subsequent guilt.

*(3) The masculine identity conflict rapist* includes a broad spectrum of offenders, "all of whom share in common an actual or felt deficiency in their masculine roles" (1978, p. 125). This is the second largest category of rapist. These men usually plan their attacks; they are among the most dangerous and violent of all types of rapists. Rada states that these rapists

> frequently show lack of feeling for the pain and suffering inflicted on the victim, and are most likely to suggest that the victim was "asking for it," "really enjoyed it," or "deserved what she got." They respond in this way not because they lack the capacity for empathy ... but because they overcompensate in their attempt to present as real men. (1978, p. 125)

*(4) The sadistic rapist,* according to Rada, comprises a very small percentage of the total. The sadistic rapist plans his assault, and "will often demand that the victim perform a variety of humiliating activities and appears to derive greater satisfaction from his ritualistic degrading of the victim than from the actual intercourse" (1978, p. 128).

*(5) The sociopathic rapist* is the most common type, constituting 30 percent to 40 percent of all rapists that Rada studied. This rapist "engages in a variety of criminal activities and has frequent encounters with the law. Rape is frequently just one of his antisocial aggressive and sexual acts" (1978, p. 129). Because his motivation is primarily sexual, these rapists may be less dangerous to the victim: "The act does not tap a conflicted reservoir of bizarre aggressive and sexual fantasies as in some other types of rapists" (1978, p. 130). Treatment for these men is difficult to prescribe, since their rape behavior does not result from intrapsychic conflict "but rather from a more pervasive personality disorder" (1978, p. 130).

Although he acknowledges that "many rapists do not show marked deviation on standard psychological testing," Rada remains convinced that psychologically "normal" men do not rape (1978, p. 131).

## Nicholas Groth's Typology

Based on his clinical experience with convicted offenders and rape victims, Groth concludes that "in *all* cases of forcible rape, three components are present: power, anger, and sexuality" (1979, p. 13). Groth emphasizes that rape, "rather than being primarily an expression of sexual desire, is, in fact, the use of sexuality to express these issues of power and anger" (1979, p. 13). This conclusion is the same as that developed by many feminist theorists, including Andra Medea and Kathleen Thompson (1974) and Susan Brownmiller (1975).

*(1) Anger rape.* Anger rape, according to Groth, is characterized by far more force than would be necessary to achieve sexual intercourse. Anger rapists commit rape rather than nonsexual assaults because they consider rape the ultimate offense they can commit against another person (1979, p. 14). Often this type of rapist may not even be sexually excited; he may be impotent, or able to achieve an

erection only by masturbating himself or having the victim do so (1979, p. 14). Typically such a rapist finds little or no sexual gratification in the attack (1979, p. 15). According to Groth, these offenders often act out their crimes on the spur of the moment, and their attacks are often of short duration (1979, p. 15)

*(2) Power rape.* In power rape, Groth suggests, "it is not the offender's desire to harm his victim but to possess her sexually. Sexuality becomes a means of compensating for underlying feelings of inadequacy and serves to express issues of mastery, strength, control, authority, identity, and capability" (1979, p. 25). These rapists use only the amount of force necessary to accomplish sexual intercourse. However, they may subject their victims to repeated assaults over an extended period of time (1979, p. 26).

Like anger rapists, Groth maintains, power rapists also tend to find little sexual gratification in rape. It never lives up to their fantasies, which often revolve around the victim's ultimate succumbing to the rapist's sexual prowess (1979, p. 26). This type of rapist often denies that he used force to achieve his ends, since he needs to believe that his victim wanted and enjoyed the experience. After the assault, he may buy the victim food or express a desire to see her again, and expect her acquiescence (1979, p. 30).

In summary, Groth writes: "The intent of the power rapist, then, is to assert his competency and validate his masculinity. Sexuality is the test and his motive is conquest" (1979, p. 31).

*(3) Sadistic rape.* Groth's view of sadistic rape is that "both sexuality and aggression become fused into a single psychological experience known as *sadism"* (1979, p. 44). Aggression becomes eroticized, and this type of offender "finds the intentional maltreatment of his victim intensely gratifying and takes pleasure in her torment, anguish, distress, helplessness, and suffering" (1979, p. 44). The victims of sadistic rapists are usually strangers, who symbolize something these men want to destroy or punish (1979, p. 45). The attacks are premeditated, not spontaneous. The victims are "stalked, abducted, abused, and sometimes murdered" (1979, p. 45).

Unlike the other two kinds of rapists, sadistic rapists are intensely sexually excited by the infliction of pain on their victims (1979, p. 45). Arousal for these men is a function of aggression. According to Groth, these offenders are often quite personable. He points out that this impression contrasts sharply with the stereotype of the vicious sexual maniac (1979, p. 46).

Groth reports that power rapes are the most common type, constituting about 55 percent of the cases referred to him. Approximately 40 percent of these cases were anger rapes, and only about 5 percent were sadistic rapes (1979, p. 58). Groth believes that there is a greater probability of conviction for anger rapes than power rapes because of the greater violence involved. He speculates that "power rapes, in fact, far outnumber anger rapes in our culture" (1979, p. 58).

## Diana Scully and Joseph Marolla's Typology

Although sociologists Scully and Marolla also based their typology on interviews with incarerated rapists, their approach is unique in many important ways. They are very aware of the highly select nature of their sample; they are very critical of the assumption that rape is the result of individual psychopathology; they used a comparison group of felons who had not been incarcerated for rape or other sexual offense; and they recognized that these men may in fact include undetected rapists (1983).

As a consequence of some of these differences, Scully and Marolla's typology is quite unique. They distinguish between rapists they describe as *admitters* and *deniers*. The former group admitted having had sexual contact with the victim and defined their behavior as rape; the latter group denied they had raped. Half of the deniers said they had had sexual contact with the victim but denied that it was rape, even when they were willing to admit to having been violent. The other half denied the sexual contact as well (1983, p. 2). Scully and Marolla point out that most of the literature has focused on the admitters (1983, p. 63); they describe the psychology of their two types of rapists as follows:

*(1) Admitters.* The rape behavior of most admitters is triggered by a crisis of everyday living. Most often it involves anger caused by a breach of their rigid double standards vis-à-vis women. In keeping with their tendency toward interpersonal violence, these men use rape to express and relieve their anger and "to dominate, humiliate, control, and get even with a woman. For these men, a rape was a purposeful, functional behavior" (1983, p. 63). However, they also considered their behavior to have been morally reprehensible. They tended to view their rape as atypical behavior caused by emotional problems and alcohol or other drug intoxication (1983, p. 63).

*(2) Deniers.* Deniers, according to Scully and Marolla, rape women "because their value system provided no compelling reasons not to do so." The behavior of these rapists shows that "when sex is viewed as a male entitlement, the result is that very few forced sexual encounters are defined as criminal" (1983, p. 63). The self-esteem of the deniers is based almost entirely on an extreme masculine identity in which a good self-image is quite consistent with hostile and violent attitudes toward women (1983, p. 38).

In contrast, the self-image of admitters suffered when they admitted to hostile or violent attitudes toward women. They also felt bad about an overly masculine or aggressive self concept (1983, p. 38).

Scully and Marolla point out that admitters and deniers also share many characteristics. For example, they do not see their victims as human beings, but as objects to be used and conquered (1983, p. 63).

## CRITIQUE OF TYPOLOGIES

There is considerable disagreement amongst the researchers cited in this section about how to categorize different types of rapists. The first three typologies focus on psychopathological factors. The latter emphasis stems from a discipline bias (psychology) that frequently denies the role of social factors, and a methodological bias that limits the rapists studied to incarcerated offenders.

Scully and Marolla aptly sum up the problems with most of this research:

> First, dominated by psychiatry and a medical model, the underlying assumption that rapists are sick, has pervaded the field. Second, with very few exceptions, the targets of research have been clinical samples of rapists within prisons. Indeed, the situation in rape research would be analogous to assuming that everyone who steals is emotionally ill and proving it by studying only psychotic burglars or, doing research on psychotic burglars to discover why people, in general, steal! (1983, p. 66)

In a rather unique study of 50 noninstitutionalized adult male rapists who were located through public media ads, Samuel Smithyman found many examples of a different kind of man. Smithyman found, for example, that 84 percent of his self-selected sample of rapists attributed their rapes solely or partly to sexual desire (1978, p. 56). Furthermore, only 4 percent believed the rape had had a negative impact on their self image, compared to 16 percent who believed it had had a positive impact, and 68 percent who said it had had no impact (1978, p. 117). This stands in contrast to Groth's notion that most rapists suffer from a poor self-image and are emotionally disturbed. As Scully and Marolla have pointed out, many of the rapists they studied *became* emotionally disturbed only *after* being arrested and incarcerated (1983, p. 54).

Smithyman also noted a remarkable absence in his 50 undetected rapists of indices to confirm popular stereotypes of rapists' inadequate, deprived social development. "As a group," Smithyman concluded, "the respondents reported having experienced relatively good family adjustment within basically 'intact' homes, appeared to have had relatively 'normal' heterosexual dating experiences during adolescence, described relatively positive social relationships with peers and so forth" (1978, p. 48).

Of course, Smithyman's sample is as self-selected and unrepresentative as are the samples of incarcerated rapists. The main value of his study is to suggest hypotheses for more rigorous testing, and to raise even more serious doubts about the validity of much of what we have learned about rapists from uncritical analyses of incarcerated sex offenders.

## Note

1. Richard Rada has summarized several typologies of rapists in his book *Clinical Aspects of the Rapist* (1978, chap. 4).

# PART II

# THE CAUSES OF RAPE

## 5

## FACTORS CREATING
## A PREDISPOSITION TO RAPE

David Finkelhor developed a four-factor model to help explain the occurrence of child sexual abuse (1981). This model also provides an excellent framework for organizing theories of rape.

When applied to rape, Finkelhor's model suggests that there are four types of preconditions that allow rape to occur:

Precondition I: factors creating a predisposition or desire to rape;
Precondition II: factors reducing internal inhibitions against acting out this desire;
Precondition III: factors reducing social inhibitions against acting out this desire;
Precondition IV: factors reducing the potential victim's ability to resist or avoid the rape.

Each of these types of preconditions will be considered in turn. Most major theories of rape causation can be fitted quite easily within one of these four factors.

### The Biological Capacity and Desire of Men to Rape

The theory of rape held by Susan Brownmiller and many other feminist theorists contains an implicit biological element. According to Brownmiller,

Man's structural capacity to rape and woman's corresponding structural vulnerability are as basic to the physiology of both our sexes as the primal act of sex itself. Had it not been for this accident of biology, an accommodation requiring the locking together of two separate parts, penis into vagina, there would be neither copulation nor rape as we know it.... [I]n terms of human anatomy the possibility of forcible intercourse incontrovertibly exists. This single factor may have been sufficient to have caused the creation of a male ideology of rape. When men discovered that they could rape, they proceeded to do it. (1975, pp. 13–14)

Further, Brownmiller writes,

Man's discovery that his genitalia could serve as a weapon to generate fear must rank as one of the most important discoveries of pre-historic times. (1975, pp. 14–15)

Brownmiller's point is well taken. Consider, for example, how different human history might be were penetration by the penis physiologically possible only when women really want to have sexual intercourse. Then women could be neither raped nor bought. What Brownmiller's theory overlooks is another, more critical biological difference between the sexes: the superior physical strength of most men over most women. It is this superior strength that enhances men's ability to protect their genitals. Without it, the latter might have become not a weapon, but a source of vulnerability. Instead of men discovering their capacity to rape, women might have discovered the vulnerability of male genitals to attack. This discovery could then have provided women with the possibility of gaining power over men.

Although Brownmiller and others have argued that women cannot "retaliate in kind" (1975, p. 14), it is in fact possible for men to be forced to have intercourse with a woman. The traditional notion of completed rape (as opposed to attempted rape) when applied to males, requires that they obtain an erection. But there have been reports of men having an erection in circumstances when intercourse was unwanted.

Aside from the direct application of force, it is also possible for women to rape by threat of force. At a certain period in the history of the United States, a white woman in the South, for instance, could force a black man to have sex with her by threatening to cry rape. Since the implementation of such a threat could result in the black man's murder, this incident would indeed qualify as rape by threat of bodily harm.

In summary: Rape is made possible by both men's capacity to rape *and* their greater physical strength vis-à-vis women as a class. This doesn't explain, however, why some men *want* to rape women or why they do so; nor does it explain why rape occurs so frequently in this country today.

Anthropologist Donald Symons argued in *The Evolution of Human Sexuality* (1979) that many differences in sexuality between males and females are probably biologically based. According to Symons, the process of natural selection has favored male attempts "to copulate with fertile females whenever this potential can be realized" (1979, p. 276). When females resist men's attempts to copulate with them, Symons maintains, this act constitutes a possible cost to males in terms of time, energy, and/or risk. Hence Symons argues,

> male attempts to force resisting females to copulate can be expected to occur only in circumstances in which the outcome cannot be "predicted" by the principals: when females are capable of very effective resistance ... selection will not favor male attempts to copulate with nonconsenting females, and when females are incapable of effective resistance, selection will not favor attempts of nonconsenting females to resist. (1979, p. 276)

Symons's theory is completely biologically deterministic. For Brownmiller, though, a biological factor is only part of the story. Brownmiller stresses a biological factor very different from Symons's notion that male animals and human beings have a built-in urge to pass on their genes to as many offspring as possible. Brownmiller assumes that men want to have power over women (otherwise why would their discovery that they can use their genitals as a weapon matter?), but she doesn't attempt to explain why men want this power.

Symons attacks the view held by Brownmiller (and many other feminists) that rape is not motivated by sexual desire, maintaining that "perhaps no major work since Lorenz's *On Aggression* has so inadequately documented its major thesis" (1979, p. 278). Because many rapists have consenting sexual partners available to them at the time of the rape, some theorists argue that they must be interested in more than sexual gratification. Symons maintains that this in no way denies the motivation of sexual desire. He points out that while many patrons of prostitutes and pornography bookstores and movies are married and therefore (he presumes) have an available consenting sexual partner, no one would or should consider this "availability" as evidence of a lack of sexual motivation (1979, p. 280).

According to Symons, men, unlike women, are biologically disposed to seek sexual variety because it increases their reproductive opportunities. In short, Symons believes that "human males tend to desire no-cost, impersonal copulations, ... and hence that there is a possibility of rape wherever rape entails little or no risk" (1979, p. 284). As one piece of evidence for this conclusion Symons cites the high prevalence of rape during war, when many normally risky behaviors can be performed at little or no risk (1979, p. 280).

Symons grants that "given sufficient control over rearing conditions, no doubt males could be produced who would want only the kinds of sexual interactions that women want" (1979, p. 285). He adds that "such rearing conditions might well entail a cure worse than the disease" (1979, p. 285). In other words, Symons believes that it would be more unpleasant for males to be socialized to please women than it would be for women to continue to be raped. Clearly Symons does not live in fear of being raped.

Several theorists agree with Symons that men have a proclivity to rape. But most have argued that this proclivity results largely from socialization and/or the imbalance of structural power between men and women. These theories will be elaborated on shortly. In brief, they hold that the crucial issue in rape prevention is not whether or not men's tendency to rape is biologically based, as Symons argues. More to the point would be the rearing of males and females in a way that minimizes both men's desire to rape, and women's vulnerability to it. Exactly what this might entail will become clear in the following sections.

### Childhood Sexual Abuse Histories
### of Sexual Offenders

In contrast to Donald Symons, psychologist Nicholas Groth regards rape as a symptom of psychological dysfunction (1979, p. 98). In his study of over 500 sexual offenders, Groth found that many of these men had histories of sexual trauma in their childhood years.

Groth defined sexual trauma rather broadly as "any sexual activity witnessed and/or experienced that is emotionally upsetting or disturbing" (1979, p. 98). Based on this definition, he reported that about one-third of the offenders (who included rapists of adult women as well as child molesters) had experienced some form of sexual trauma in their formative years. He noted that this was significantly higher than the percentage (10 percent) of males reporting childhood experinces of sexual abuse in David Finkelhor's survey of college students. He noted also that the incidence of childhood sexual trauma was the same for both rapists and child molesters (1979, p. 98).

Groth reported that of those offenders who reported a childhood sexual trauma, 45 percent were victims of sexual assault, 18 percent were pressured into sexual activity by an adult, 18 percent "participated in a sex-stress situation where the anxiety resulted from family reaction to the discovery of the subject's involvement in sexual activity" (1979, p. 99), 3 percent witnessed upsetting sexual activities, and 2 percent suffered some sexual injury or physiological handicap

(1979, pp. 99-100).[1] It is important to note that the usual definition of sexual abuse would include only sexual assault and sexual activity with an adult. This might partially explain Groth's finding that about one-third of all offenders had experienced some form of sexual trauma in childhood, compared to Finkelhor's 10 percent figure for sexual abuse.

Groth goes on to say that the early sexual victimization experiences reported by the rapists were more frequently incestuous than those reported by the child molesters; the rapists were also more often abused by females than males. In addition, although the age of trauma for both child molesters and rapists was predominantly preadolescent, 40 percent of the rapists were adolescent at the time of the trauma, as compared with only 25 percent of the child molesters (1979, p. 101).

Finally, 46 percent of the sexual offenders who showed a persistent and exclusive preference for children reported being sexually victimized. This is double the number (23 percent) of those whose involvement with a child was a clear stress-precipitated departure from their preferred sexual relationships with adult women (1979, p. 101).

There are serious limitations inherent in Groth's methodology, which result in the tentativeness of his findings. Not only is any kind of control group of nonoffenders lacking, but Groth's sample of offenders is an exceedingly select group. Groth shows extraordinary naivete when he optimistically states the following:

> There is no way of determining whether the subjects we have worked with and studied constitute a random sample of all men who rape. They are representative, however, of those offenders who directly or indirectly come to the attention of criminal justice and mental health agencies and with whom law enforcement officials and providers of social services are expected to deal in some effective manner. (1979, p. xiii)

First, we can indeed be sure that Groth's sample is not a random one, because he did not apply random sampling techniques. Second, identified sexual aggressors—as he sometimes refers to them—are a unique group who in no way represent the population of rapists at large. The psychological and social characteristics (e.g., race, social class) of rapists who are not apprehended are likely to be very different from their less fortunate brothers. Susan Brownmiller is among those suggesting that it is only the most disturbed rapists who are convicted, though studies on this issue are inconsistent (1975).[2]

Second, as the Russell survey findings cited in Chapter 3 demonstrated, reported cases are not representative of unreported cases.

Further, only a fraction of the reported cases of rape ever result in offenders who "come to the attention of criminal justice and mental health agencies" (Groth, 1979, p. xiii). If reported rape is the tip of the iceberg, the rapist who becomes an offender known to the criminal justice system is the speck of dust on the tip of the iceberg.

Groth conceded that his methodology was far from rigorous and that no control group was available. He nevertheless saw fit to conclude that the sexual offender's adult crime "may be in part a repetition and an acting out of a sexual offense he was subjected to as a child" (1979, p. 102). The child molester in particular, Groth observed, appeared to duplicate his own early victimization in his later offenses.

These observations may be applicable to the majority of sex offenders who are never apprehended or incarcerated. However, it would be more appropriate to regard this and other findings based on such highly skewed samples as very tentative. This also applies to the research results of psychologists Theoharis Seghorn and Richard Boucher (to be cited next).

Seghorn and Boucher report that more than 50 percent of a sample of aggressive and/or recidivist sexual offenders they studied were sexually victimized prior to adolescence (1980, p. 705). These offenders were among 10 percent of the most severely disturbed patients committed to a treatment center; because of this selective factor, as well as the lack of a control group, the authors urge caution in generalizing their findings (1980, p. 705). Nevertheless, their research led them to hypothesize that "under specific conditions, men who have been victims of sexual abuse will themselves be at higher risk for committing sexual offenses as adults" (1980, p. 706).

Seghorn and Boucher drew a sample of 50 records of committed patients who reported some experience of childhood sexual victimization. Prior to the sexual crime that brought them to the Treatment Center, 60 percent had committed previous nonsexual offenses as adults; 80 percent had committed at least one prior sexual offense—often many offenses (1980, p. 707). A striking finding reported by these researchers was that "Those men who were molested by a relative were much more likely to have assaulted, brutally and sadistically, adolescent and adult women, while those men who had been molested by nonrelatives were more likely to molest males and less likely to subscribe to one extreme form of aggression" (1980, p. 707).

In addition, the men who had been molested by a nonrelative were four times more likely to have victimized a child under the age of 5; 97 percent of their victims were under 16 years of age (1980, p. 707). These men, Seghorn and Boucher reported, used only the amount of force necessary to obtain the "cooperation" of the child. When the child was female, penetration was rarely attempted: "rather, the behavior remains exclusively pregenital, that is, sexually immature, and at the level of what would be for adults, foreplay" (1980, p. 708). According to Seghorn and Boucher, these men had never made an adequate sexual adjustment to adults, and were socially comfortable only with children. The child was usually known to the offender, and the relationship often began "by a type of disarming courtship which engages the child and even his or her parents" (1980, p. 708). Seghorn and Boucher refer to many of the men in this group as fixated pedophiles.

In contrast, the men who were molested as children by a relative, either female or male, were three times more likely to choose a victim who was a postpubescent female. These men were also more likely to be violent toward their victims and to injure them. All of the victims who were beaten during or after the sexual assault were attacked by men in this group. The sexual offense frequently appeared to be an isolated loss of control. But despite their sexually active social lives, Seghorn and Boucher report that these men had a long history of difficulty in heterosexual relationships (1980, p. 709). Women were seen by them as "hostile, demanding, ungiving, and unfaithful" (1980, p. 709).

While Seghorn and Boucher appropriately conclude that generalizing from their highly elect sample is not possible, they nevertheless maintain that "in at least some children who are at risk, sexual victimization in childhood can have long lasting and devastating effects on their subsequent development, including a potential for aggressive sexual acting out" (1980, p. 710).

## Male Sex-Role Socialization

### THE MASCULINITY MYSTIQUE

[Rape] is so exclusively an act of the male that it expresses aggressive masculinity better than any other type of sadistic activity. (Desmond Morris)

A little bit of rape is good for a man's soul. (Norman Mailer)

"I was seventeen, and I was trying to prove that I was a man. I didn't fit into a John Wayne image, so I had to do something to prove my manhood." (Rapist; Russell, 1975, p. 249)

In *The Politics of Rape,* based on interviews with 90 rape victims and a handful of rapists, I concluded that rape is not so much a deviant act as an over-conforming one (1975, p. 260). It is an extreme acting-out of qualities that are regarded as masculine in this and many other societies: aggression, force, power, strength, toughness, dominance, competitiveness. To win, to be superior, to conquer, and to control demonstrate masculinity to those who subscribe to common cultural notions of masculinity; this constitutes the *masculinity mystique*.

It would be surprising if these notions of masculinity did not find expression in men's "normal" sexual behavior. Indeed, sex may be the arena where these notions of masculinity are most intensely played out, particularly by men who feel powerless in the rest of their lives and whose masculinity is threatened by this sense of powerlessness.

One respondent's three rapists, for example, told her that she was only getting what she deserved for walking on the street without a man at night. They saw themselves as decent for letting her get away so lightly. She felt that they did not particularly enjoy themselves, but were behaving in a way they saw as natural for men to whom a woman has given the opportunity (by being unprotected) that men are not supposed to be given (1975, pp. 260–261).

### FUSION OF SEX AND AGGRESSION

"Some women are really well built and good-looking but they are also snotty as hell. Those are the kind I would like to just rape the hell out of."

"I have wanted to rape a particular woman I know who was in a position of authority over myself and several hundred other Americans at the school I attended. She was/is hard, cold, cruel, and sadistic. We often talked about raping her to degrade her, gang-bang style.... I'm surprised she is still alive, to be honest!" (Male respondents; Hite, 1981, pp. 712, 713)

In *Against Our Will* (1975), Brownmiller provided a thorough and chilling documentation of the ubiquity and antiquity of rape as a concomitant of war. She argues that rape of enemy women is commonly considered natural soldierly behavior. This view presumes acceptance of men's capacity to express aggression and hatred through sex (Russell, 1975, p. 261). If men can express their hatred and aggression through war-time rape, it would be remarkable if they could not do it at home too.

For many men, it seems, aggression and sex are closely related. The unconscious rationale goes as follows: Being aggressive is masculine; being sexually aggressive is masculine; rape is sexually aggressive behavior; therefore, rape is masculine behavior (Russell, 1975, p.

261). How else can one explain statements like Ogden Nash's, "Seduction is for sissies; a he-man wants his rape" (Russell 1975, p. 264)?

## THE VIRILITY MYSTIQUE

> "I have had fantasies of doing it [rape] as a form of 'proving' to the woman that I am really all 'man,' able to get and keep a hard-on and use it to force myself on her, whether she wants me or not."

> "Two previous girl partners (separately) said 'no' and I did it [rape] anyway. I was thrilled out of my mind that I could be such a beast and it was really satisfying." (Male respondents; Hite, 1981, p. 718)

In *The Politics of Rape,* the impact of the masculinity mystique on male sexuality is referred to as "the virility mystique" (Russell, 1975, p. 263). This mystique dictates that males separate their sexual responsiveness from their needs for love, respect, and affection. They are expected to get an erection in the presence of a "sexy" woman, or upon seeing pictures of naked female bodies. A man is not supposed to be impotent if he is angry with his wife or lover. He is supposed to be able to perform despite the most chilling circumstances (Russell, 1975; also see Hite, 1982, and Stoltenberg, 1977).

The virility mystique causes some men to be threatened by women who take the initiative in sexual relations, or who want a lot of sex. One reason may be that these situations force men to realize that they *can't* perform whenever the opportunity arises. This fact is masked when sex occurs only at the man's initiative. Hence many men feel "castrated" by women who demand "equal time" in the making of sexual overtures (Russell, 1975, p. 263).

Males are trained from childhood to separate sexual desire from caring, respecting, liking, or loving. One of the consequences of this training is that many men regard women as sexual objects, rather than as full human beings. The virility mystique attaches status to attaining access to (and keeping score of) many women—the more the better. This approach dominates men's perspective on women (Russell, 1975). Indeed, making it clear to male companions that he views women in this way is important to the man who wants to appear virile (Hite, 1981).

The virility mystique, currently expounded by such popular magazines as *Playboy, Penthouse,* and *Hustler,* makes no provision for the inexperienced or virgin male. Further, experience is determined by the quantity of partners and their attractiveness as sex objects, rather than by the attractiveness of their personalities and the quality of the total relationships (Russell, 1975, p. 264). According to the virility mystique, until a man has "made it" with a woman, his manhood is in question. How he "made it" is not as important as having done so. And a man must continue "making it" with women (Russell, 1975, p. 264; and Hite, 1981). "It's better to commit rape than masturbate," said Norman Mailer (1962, p. 20). With such values to guide men, it is no wonder that so many are strongly tempted to rape, and that so many succumb to the temptation.

According to this theory, it is the virility mystique that predisposes men to rape. Even if women were physically stronger than men, it is doubtful that there would be many instances of female rapes of males: Female sexual socialization encourages females to integrate sex, affection, and love, and to be sensitive to what their partners want (Russell, 1975, p. 264; Hite, 1976). Of course, there are many women who deviate from this pattern, just as there are many men who have managed not to become victims of their sexual socialization. But for purposes of this analysis, the generalities are of greater significance than the exceptions.

Among the Arapesh of New Guinea, males are reared to be gentle and nurturant. According to Margaret Mead, "Of rape the Arapesh know nothing beyond the fact that it is the unpleasant custom of the Nugum people to the southeast of them" (1935, p. 110).

### THE RELATIONSHIP BETWEEN RAPE AND NORMATIVE MALE SEXUAL BEHAVIOR

In lovemaking, the woman must be able to follow the man's lead and tune into his body rhythms and style. While occasionally nothing will delight him more than your taking the initiative, breaking rhythm and turning him into the follower, in the main he will not be happy unless he is controlling the lovemaking. He wants you to do everything imaginable to him, but he also wants to tell you when ... Now, as never before, even the most fantastic lover needs to know that he is in full command of the scene sexually. ("J," 1971, pp. 35-36)

Rape is simply at the end of the continuum of male-aggressive, female-passive patterns, and an arbitrary line has been drawn to mark it off from the rest of such relationships. (Medea & Thompson, 1974, p. 11)

Women's alienation from her own sexuality, man's resentment at having to purchase sexual fulfillment, the unequal bargaining that trades security for sex—all of these distortions of human sexuality make it inevitable that much sexual contact between men and women will necessarily be coercive in nature. (Clark & Lewis, 1977, pp. 128-129)

Since Kate Millett's brilliant analysis of sexual politics was published in 1970, feminists have emphasized that rape must be viewed within the context of other sexual abuses of women. Germaine Greer pointed out connections between seduction and rape (1973), and Andra Medea and Kathleen Thompson wrote about a continuum that included the "little rapes" as well as legally defined rape (1975). In *The Politics of Rape*, I have suggested that if one were to see sexual behavior as a continuum with rape at one end and sex liberated from sex-role stereotyping at the other, much of what passes as normal heterosexual intercourse would be seen as close to rape (1975, p. 261).

Of course, the connection between sex and aggression does not necessarily express itself in rape; less extreme ways of expressing the connection are more common. For example, some men prefer women to be passive, leaving all the action to them. These men *do* things *to* women; the act is not a mutual one (1975, p. 261).

Although this is not rape, this classic pattern would be near the rape end of the hypothesized continuum of sexual behavior. This is true of much conventional sexual behavior. As Germaine Greer so aptly put it, "A man is, after all, supposed to seduce, to cajole, persuade, pressurize and even actually overcome" (1973, p. 178). Consider also "J's" advice to women in her bestselling book *The Sensuous Woman:*

> no woman of any sensitivity would refuse to make love to a man she cares for, just because she "doesn't really feel like it." You focus like mad on all the fantasies that stir your sexual juices, concentrate on making your body respond to the highest point possible, and, if you really can't get to orgasm, to avoid disappointing and spoiling his plateau of excitement and sexiness, you fake that orgasm. (1971, p. 179)

Marriage is the only relationship in which a woman's acquiescence to sexual demands was, until very recently, sanctioned by law in this country and in most others as well. So it should not surprise us that even where rape in marriage does not occur, much rape-like behavior does (Russell, 1982).

In *Rape: The Price of Coercive Sexuality,* Lorenne Clark and Debra Lewis articulate the same idea. They argue that the unequal power relationship between men and women has resulted in coercive sexuality becoming the norm (1977). In a chapter titled "Rapists and Other Normal Men," Clark and Lewis point out that

> men are unwilling to acknowledge that there is anything abnormal about wanting sexual relations with an unwilling partner, because they fear that if full, consensual sexuality were to become the standard of acceptable sexual relations, they would be deprived of many . . . of the sexual acts they enjoy. (1977, p. 142)

Out of this perspective comes their rhetorical question: "If misogyny and sexual aggression are the rule rather than the exception, then why are not all men seen as real or potential rapists?" (1977, p. 140). Clark and Lewis conclude that "all men are shaped by the same social conditioning . . . and they are all sexually coercive to some degree—at least, at some point in their lives" (1977, p. 145).

Two teams of contemporary researchers have empirically verified the validity and utility of this concept of a continuum.[3] John Briere, Neil Malamuth and Joe Ceniti asked 356 subjects the following question: "If you could be assured that no one would know and that you could in no way be punished for engaging in the following acts, how likely, if at all, would you be to commit such acts?" (1981, p. 4). Among the sexual acts listed were the two of interest to these researchers: "forcing a female to do something she really didn't want to do" and "rape" (1981, p. 5).

On the basis of answers to these two items, subjects were allocated to one of four groups: (1) no likelihood of force, (2) no likelihood of force but a likelihood of rape, (3) a likelihood of force but no likelihood of rape, and (4) a likelihood of both force and rape (1981, p. 5).

Of the male students 99 (28 percent) reported some likelihood of both force and rape. Six (2 percent) reported some likelihood of rape but not force. A likelihood of force but not rape was reported by 108 (30 percent). And 143 (40 percent) reported no likelihood of rape or force. This means that *60 percent of the sample indicated that under the right circumstances, there was some likelihood that they would use force, or rape, or both.*

Briere et al. designed this study to examine the attitudinal and sexual correlates of self-reported likelihood to rape, and self-reported likelihood to force a woman to perform sexual acts against her will. The most significant finding of this study is the linear relationship it uncovered between degree of force/rape inclination, and rape-supportive beliefs. This confirms the validity of an "aggression toward women" continuum "rather than a view of rape as a discrete, specific phenomenon with its own characteristic antecedents" (1981, p. 7). This research highlights the importance of recognizing sexual abuse as a continuous variable. Many women who are not raped as legally defined may nevertheless be seriously sexually violated.

It is also significant that no relationship was found between the likelihood of force or rape and numerous sexual variables (for example, the subjects' rating of their sex lives, the importance of sex to them, or the extent of their sexual inhibitions). The only sexual variable that distinguished each of the three groups of men was sexual experience; the men who denied any likelihood that they would rape or use force reported significantly *less* sexual experience than did the other two groups (1981, p. 13, Table 1). Briere et al. conclude that this "supports a view of rape as unrelated to sexual frustration or sexual maladjustment." They speculate that "the antecedents to rape are primarily social or attitudinal in nature" (1981, p. 8).

## Effects of Exposure to Pornography

"I felt like I was expected to live up to the 'manly' image of the porno magazines.... Anyone who doesn't like *Playboy* is obviously not a real man—must be a weirdo." (Male respondent; Hite, 1981, p. 777)

"I went to a porno bookstore, put a quarter in a slot, and saw this porn movie. It was just a guy coming up from behind a girl and attacking her and raping her. That's when I started having rape fantasies. When I seen that movie, it was like somebody lit a fuse from my childhood on up.... I just went for it, went out and raped. ... The movie was just like a big picture stand with words on it saying go out and do it, everybody's doin' it, even the movies." (Rapist; Beneke, 1982, pp. 73-74)

This and the next factor, media violence, are difficult to categorize within any one of the four preconditions. As the data to follow will show, pornography appears to foster rape fantasies and desires in the men who view it, and therefore should be categorized in Precondition I. However, recent research suggests that pornography also plays a role in overcoming internal barriers against acting out these desires (Precondition II), as well as in eroding external barriers by contributing to the cultural supports for rape (Precondition III). And finally, it seems that pornography may contribute to the undermining of some women's assertiveness about what sexual acts they do not wish to engage in, and therefore has a place in Precondition IV. Rather than trying to subdivide the analysis and review the literature on the effects of pornography according to this scheme, this factor will be dealt with here.

The task of evaluating existing research on the effects of pornography is fraught with difficulties.[4] First, distinctions are rarely made between "explicit, sexual materials," "erotica," and "pornography." Second, precise descriptions of the films, pictures, or stories used in experiments are usually lacking, making it impossible to know whether the findings are relevant to the effects of pornography or not. Third, although many researchers have focused on the effects of "erotica" on sexual behavior, a distinction is rarely made between degrading images of sex and respectful, tender images.

Before arriving at her excellent definition of pornography, philosopher Helen Longino points out what it is not. "Pornography," she writes, "is not just the explicit representation or description of sexual behavior, nor even the explicit representation or description of sexual behavior which is degrading and/or abusive to women." Rather, *pornography is "material that explicitly represents or describes degrading and abusive sexual behavior so as to endorse and/or recommend the behavior as described"* (Longino, 1980, p. 44, emphasis added). In addition, Longino maintains that the contextual features that communicate such endorsement "are intrinsic to the material; that is, they are features whose removal or alteration would change the representation or description" (1980, pp. 44–45).

*Erotica are representations or descriptions that are intended to stimulate sexual or sensual feelings that are not degrading or abusive.* Like pornography, then, erotica are often intended to turn people on sexually. And like pornography, erotica may also be sexually explicit—although they often tend to be more subtle and/or artistic than is usual for sexually explicit materials.

*Sex education materials* differ from erotica in that they are designed not to stimulate, but to educate. Of course, they may be sexually stimulating to some people, and they are usually sexually explicit as well. Sex education materials are not supposed to be degrading and abusive; when they are, they become pornography as defined here.

In the Russell survey the 930 women were asked the following question: "Have you ever been upset by anyone trying to get you to do what they'd seen in pornographic pictures, movies, or books?" Eighty-nine women—approximately 10 percent of the total number—answered that they had been upset by such an experience at least once.

Since the sample is a representative one, it is permissible to predict that approximately 10 percent of the adult female population in San Francisco would report upsetting experiences with people who have tried to get them to do something sexual they'd seen in pornography.

Of course, it is possible that the women may be wrong in thinking that the men were inspired by what they had seen in the pornographic pictures, movies, or books. On the other hand, there may have been some or many upsetting sexual experiences in which the women were unaware that the men's desires came from pornography; these cases could not be elicited by this question.

The women who answered "yes" to the question were then asked to describe the experience that upset them the most. As the answers cited below show, many of the women were able to avoid doing what was asked or demanded of them, but others were not so fortunate. And even in cases where the behavior was avoided, the women often ended up feeling harassed and/or humiliated.

## SELECTED ANSWERS TO PORNOGRAPHY QUESTIONS IN THE RUSSELL SURVEY OF 930 WOMEN

*Question:* "Have you ever been upset by anyone trying to get you to do what they'd seen in pornographic pictures, movies, or books?"

*If yes:* "Could you tell me briefly about the experience that upset you the most?"

*Ms. A:* Urinating in someone's mouth.

*Ms. B:* It was a three-girls-and-him situation. We had sex. I was really young—like fourteen.

*Ms. C:* He was a lover. He'd go to porno movies, then he'd come home and say, "I saw this in a movie. Let's try it." I felt really exploited, like I was being put in a mold.

*Ms. D:* I was staying at this guy's house. He tried to make me have oral sex with him. He said he'd seen far-out stuff in movies, and that it would be fun to mentally and physically torture a woman.

*Ms. E:* It was physical slapping and hitting. It wasn't a turn-on; it was more a feeling of being used as an object. What was most upsetting was that he thought it would be a turn-on.

*Ms. F:* He'd read something in a pornographic book, and then he wanted to live it out. It was too violent for me to do something like that. It was basically getting dressed up and spanking. Him spanking me. I refused to do it.

*Ms. G:* He forced me to have oral sex with him when I had no desire to do it.

*Ms. H:* This couple who had just read a porno book wanted to try the groupie number with four people. They tried to persuade my boyfriend to persuade me. They were running around naked, and I felt really uncomfortable.

*Ms. I:* It was S & M stuff. I was asked if I would participate in being beaten up. It was a proposition, it never happened. I didn't like the idea of it. *Interviewer:* Did anything else upset you? *Ms. I:* Anal intercourse. I have been asked to do that, but I didn't enjoy it at all. I have *had* to do it, *very* occasionally.

*Ms. J:* My husband enjoys pornographic movies. He tries to get me to do things he finds exciting in movies. They include twosomes and threesomes. I always refuse. Also, I was always upset with his ideas about putting objects in my vagina, until I learned this is not as deviant as I used to think. He used to force me or put whatever he enjoyed into me.

*Ms. K:* He forced me to go down on him. He said he'd been going to porno movies. He'd seen this and wanted me to do it. He also wanted to pour champagne on my vagina. I got beat up because I didn't want to do it. He pulled my hair and slapped me around. After that I went ahead and did it, but there was no feeling in it.

*Ms. L:* I was newly divorced when this date talked about S&M and I said, "You've got to be nuts. Learning to experience pleasure through pain! But it's your pleasure and my pain!" I was very upset. The whole idea that someone thought I would want to sacrifice myself and have pain and bruises. It's a sick mentality. This was when I first realized there were many men out there who believe in this [S & M].

*Ms. M:* Anal sex. First he attempted gentle persuasion, I guess. He was somebody I'd been dating a while and we'd gone to bed a few times. Once he tried to persuade me to go along with anal sex, first verbally, then by touching me. When I said "No," he did it anyway—much to my pain. It hurt like hell.

*Ms. N:* This guy had seen a movie where a woman was being made love to by dogs. He suggested that some of his friends had a dog and we should have a party and set the dog loose on the women. He wanted me to put a muzzle on the dog and put some sort of stuff on my vagina so that the dog would lick there.

*Ms. O:* My old man and I went to a show that had lots of tying up and anal intercourse. We came home and proceeded to make love. He went out and got two belts. He tied my feet together with one, and with the other he kinda beat me. I was in the spirit, I went along with it. But when he tried to penetrate me anally, I couldn't take it, it was too painful. I managed to convey to him verbally to quit it. He did stop, but not soon enough to suit me. Then one time, he branded me. I still have a scar on my butt. He put a little wax initial thing on a hot plate and then stuck it on my ass when I was unaware.

*Ms. P:* My boyfriend and I saw a movie in which there was masochism. After that he wanted to gag me and tie me up. He was stoned. I was not. I was really shocked at his behavior. I was nervous and uptight. He literally tried to force me, after gagging me first. He snuck up behind me with a scarf. He was hurting me with it and I started getting upset. Then I realized it wasn't a joke. He grabbed me and shook me by my shoulders and brought out some ropes, and told me to relax, and that I would enjoy it. Then he started putting me down about my feelings about sex, and my inhibitedness. I started crying and struggling with him, got loose, and kicked him in the testicles, which forced him down on the couch. I ran out of the house. Next day he called and apologized, but that was the end of him.

From the women's answers, it can not be concluded that pornography *caused* the behavior described, merely that the women believed there was a connection between them. The answers, though, certainly *do* indicate that pornography *did* have some effect. Most notable is that 10 percent of the women interviewed felt they had been personally victimized by pornography. It also appears that some men these women described had indeed attempted to use pornography to get them to do what they wanted.[5] It seems likely that pornography may have reinforced and legitimized these acts, including the assaultive behavior, in these men's minds. In some cases the actual *idea* of doing certain acts appears to have come from viewing pornography—as in the suggestion involving a dog, and in some of the sadomasochistic proposals.

In recent years several researchers have been exploring the effects on aggressive behavior of sexual arousal by "erotic" stimuli. Edward Donnerstein, one of the most noted of these researchers, emphasized that as recently as 1980, the kind of research that would be most relevant to women—namely, investigation of the effects of aggressive cues juxtaposed with "erotica"—was still rare (1980).

Psychologists Seymour Feshbach and Neil Malamuth are two researchers who *have* conducted experiments in this area that are relevant to women. They describe one of the most common experimental designs used in this kind of research as follows:

> The typical procedure is to expose some subjects to a sexually arousing stimulus—an erotic film or written passage—and then provide them with an opportunity to act aggressively against someone else, usually a confederate of the experimenter who makes a preset number of errors in a guessing game. For each error, the subject may administer an electric shock to the confederate that ranges in intensity from the barely perceptible to the quite strong. (Unknown to the subject, the shock leads to the confederate are disconnected.) The average level of shock the subject administers over the series of error trials provides researchers with an index of the level of aggression. (1978, p. 112)

In one of Edward Donnerstein's experiments, aggressive behavior was measured by the "typical procedure" described by Feshbach and Malamuth. Some of the students in the study were subjected to insults designed to arouse their anger, to test the impact of anger on their behavior prior to viewing "erotic" movies. Donnerstein used two neutral, two "erotic," and two "aggressive-erotic" films, each four minutes long. The neutral films were of a talk-show interview; the "erotic" films "depicted a young couple in various stages of sexual intercourse"; the aggressive-erotic films contained scenes in which an individual with a gun forces himself into the home of a woman and forces her into sexual intercourse (1980, p. 9). The subjects were 120 male undergraduates.

Donnerstein (1980) reported that an important difference emerged, depending on whether the "victim" of aggression was male or female:

When angered subjects were paired with a male, the aggressive-erotic films produced no more aggression than exposure to the erotic film. Those subjects paired with a female, however, *only* displayed an increase in aggression after viewing the aggressive-erotic film. In fact, this increase occurred even if subjects were not angered, although the combination of anger and film exposure produced the highest level of aggressive behavior. (1980, p. 22)

Donnerstein's explanation for these results is that the "female's association with observed violence was an important contributor to the aggressive responses toward her" (1980, p. 22). In other words, the male subjects associated the victimized woman in the film with the woman in the experiment, making her "an aggressive stimulus which could elicit aggressive responses" (n.d., p. 13).

Donnerstein concludes that if his interpretation is correct, "it would be expected that films which depict violence against women, even without sexual content, could act as a stimulus for aggressive acts toward women" (n.d., p. 13). Later Donnerstein goes a step further.

"There is ample evidence," he maintains, "that the observation of violent forms of media can facilitate aggressive responses, yet to assume that the depiction of sexual-aggression could not have a similar effect, particularly against females, would be misleading" (n.d., p. 14). The word "misleading" is quite an understatement. In fact, it is inconsistent and dangerous.

Seymour Feshbach and Neil Malamuth found in an experiment that even "one exposure to violence in pornography can significantly influence erotic reactions to the portrayal of rape" (1978, p. 116). In this experiment, a group of college students were asked to read a mildly sadomasochistic story taken from *Penthouse*. Another group of students read a similar but nonviolent version of the story. Both groups then read a story about rape in which the terrified victim was compelled to yield at knife point (this story was quoted earlier in Chapter 1).

The experimenters found that men who had read the sadomasochistic story tended to be more sexually aroused in response to the account of rape than those who had read the nonviolent story. Feshbach and Malamuth concluded that, "The inhibitions that are ordinarily a response to pain cues were somehow altered because of exposure to sadomasochistic material" (1978, p. 116). Furthermore they observed that "for these males the greater their judgment of the victim's pain, the greater their sexual excitement" (1978, p. 116).

In another study by Neil Malamuth, 29 male students were classified as sexually force-oriented or nonforce-oriented on the basis of their responses on a questionnaire (1981a). These students "were randomly assigned to exposure to rape or mutually-consenting versions of a slide-audio show. All subjects were then exposed to the same audio description of a rape read by a female. They were later asked to create their own fantasies" (1981a, p. 33).

Malamuth regarded the most significant finding of this experiment to be that "those exposed to the rape version, irrespective of their sexual classification, created more violent sexual fantasies than those exposed to the mutually-consenting version" (1981a, p. 33). He concluded that there was reason to be concerned about the violent fantasies that may be stimulated by the mass media. More specifically, Malamuth argued that

> To the extent that such fantasies persist beyond the confines of the laboratory, they may contribute to deviant behavior. ... [I]n keeping with the possibility that violent sexual fantasies may have undesirable effects is the consistent finding that sexual responsiveness to sexual violence is associated in college students with a callous attitude towards rape and rape victims and with a self-reported possibility of raping. (1981a, p. 44).

Briddell et al. designed an ingenious experiment to test the effects of alcohol and cognitive set on sexual arousal to vivid, two-minute audiotaped descriptions of rape and nonrape sexual scenes. They found that alcohol did not significantly influence levels of sexual arousal. However,

> Subjects who *believed* they had consumed an alcoholic beverage evidenced significantly more arousal to the forcible rape recording and to the sadistic stimuli than subjects who believed that they had consumed a nonalcoholic beverage, regardless of the actual contents of the beverage. (1978, p. 418, emphasis added)

Briddell et al. conclude that "these feelings ... suggest that normal heterosexual males who have been drinking (or believe they have been drinking) may exhibit sexual arousal patterns indistinguishable from those patterns reported for identified rapists" (1978, p. 427).

Don Smith did a content analysis of 428 "adults only" paperbacks published between 1968 and 1974. His sample was limited to books that were readily accessible to the general American public, excluding paperbacks that are usually available only in so-called "adult bookstores" (1976). He reported the following:

- One-fifth of all the sex episodes involved completed rape (p. 5);
- the number of rapes increased with each year's output of newly published books (p. 12);
- of the sex episodes 6 percent involved incestuous rape (p. 10);
- the focus in the rape scenes was on the victim's fear and terror, which became transformed by the rape into sexual passion. Over 97 percent of the rapes portrayed resulted in orgasm for the victims. In three-quarters of these instances, multiple orgasm was achieved. (p. 10);
- less than 3 percent of the rapists experienced any negative consequences, and many were rewarded (p. 11).

Neil Malamuth and Barry Spinner also report that "in 1977 an individual examining the two best-selling erotic magazines would have been exposed to sexual violence in about 10 percent of the cartoons and close to 5 percent of the pictorial stimuli" (1980, p. 235). They also observe that "the information conveyed in much of the sexually violent materials is that women are basically masochistic and in need of male domination."

Further, Malamuth and Spinner point out the following: "The effects of such materials cannot be considered only within the limited context of other mass-media and nonmedia 'messages.' A message of female subordination communicated in varied forms may have summative effects in promoting a sexist ideology" (1980, p. 235).

Such pornography conveys the message that many ordinary men commit rape, and that when they do, they experience not remorse, but sexual, ego, and other gratifications. Consumers of this pornography may come to believe that rape is not a breach of norms. By making rape appear easy to accomplish and easy to get away with, pornography may affect inhibitions based on fear of being caught. Most important, pornography of this kind may inhibit the conscience. If a man can persuade himself that women really *like* being raped—that they don't really mean "no"—what reason is there for guilt?

Another approach to examining the effects of pornography is simply to point out that learning by imitating others' behavior (a form of learning that has been established after decades of psychological research) applies to pornography. As Victor Cline writes with some exasperation, "Are the laws of learning somehow repealed or inoperative here but not in the rest of life?" (1974, p. 208).[6]

In addition to imitative or observational learning, Cline points out that the laws of learning referred to as "classical" and "instrumental conditioning" are also highly relevant to an analysis of pornography's effects. He cites work by S. Rachman of the Institute of Psychiatry,

Maudsley Hospital, London, who has demonstrated repeatedly that sexual fetishism can be created in the laboratory using sexually explicit pictures. Rachman

> exposed male subjects to colored photographic slides of nude females in sexually arousing positions along with a picture of female boots. Eventually, through simple conditioning, the male subjects were sexually aroused at merely seeing only the picture of the female boot. (Cline, 1974, p. 208)

The point is not that such a fetish is necessarily harmful. However, these same laws of conditioning suggest that men who are sexually aroused by watching pornographic movies or pictures that depict rape, can come to associate rape with sexual arousal.

Even if men are not sexually excited during the movie, subsequent masturbation to movie images that have included rape reinforces the association, constituting what McGuire and his colleagues refer to as "masturbatory conditioning" (Cline, 1974, p. 210). The pleasurable experience of masturbation can thereby make the image as well as the act of rape more sexually exciting.

The movie *A Clockwork Orange* dramatized the use of aversive conditioning by the association of electric shocks with pictures of rape. In the real world, these techniques have been probably been as frequently used to try to change homosexuals into heterosexuals as to try to change the behavior of rapists. After citing many such studies, Cline concludes that

> this literature suggests that erotic materials have great potetial power to assist in the shift of sexual orientation when used under certain prescribed conditions. The possibility of deliberate or accidental real-life conditionings in the reverse direction has to be given due consideration here. (1974, p. 210)

Given that both erotica and pornography can elicit behavioral changes of any kind in a doctor's office, its potential to effect change in other circumstances is unquestionable.

More recently, Hans Eysenck and D.K.B. Nias have made similar arguments in their book *Sex, Violence and the Media* (1978). After reviewing Rachman's research cited above, they suggest that "the theory of conditioning, combined with the evidence from the above studies, indicates that it might be possible to create a rapist or sadist in the laboratory by presenting scenes of rape or sadism immediately prior to normally arousing scenes" (1978, p. 190).

*Conclusion*

Recent research and analysis indicates that a large percentage of the male population has a propensity to rape. Important inhibitors to the acting out of this propensity are, first of all, *social controls* such as the possibility of being caught and apprehended.

*Social norms* that define rape as unacceptable behavior constitute a second source of inhibition. When social norms do not define rape as unacceptable—as during times of war, or in certain subcultures (for example, the Hell's Angels), or where group rape is seen as an acceptable way to punish deviant women—one would anticipate a greater percentage of men being willing to rape.

The third and crucial inhibitor is *conscience.* Some men clearly abhor the idea of rape because they see it as immoral and brutal behavior.

Male consumers of the violent pornography so prevalent today, have their inhibitions against rape undermined on all three levels.

## Effects of Exposure to Mass Media that Encourage Rape

The growing strength and demands of women in real life, spear-headed by women's liberation, obviously provoked a backlash in commercial film: a redoubling of Godfather-like machismo to beef up man's eroding virility or, alternately, an escape into the all-male world of the buddy films from *Easy Rider* to *Scarecrow*. With the substitution of violence and sexuality (a poor second) for romance, there was less need for exciting and interesting women; any bouncing nymphet whose curves looked good in catsup would do. (Haskell, 1974, pp. 323–324)

On the basis of its research, the National Commission on the Causes and Prevention of Violence concluded in 1969 that media violence can induce people to act aggressively. One year later, the Commission on Obscenity and Pornography concluded that exposure to pornography does not have a harmful effect (1970). The latter conclusion was not limited to nonviolent pornography. This glaring contradiction was pointed out by political scientist Irene Diamond, one of the very few women currently doing research on pornography (1980).

Psychologists Neil Malamuth and James Check designed a field experiment to examine the effects of violent sexuality portrayed in feature-length movies in a nonlaboratory setting. Their goal was "to directly test the feminist contention that mass media exposures that portray violence against women as having favorable consequences contribute to greater acceptance of sexual and nonsexual violence against women" (1981).

Two hundred and seventy-one males and females were the subjects in this experiment. Some of them had signed up to participate in a study on movie ratings. They were randomly assigned to view either a feature-length film that included violent sexual scenes or one that did not. These movies were being shown as part of the regular campus film program. Members of the subjects' class who had not volunteered to participate were used as a comparison group.

The movies *Swept Away* and *The Getaway* were chosen "because they portray violence against women as having justification and positive consequences" (1981). The two control films, *A Man and a Woman* and *Hopper* do not portray any form of sexual violence. After viewing the movies, the subjects completed a brief questionnaire as well as an evaluation of the film.

Within a week, an attitude survey was administered to all students in the class from which the subjects had been recruited. Embedded within this survey were an Acceptance of Interpersonal Violence Scale (for example: "A man is never justified in hitting his wife"), and a Rape Myth Acceptance Scale (for example, "Many women have an unconscious wish to be raped and may then unconsciously set up a situation in which they are likely to be attacked"; 1981).

This experiment showed that exposure to the sexually violent movies increased the male subjects' acceptance of interpersonal violence against women (this relationship was statistically significant). Their acceptance of rape myths also increased (this relationship did not reach statistical significance). In contrast, female subjects exposed to the violent sexual films were less accepting of interpersonal violence and rape myths than the control subjects (these relationships did not reach statistical significance).

These results might appear to cancel each other out because of the opposite effects on males and females. But the fact remains that it is almost always men who rape and beat women, not vice-versa. Hence, men's attitudes about these behaviors are more significant to the incidence of violent sexual abuse.

Malamuth and Check concluded as follows:

> In considering the generalizability of the present findings, it is important to evaluate the comparability of the "dosage levels" used to those of nonexperimental settings. Is exposure to two films portraying violent sexuality within a four-day period an event unlikely to occur in daily life? In the present authors' view, such "dosage levels" are not very unusual. (1981)

It seems difficult to refute this conclusion. Indeed there is evidence that the "dosage levels" of violence against women in movies may be increasing. In 1980, PBS-TV devoted a special edition of *Sneak Previews* to a discussion of movies depicting "extreme violence directed at women." This program was in response to the enormous number of commercials "exploiting the plight of women in danger" that had been "saturating television for the past two years" (transcript, *Sneak Previews* #304).

Film critics Roger Ebert and Gene Siskel decided to evaluate a new genre of films featuring extreme violence against women. Most of them involved "teenage girls being raped or stabbed to death, usually both," for example, *Prom Night, Don't Go in the House, The Howling, Terror Train, The Boogeyman, He Knows You're Alone, Motel Hell, Silent Scream, I Spit on Your Grave* (transcript, *Sneak Previews* #304).

In answer to the question as to why these movies had become so popular, Siskel replied:

> I'm convinced it has something to do with the growth of the women's movement in America in the last decade. I think that these films are some sort of primordial response by some very sick people saying, "Get back in your place, women."

Siskel pointed out that the women in these films "are typically portrayed as independent, as sexual, as enjoying life. And the killer, typically ... is a man who is sexually frustrated with these new aggressive women, and so he strikes back at them" (transcript, *Sneak Previews* #304). Siskel observed that decapitations are quite common in these movies, and repeated stabbing shots of all parts of women's bodies "are grotesquely routine." Furthermore, the movies encourage the audience to identify with the killer, not the victim. Siskel concludes that the filmmakers are "picking up on the notion that a lot of men are angry at women, don't know how to cope with women—and they're pandering, exciting, inflaming men" (transcript, *Sneak Previews* #304).

This analysis by Siskel and Ebert is consistent with the way some theorists interpret the occurrence of rape itself. They see it as a means of controlling women. These theories will be presented next.

### Rape as a Means of Social Control

He said, "Listen, any time any man wants to rape you, he can, and I'm telling you this for your own good." (Rapist; Russell, 1975, p. 231)

"Rape is like smoking—you can't stop once you start. ... I knew what I
was doing. I was angry. I could have stopped but I didn't want to. I
wanted to hurt their pride, put them in their place." (Rapist; Scully &
Marolla, 1983, p. 56)

Susan Brownmiller offers several theories about the causes of rape.
Her biological theory was cited previously; the violent subculture
theory, to which she also subscribes, will be described shortly. Her
best-known theory is that the function of rape is to keep women subordinate to men. This is how she put it:

> From prehistoric times to the present, I believe, rape has played a
> critical function. It is nothing more or less than a conscious process of
> intimidation by which *all* men keep *all* women in a state of fear. (1975,
> p. 15; emphasis in original)

If Brownmiller is saying here that all men consciously use rape to
intimidate women, she seems to be guilty of overstatement.

If, on the other hand, Brownmiller means that all men benefit from
the state of fear that affects all women because some men consciously
intimidate women by raping them, then she contributes a brilliant
insight. Since Brownmiller makes the latter point elsewhere in her
book, it seems to be the best interpretation of her rather ambiguous
statement. More specifically Brownmiller summarizes her analysis of
what she calls "the police-blotter rapist" (the portrait of rapists that
emerges from the relatively few cases that are reported to the police):

> Police-blotter rapists in a very real sense perform a myrmidon function
> for all men in our society. Cloaked in myths that obscure their identity,
> they, too, function as anonymous agents of terror. Although they are
> the ones who do the dirty work, the actual *attentat,* to other men, their
> superiors in class and station, the lasting benefits of their simple-
> minded evil have always accrued.

> A world without rapists would be a world in which women moved
> freely without fear of men. That *some* men rape provides a sufficient
> threat to keep all women in a constant state of intimidation, forever
> conscious of the knowledge that the biological tool must be held in awe
> for it may turn to weapon with sudden swiftness borne of harmful
> intent. Myrmidons to the cause of male dominance, police-blotter
> rapists have performed their duty well, so well in fact that the true
> meaning of their act has largely gone unnoticed. Rather than society's
> aberrants or "spoilers of purity," men who commit rape have served in
> effect as front-line masculine shock troops, terrorist guerrillas in the
> longest sustained battle the world has ever known. (1975, p. 209)

**CONCLUSION**

Clearly if the desire to rape was as foreign to men in the United States as Margaret Mead claimed was the case for the Arapesh in New Guinea (1935), then the factors that reduce men's internal and social inhibitions against rape, as well as the factors that reduce the potential victim's ability to avoid rape, would be irrelevant. So, for example, since a predisposition to rape appears to be largely absent in women, examination of these other three factors becomes redundant for them.

The next three chapters will focus on theories of causation that fit into the remaining three preconditions of rape by men.

*Notes*

1. Groth does not explain why these percentages add up to only 86.

2. For a recent summary of some of these studies, see Mary Koss et al. (1981a).

3. The research of one of these teams (Mary Koss et al., 1981) will be discussed in Chapter 6.

4. The analysis of the relationship between pornography and violence to follow has drawn extensively from "Pornography and Violence: What Does the New Research Say?" (Russell, in Lederer, 1980).

5. Donald Mosher reported that 16 percent of a sample of 256 male college students had "shown a girl pornography, or taken a girl to a sexy movie to induce her to have intercourse" (1971, p. 318).

6. Cline, a psychologist, edited a book on pornography entitled *Where Do You Draw the Line?* (1974). While he deserves to be commended for his strenuous and informed critique of the National Commission on Obscenity and Pornography, it is as difficult to sift through his biases as it is to sift through the very different biases in the ten volumes of the commission reports (1971). The commission's reasoning appears to have been that sex is good, that sex and pornography are synonymous, and that therefore pornography is harmless. Cline's reasoning, on the other hand, is that sex is bad, that sex and pornography are synonymous, and that therefore pornography is bad. In addition, he is quite homophobic.

# 6

# FACTORS REDUCING INTERNAL INHIBITIONS AGAINST RAPE

## Cultural Values that Encourage Rape

"In recent months, I have become more sympathetic toward rapists, because I see in myself the other side of the sexual revolution: it is all well and good for the Beautiful People to decide to bring their fantasies out of the closet and talk about the joys of sex in public—it is another to be tantalized day after day by the sight of beautiful women you desire but can't have. Apparently every one of them is experiencing the wildest sexual pleasures and fulfillment, because the media are everywhere saying so."

"I have never raped a woman. But I have been mad enough at women's behavior toward me to want to at least think about it. There is *provocation for the act of rape* in a man's life and it isn't necessarily the provocation of the rape victim. The provocation can be a generalized frustration and feeling of *personal* impotence. The media proclaim that everyone is having sex. If you are not having sex, these media statements mean *everyone but you*. As in propaganda, the Big Lie, if told often enough, begins to be believed. When it is believed, a man may start to wonder about himself—'What's wrong with me? Why aren't I getting any?'" (Male respondents; Hite, 1981, p. 717)

### FEMALE SEXUALITY VIEWED AS A COMMODITY

"I've seen a lot of women who seem to be asking for it ... just as a person with a fistful of money is asking for robbery by flaunting his money, especially in a gin mill or dark alley. I also feel sympathy for women. After all, when someone wants to protect one's money from being stolen, the money can be placed in a bank. But how does a woman protect her body from being raped? I wish I knew. A little more prudence, I guess. I'm glad I'm a man." (Male respondent; Hite, 1981)

Canadian researchers Lorenne Clark and Debra Lewis believe that when women are viewed as private property, their sexual and reproductive capacities became the sole qualities that gave them value (1977, p. 115). Looking at this situation through men's eyes, Clark and Lewis offer a chilling though probably accurate picture:

> From the male point of view, female sexuality is a commodity in the possession of women, even if it is something men will come to own and control under the appropriate circumstances. Women are seen as the hoarders and miserly dispensers of a much desired commodity, and men must constantly wheedle, bargain, and pay a price for what they want. And if anything lies at the root of misogyny, this does. Men naturally come to resent and dislike women because they see them as having something which they want and have a perfect right to, but which women are unwilling to give them freely.... Woman's alienation from her own sexuality, man's resentment at having to purchase sexual fulfillment, the unequal bargaining that trades security for sex—all of these distortions of human sexuality make it inevitable that much sexual contact between men and women will necessarily be coercive in nature. (1977, pp. 128–129)

Interviews with rapists or men who express a desire to rape women suggest that these men are particularly apt to view female sexuality as a commodity (Hite, 1981; Beneke, 1982). This is part of the more general tendency so common in this culture to objectify women. One would-be rapist described his thoughts during the attack as follows: "[A]ll of a sudden it came into my head, 'My God, this is a human being!' I came to my senses and saw that I was hurting this person" (Russell, 1975, p. 249). Objectification of people is a key defense mechanism in the facilitation of brutal or inhumane behavior, whether it be torturing those defined as the enemy during a war, or raping women.

### RAPE AS A CONSEQUENCE OF A RAPE-SUPPORTIVE CULTURE

> "I have never raped a woman, or wanted to. In this I guess I am somewhat odd. Many of my friends talk about rape a lot and fantasize about it. The whole idea leaves me cold." (Male respondent; Hite, 1981, p. 719)

> "She said 'no' but it was a societal 'no,' she wanted to be coaxed ... all women say 'no' when they mean 'yes,' but it's a societal 'no' so they won't have to feel responsible later." (Rapist; Scully & Marolla, 1983, p. 43)

In the early seventies feminists observed that many beliefs in this culture deny that rape of a woman is possible (Russell, 1975, pp. 257–259). The belief that all women secretly want to be raped implies that rape victims must have wanted or enjoyed being raped. Consequently the victims are blamed for being raped. If women can be blamed for rape, men can more readily indulge their desires to rape them. Many victims never report being raped, because they too blame themselves or fear they will be blamed by others. Blaming the victim also results in prejudicial and hostile treatment toward some of the victims who do report. Another consequence is that many rapists fail to see themselves as such (Russell, 1975, p. 259).

Sociologist Martha Burt undertook a study to test the feminists' theory that such myths support rape and even play a causative role in rape. Burt defined rape myths as prejudicial, stereotyped, or false beliefs about rape, rape victims, and rapists. The following are examples of these rape myths, as Burt phrased them (1980, pp. 217–230): "Any healthy woman can resist a rapist." "In the majority of rapes, the victim was promiscuous or had a bad reputation." "If a girl engages in necking or petting and she lets things get out of hand, it is her fault if her partner forces sex on her." "One reason that women falsely report a rape is that they frequently have a need to call attention to themselves." Burt found that over half of a representative sample of 598 residents of Minnesota agreed with these and other rape myths.

Burt also found that belief in these rape myths formed part of a larger interrelated structure of beliefs and attitudes that included "sex role stereotyping, sexual conservatism, acceptance of interpersonal violence, and beliefs that sexual relationships between men and women are adversarial in nature (a 'battle of the sexes' philosophy)" (1978, p. 3). She argued that "these attitudes effectively support rape."

With regard to the causative role of the attitudes measured by Burt in the occurrence of rape, she pointed out that

> rapists themselves hold rape-supportive attitudes and use them to excuse or deny their behavior after the fact. Their attitudes may also serve as psychological releasers or neutralizers, allowing potential rapists to turn off social prohibitions against injuring or using others when they want to commit an assault. (1978, p. 5)

In a paper designed "to present selected aspects of the feminist viewpoint as empirically testable hypotheses about rape and to review the research relating to each," James Check and Neil Malamuth replicated Burt's findings on college students. They found there to be considerable empirical support for Burt's findings regarding the attitudinal structure of rape myth acceptance (1981, p. 11).

Check and Malamuth then designed an experiment to determine whether these attitudes would be predictive of reactions to the following: a pornographic depiction of rape; a real rape; and males' actual predictions about their own likelihood of raping. They used Burt's scales to measure rape myth acceptance, acceptance of violence against women, and adversarial beliefs about sexual relationships by 126 college students (1981, p. 12).

Three weeks later, some of these students were given what the researchers described as "pornographic rape portrayals" to read. The students were asked to report their perceptions of the victim's experience in terms of her willingness, sexual pleasure, and pain. The male students were also asked how likely they would be to rape. A few days later these same students were asked to read a newspaper report of what purported to be an actual rape, and to report their perceptions of the causes of rape in the real world (1981, p. 12).

Check and Malamuth report the following results of this experiment:

- The male students who perceived the rape victim's experience in the pornographic depiction as positive were more likely to accept rape myths, violence against women, and adversarial sex beliefs.
- Male students with high acceptance of violence against women and high adversarial sex beliefs were less likely to think that the rapist in the newspaper account of rape should be charged for his crime.
- Male students who subscribed to the rape myths were more inclined to believe that the rape victim in the newspaper account was responsible for being raped.
- Male students who were high on all three scales were more inclined to believe that women secretly desire to be raped, and that natural masculine tendencies as well as women's behavior in general are important in causing rape.
- Finally, all three scales were also predicative of male students' self-reported likelihood of raping women (1981, p. 13).

Check and Malamuth cite other research showing that rape myth acceptance is associated with aggressive behavior. This includes actual aggression against women under laboratory conditions (1981, p. 14). Research by Mary Koss, Kenneth Leonard, Dana Beezley, and Cheryl Oros confirms these conclusions (1981b). They classified male students into four groups:

(1) *Highly sexually aggressive.* Males who admitted obtaining sexual intercourse, including oral or anal intercourse, through the threat or use of force.

(2) *Moderately sexually aggressive.* Males who admitted to using some degree of physical force (twisting her arm, holding her down, etc.) to force a woman to engage in kissing or petting when she didn't want to; or, where rape was attempted but not completed.

(3) *Somewhat sexually aggressive.* Males who admitted to obtaining intercourse with a woman who didn't want to by saying things they didn't mean, or threatening to end the relationship if she didn't submit, or using other forms of verbal pressure.

(4) *Nonsexually aggressive.* Males who denied all the sexually aggressive items, and admitted only to mutually desired intercourse (1981b, pp. 11–12).

Koss et al. found that the "higher levels of sexual aggression were associated with views of sexual aggression as normal, heterosexual relationships as gameplaying, traditional attitudes toward female sexuality, and the acceptance of rape myths" (1981b, p. 16).

For example, the highly sexually aggressive men tended to agree to items such as these:

"Sometimes the only way a man can get a cold woman turned on is to use force."

"Being roughed up is sexually stimulating to many women."

"Most women are sly and manipulating when they are out to attract a man."

The sexually aggressive men tended to disagree with items such as these:

"Most women who say 'No' to a man's sexual advances mean it."

"Most men would not pretend to be emotionally involved with a woman just in order to have sex with her."

These men also tended to accept rape myths as factual, and to uphold traditional attitudes toward women and female sexuality. For example, they disagreed with items such as the following:

"Any female can get raped."

"Women who have rape fantasies which sexually arouse them would probably not enjoy the real thing." (1981b, p. 18)

As their measure of traditional attitudes toward females, Koss et al. used the 25-item Spence-Helmreich Attitudes Toward Women Scale. This scale gauges the degree to which individuals accept traditional sex role stereotypes (1981b, p. 13). Male subjects with a higher level of sexual aggression tended to subscribe to more traditional attitudes toward females than those with lower levels of sexual aggression (1981b, p. 17).

Although correlation does not prove causation, Koss et al. conclude that their findings are nevertheless consistent with the theory that rape-supportive attitudes (1) serve to facilitate the act of rape, and (2) serve as a subsequent justification of the rape (1981b, p. 17). The relationship between attitudes and behavior has been a matter of dispute in psychology for a long time. The research discussed in this section addresses the connection between them and strongly suggests that rape-supportive attitudes do indeed affect behavior. Although many people have not waited for researchers to confirm what they consider common sense, this research does significantly advance rape theory in this area.

## RAPE AS A CONSEQUENCE OF SUBCULTURAL NORMS

Marvin Wolfgang and Franco Ferracuti developed the notion that "the urban ghetto produces a subculture in which aggressive violence is accepted as normative and natural in everyday life" (Mulvihill et al., 1969, vol. 11, p. xxxiv; Wolfgang & Ferracuti, 1967). They believe this theory to be most helpful in explaining aggressive violence in the United States. They particularly addressed the fact that black urban-dwelling males are so overrepresented amongst those arrested for violent crimes, and that black men and women are so overrepresented amongst those victimized by violent crime.

The authors of the summary to the National Commission reports (who are presumably Wolfgang and Ferracuti, since it is their theory that is cited, although no specific authors are mentioned) hasten to add that

Not everyone in the ghetto accepts an ethos of violence. Even among those who do, primarily young males, violence is not the only or predominant mode of expression. When it is used, the context often involves the desire to prove one's masculinity and to become a successful member of ghetto society. (Mulvihill et al., 1969, vol. 11, p. xxxiv)

Wolfgang and Ferracuti were among the few nonfeminist scholars who emphasized the connection between violence and ideals of masculinity prior to the 1970s. It is also significant that they saw the subculture of violence as being caused by the poverty, unemployment, and lack of options imposed on black people by white society (Mulvihill et al., 1969, vol. 11, p. xxxiv).

Susan Brownmiller finds the subculture of violence theory most useful in explaining what she calls "the police-blotter rapist." "There is no getting around the fact," Brownmiller boldly states, confronting the desire of many liberals and radicals to do just that, "that most of those who engage in antisocial, criminal violence (murder, assault, rape and robbery) come from the lower socioeconomic classes" (1975, p. 181). There is also no doubt, she continues, that because of centuries of oppression by white people, black people are disproportionately in the lower socioeconomic classes, and hence contribute a disproportionate number of the crimes of violence (1975, p. 181).

Be this as it may, the Russell survey data have shown that when the focus is shifted from stranger rape to rape by intimates, and reported to unreported rape, the correlation between social class, race and ethnicity, and the perpetration of rape becomes significantly weaker (see Chapter 3 for a fuller discussion of these findings).

## RAPE AS A SYMPTOM OF A VIOLENT CULTURE

Some theorists see rape as one crime of violence among many, (homicide, aggravated assault, and robbery), all of them caused by unemployment, poverty and marginality (for example, Schwendinger & Schwendinger, 1983). Reported rapes have been increasing at a more rapid rate than have other crimes of violence, but until 1981 *all* these crimes had been increasing alarmingly over the years. As already mentioned, the recent decline appears to be due to a decline in the number of men in the most violence-prone age groups concomitant with the aging of males born during the baby boom. (See Chapter 1 for a more thorough discussion of these statistics.)

Since the most reliable crime statistics are available on reported homicides, Table 6.1 presents the homicide rate per 100,000 inhabitants in the United States over the last 24 years. The actual number of homicides has more than doubled during these years (from 8,580 in 1959 to 21,012 in 1982), while the rate per 100,000 has nearly doubled during that period (from 4.8 to 9.1).

The fact that the perpetrators of violent crimes are disproportionately black and poor is consistent with this theory. To the extent that this theory is correct, the implication for social policy is clearly in favor of programs that create full employment, job training, and a guaranteed annual income.

This theory, like many other theories that relate crime to lack of economic well-being and opportunities (as well as other deprivations), overlooks a crucial fact: Black women should then be the most overrepresented group among criminals, and by some measures (such as annual earnings), white women should be the next most overrepre-

**TABLE 6.1**

**Homicide Rates in the United States 1959-1982**

| Year | Total Number Homicides | Homicide Rate per 100,000 Inhabitants |
|------|------------------------|----------------------------------------|
| 1982 | 21,012 | 9.1 |
| 1981 | 22,516 | 9.8 |
| 1980 | 23,044 | 10.2 |
| 1979 | 21,456 | 9.7 |
| 1978 | 19,555 | 9.0 |
| 1977 | 19,120 | 8.8 |
| 1976 | 18,780 | 8.8 |
| 1975 | 20,510 | 9.6 |
| 1974 | 20,600 | 9.7 |
| 1973 | 19,510 | 9.3 |
| 1972 | 18,520 | 8.9 |
| 1971 | 17,630 | 8.5 |
| 1970 | 15,810 | 7.8 |
| 1969 | 14,590 | 7.2 |
| 1968 | 13,650 | 6.8 |
| 1967 | 12,090 | 6.1 |
| 1966 | 10,920 | 5.6 |
| 1965 | 9,850 | 5.1 |
| 1964 | 9,250 | 4.8 |
| 1963 | 8,500 | 4.5 |
| 1962 | 8,400 | 4.5 |
| 1961 | 8,600 | 4.7 |
| 1960 | 9,140 | 5.1 |
| 1959 | 8.580 | 4.8 |

SOURCE: *Uniform Crime Reports*, 1960-1983.

sented group. But in fact, rape as well as other violent crimes and other violent acts are perpetrated predominantly by males.

Statistics on crimes of violence clearly indicate that violence is overwhelmingly a male problem in this society—and that both women and men suffer the consequences. Sixty-two percent (62 percent) of homicides involve men murdering other men; only 4 percent involve women murdering other women (Mulvihill et al., 1969, vol. 11, p. 210). In 1979, 99 percent of the arrests for forcible rape, 88 percent of the arrests for aggravated assault, and 86 percent of the arrests for homicide were of males (FBI, 1980). When crimes of murder, rape, aggravated assault, and robbery with violence or threat of violence are added together, 90 percent of those arrested for these crimes in 1979 were men, and only 10 percent were women. This 9:1 ratio has changed little in recent years.

The homicide rate per 100,000 people in the United States is sub-stantially higher than that of any other Western nation (Wolfgang & Ferracuti, 1967). In 1960, for example, when the homicide rate in the United States was 4.5 per 100,000, it was 1.8 in West Germany, 1.7 in France, 1.5 in Australia, 1.5 in Greece, 1.4 in Canada, 1.4 in Italy, 1.1 in New Zealand, .9 in Portugal, .9 in Switzerland, .8 in Spain, .7 in Belgium, .7 in Sweden, .6 in England, .5 in Denmark, .5 in Norway, .3 in the Netherlands, and .2 in Ireland (1967, p. 275). This means that the homicide rate in 1960 was 23 times higher in the United States than in Ireland.

It is in the interests of the well-being and survival of the entire population of this country to recognize the magnitude and serious-ness of the problem of male violence in the United States today.

## Irresistible Impulse and Rape

According to Joseph Marolla and Diana Scully, "psychiatric litera-ture has been filled with the assertion that irresistible impulse is at the root of rape" (1979, p. 303). These authors cite the following two examples (1979, p. 303, emphasis added):

Whether it is comparatively mild as in the case of simple assault, or whether it is severely aggravated assault, *it is, as a rule, an expression of an uncontrollable urge, committed without logic or rationale, under the influence of a strong, overpowering drive.* (B. Karpman, 1951, p. 185)

It is not intended to suggest that all recidivous sex offenders are physically dangerous, but experience shows that some of them are compulsively so, and that *most of them are driven by uncontrollable impulsions* that do not respond to customary procedures. (J. Reinhardt & E. Fisher, 1949, p. 734)

B. Karpman also argued that "uncontrollable instinct is beyond punishment"; he used this "fact" to explain why punishment was so ineffective with sexual psychopaths (Marolla & Scully, 1979, p. 303).

Marolla and Scully offer the following critique of the irresistible impulse theory: First, they cite studies reporting a low recidivism rate for rape, for example, T. Gibbens, C. Way, and K. Soothill found only 3 percent over a 12-year period (1977). Second, they cite Mena-chem Amir's study in which 71 percent of the rapes were premedi-tated (1971). They point out that "if the act was impulsive, by definition, the offender should not have been able to delay his response" (1979, p. 304).

Finally, these researchers observe that "since impulse theory could hypothetically be applied to any behavior, it is interesting to question why it has been used as an appropriate motive for crimes against women and not for other types of criminal behavior" (1979, p. 304). They suggest that although the theory does not explain rape, it does fit psychiatric assumptions about male and female sexuality.

## Psychopathology and Rape

According to Marolla and Scully, when psychoanalysts employ the disease model, they usually make one or more of the following assumptions about rape:

> Rape is directly or indirectly sexual in nature. It is perpetrated by a perverted or sick individual who often has latent homosexual tendencies. He has experienced an abnormal childhood which has resulted in a sadistic personality. And finally, rape is often an attack on a mother figure and should be considered as symptomatic of inner conflicts which are the real problem. (1979, p. 305)

Marolla and Scully refute each of these assumptions. They argue that when rape is viewed as a sexual act, "victim seduction becomes a possible element in the crime" (1979, p. 306). They add that

> since sex is generally thought of as a reciprocal process, the role of the other and the issue of consent become relevant. However, when rape is defined as physical assault, the motive "sexual provocation" is hardly appropriate. Unless it could be proven that the woman was a practising masochist there would be no case. When defined sexually a husband cannot be accused of rape nor can a prostitute or allegedly "promiscuous" woman be victimized since in both cases consent has been bought or exchanged for material goods. All of these arguments appear absurd when rape is viewed as a violent attack against a person. (1979, pp. 306–307)

Marolla and Scully are two of the many researchers who view rape as an act primarily of violence or aggression.

Many psychologists (as well as laypeople) believe that rapists are sick, and that their behavior is symptomatic of a mental disorder. Marolla and Scully refute this belief, arguing that "research comparing convicted rapists to other groups, including convicts, other sex offenders, and college males, has been, at best, inconclusive and, at worst, from the disease model perspective, nonsupportive of psychological differences" (1979, p. 307).

Mary Koss and her associates report on a study in which they used two different measures of psychopathology[1] on "men who admitted to sexual acts congruent with the legal definition of rape." These men were not incarcerated rapists, but students selected from a university population (1981a, p. 9). The scores of these undetected rapists were compared with those of three other groups: students who were sexually aggressive, but less so than the most aggressive group of rapists; students who were low on sexual aggressiveness; and sexually non-aggressive students. No differences in the levels of psychopathology were found between these four groups of students (1981a, p. 15).

Koss et al. point out that studies reporting rapists as suffering from psychopathology are almost always based on incarcerated rapists. They suggest that the simplest explanation for the discrepancy between the findings of researchers who use incarcerated rapists as subjects and those who do not

> may be that psychopathology in the assailant may facilitate his prosecution and conviction of the crime. From this perspective, psychopathology influences the consequences of the rape, but is not a necessary precursor to the actual rape. (1981a, p. 21)

Marolla and Scully observe that the disease model has several obvious functions: "It places the behavior in a 'special' category and thus protects the interest of 'normal' males. Additionally, it casts offenders in the sick role.... Ultimately, the offender is returned to psychiatry's domain" (1979, p. 309).

According to Marolla and Scully, many psychologists start with the assumption that rapists are sick, then go on to conclude that "rape is merely symptomatic of the real disorder or disease" (1979, p. 309). Some psychologists identify the true or underlying problem as being "latent homosexuality or hostility toward a mother figure" (1979, p. 309). Marolla and Scully cite N. Littner's (1973) claim that "the nature of the illness is far more important than the crime, which is only a symptom" (1979, p. 309). Similarly, M. Guttmacher and H. Weihofen (1952) argued that the actual behavior of sex offenders "cannot be taken seriously because very often a sex offense is not really committed by a sexual deviate" (1979, p. 309). To illustrate this conclusion, Guttmacher and Weihofen cite the case of a man who became very nervous and agitated while riding on a bus:

> He solved his problem by getting off the bus and approaching a woman who he demanded have oral sex with him. The analysts explained that the man had a claustrophobic experience (noxious circumstance) on

the bus and was merely trying to get his mind off his "self." This type of interpretation is frequently found in psychiatric literature. They do not explain why the man chose to free his psyche by assaulting a woman rather than a man. (1952)

In the book that is considered by many to be the major contemporary work on sexual offenders—*Men Who Rape*—Nicholas Groth reaffirms this model of the rapist as sick. Groth states, "Although there is a wide variety of individual differences among men who rape, there are certain general characteristics that men who are prone to rape appear to have in common" (1979, p. 106). He enumerates these supposedly common characteristics at length:

> His overall mood state, then, is dysphoric, characterized by dull depression, underlying feelings of fear and uncertainty and an over-whelming sense of purposelessness. At the root of all this are deep-seated doubts about his adequacy and competency as a person. He lacks a sense of confidence in himself as a man in both sexual and nonsexual areas—a feeling that is often unacknowledged since he exhibits little capacity for self-awareness. (1979, p. 107)

Groth describes 10 percent of these men as being in a psychotic state at the time of the offense, and 56 percent as "belonging to various types of personality disorders (inadequate, antisocial, passive-aggressive, borderline, and the like)" (1979, p. 109). This picture may well be appropriate for incarcerated rapists; it is, however, a hopelessly limited and inadequate description of the many different types of men who rape women in a culture that has itself been described as a "rape culture."

Groth's conclusions are based on clinical interviews with 500 convicted sexual offenders. The limitations of his methodology have been described in some detail in Chapter 5; they will not be repeated here. As previously mentioned, Mary Koss et al. have also emphasized that incarcerated rapists are a very unique group. These researchers correctly point out that such men are likely to be totally unrepresentative of nonconvicted rapists in terms of race and socioeconomic status, as well as mental health (1981a).

There is no denying that some rapists are mentally ill; the psychopathological model only becomes objectionable when it is used to apply to all or most rapists, as is done so often.

## Alcohol Consumption and Rape

> Whereas it [alcohol] functions to the advantage of rapists, as an excuse for their behavior, it is used to discredit the victim and make her more responsible. (Scully & Marolla, 1983, pp. 45–46)

Several studies of sex offenders have emphasized the important role of alcohol in the occurrence of rape (Katz & Mazur, 1979, p. 84; Guttmacher, 1951; Gebhard et al. 1965; Rada, 1975). Richard Rada cites a study published as early as 1919 whose author, M.J. Rowe, estimated that 50 percent of sex crimes resulted from the use of alcohol (1978, p. 48). Since then, estimates have ranged from 0 percent to 50 percent (1978, p. 48). In his own studies of offenders, Rada reports,

> We have consistently found that 50 percent of rapists were DATCO (drinking at the time of the commission of the offense), the great majority of them were drinking heavily, defined as ten or more beers or the equivalent. In additon, 33 percent are alcoholic by history, using stringent criteria. (1978, p. 49)

Rada concedes that the association between alcohol consumption and rape does not prove that the alcohol causes rape. He does argue, however, that treatment programs focusing only on the offender's sexual adjustment and not on his alcohol problem are inadequate (1978, p. 49).

In another article Rada describes three different alcohol-rape situations: rape involving an offender who was drinking at the time; rape by an alcoholic offender; and rape that may be triggered by alcohol (1975). Rada argues that for some rapists who were drinking just prior to the rape, the rape dynamic is primary; the alcohol acts to reinforce and promote the rape behavior (1978, p. 50). In contrast, for the alcoholic rapist, the rape is often but one further manifestation of his social disorganization and is secondary to alcoholism. Finally, Rada describes rapists in whom the desire to rape is only present when they are drinking (1978, p. 50).

Paul Gebhard et al. from the Institute for Sex Research in Indiana reported in their study of incarcerated sex offenders that 54 percent of the rapes of adult women by heterosexual men were associated with alcohol consumption. Of those who raped minors (females 12 to 15 years old), 37.5 percent were associated with alcohol; of those who raped children under the age of 12, fully 76 percent were alcohol related (1965, p. 813). (See Table 6.2)

That there is a significant relationship between alcohol consumption and rape seems clearly demonstrated by the research.

## Peer Pressure in Pair and Gang Rape

"I'm against hurting women. She should have resisted. None of us were the type of person that would use force on a woman ... my weakness is

**TABLE 6.2**

**Alcohol Use by Types of Sex Offense (in percentages)**

| Offense Type | Alcohol Present | Offender Drunk | Total Alcohol Consumption |
|---|---|---|---|
| (1) Heterosexual Offenses versus | | | |
| Children | 5.9 | 22.7 | 29 |
| Minors | 8.9 | 8.9 | 18 |
| Adults | 8.0 | 9.2 | 17 |
| (2) Heterosexual Aggressions versus | | | |
| Children | 9.5 | 66.7 | 76 |
| Minors | 12.5 | 25.0 | 37 |
| Adults | 14.6 | 39.4 | 54 |
| (3) Incest Offenses versus | | | |
| Children | 7.7 | 30.8 | 38 |
| Minors | 3.0 | 21.2 | 24 |
| Adults | 5.0 | 20.0 | 25 |
| (4) Homosexual Offenses versus | | | |
| Children | 9.9 | 25.3 | 35 |
| Minors | 5.4 | 11.4 | 17 |
| Adults | 9.0 | 15.3 | 24 |

SOURCE: Adaptation of Table 142, Gebhard et al., 1965, p. 813. Reprinted by permission.

to follow. I never would have stopped, let alone picked her up without the others." (Rapist; Scully & Marolla, 1983, pp. 50–51)

Most of the literature on group rape has focussed on the psychological and social dynamics of the offenders (Katz & Mazur, 1979, p. 167). According to Gilbert Geis and D. Chappell, most group rapes are committed by young men. Typically, a night of drinking ends with the rapists' selecting a victim from the bar or street (Geis & Chappell, 1971, p. 431).

According to two other researchers, most group rapes are planned in advance (Amir, 1971; Peters et al., 1976). Some gang rapes actually serve as initiation rites for would-be members of a gang (Katz & Mazur, 1979, p. 167). Peer pressure in these situations appears to play a significant role in reducing whatever inhibitions against rape a gang member might otherwise feel. Perhaps peer pressure also explains why group rapes often involve more violence and sexual perversion than individual rapes do (Amir, 1971, pp. 218, 222).

Peer groups are influential in two of the three types of rapists distinguished by Menachem Amir and described as follows in *Patterns in Forcible Rape:*

(1) Rapists for whom the crime is mainly a *role-supportive act,* usually in the context of a youth culture. The act is performed for the purpose of maintaining membership in a group, or for sheer sexual gratification. Pathology is absent.

(2) Rapists for whom the crime is mainly a *role-expressive act.* "It is performed not so much for the sexual satisfaction as because of participation in the context (within) which it occurred, for example, group rape." (1971, pp. 318–319)

Amir believes that the aggressive behavior of these two types of rapists does not result from deviant sexuality; it is simply an outcome of their participation in a group that condones the use of force to achieve its goals.

**CONCLUSION**

This chapter has presented some of the key theories of rape causation that stress the role of different factors in the reduction of some men's internal inhibitions against acting out their desire to rape women. In order for rape to occur, social inhibitions against rape must also be surmounted. The next chapter will focus on some of the factors that reduce these social inhibitions.

*Note*

1. These measures were the Psychopathic Deviate Scale of the MMPI and the Social Anxiety Scale of Lykken's Activity Preference Questionnaire.

# 7

# FACTORS REDUCING SOCIAL INHIBITIONS AGAINST RAPE

The distinction made by anthropologist Robert Le Vine between internal and external inhibitions to rape helps clarify the difference between them. He defines an external inhibition as one created by structural barriers (such as physical or social arrangements in the individual's environment) that prevent a person from obtaining their sexual objective (1959, p. 222).

Le Vine defines internal inhibitions as learned tendencies "to avoid performing sexual acts under certain conditons" (Le Vine, 1959, p. 222). These result from socialization in the early years.

## The Power Disparity Between Men and Women

*Question:* "Have you ever raped a woman?"

"No. But I've wanted to—especially ones who think that they're so high and mighty on a pedestal that nobody can touch them. I would like to rape them to show them that they're no better than any cunt walking down the street."

"Why do I want to rape women? Because I am basically, as a male, a predator and all women look to men like prey. I fantasize about the expression on a woman's face when I 'capture' her and she realizes she cannot escape. It's like I won, I own her." (Male respondents; Hite, 1981)

Susan Brownmiller argues that rape is used to keep women in their place, below men. A slightly different theory is that rape, like other violence against and abuse of women by men, is a *consequence* of the power disparity between the sexes that has existed as long as recorded history (Russell, 1975). There are many variants of this theory. One states simply that power corrupts, and that abuses result from this corruption. This interpretation views rape as a form of corruption whereby some men simply take what they want because they want it;

they expect to get away with it because of their power relative to women in society.

Some rape myths may result from the power men have wielded over women for such a long time. One such myth is that women enjoy being raped—that even when women cry, struggle, and fight to get away, ultimately the penis is irresistible. It is not unusual for group rapists to ask their victims afterward a question like "Which one of us did you like best?" Some rapists expect their victims to climax. Many simply don't understand that they have raped a woman, since they believe women enjoy being forced (Russell, 1975; Scully & Marolla, 1983).

Pauline Bart's notion of "male entitlement" describes men's sense that they are entitled to domestic and sexual services from women as a class (personal communication, 1983). The institution of female prostitution is frequently justified on the grounds of male entitlement. An even more obvious example is the fact that only recently have a few states outlawed rape in marriage. For centuries women lost their right to sexual autonomy when they married (Russell, 1982). The idea of male entitlement may be a consequence of the power disparity between men and women.

Lorenne Clark and Debra Lewis' theory of rape seems to fit best in this category. They argue in *Rape: The Price of Coercive Sexuality* that it is the status of women as the sexual and reproductive private property of men that "has created the problem of rape as we know it" (1977, p. 174). Clark and Lewis see rape as but one form of coercive sexuality, a "by-product of a system of institutionalized inequalities" (1977, p. 175).

Clark and Lewis are adamant in their view that sexism, and hence the problem of rape, is structural. This is how they put it:

> Though our society is male dominated, male domination cannot be explained by the theory that each and every man wants to dominate women, or by the statement that we are simply socialized into different and unequal roles. Our society is characterized by institutions and practices (and the socialization processes necessary to support them), which consistently and systematically ensure that only men rise to positions of power and authority in the public world, while women remain at home, in the private sphere, under the legal ownership and control of their husbands. (1977, p. 176)

Clark and Lewis are particularly emphatic that socialization per se is neither the cause nor the remedy of rape and sexism.

> Socialization processes prepare us for structurally predetermined posi-
> tions, but do not by themselves create those positions ... No amount of
> resocialization of individuals, either male or female, will alter the struc-
> ture which creates unequal status, and to believe that it does, or can, is
> a dangerous illusion. (1977, p. 176)

Clark and Lewis's view that the problem is greater than one of
faulty socialization is an important one. Socialization is what it is
because males and females are trained to take unequal places in the
society. Thus, making efforts to change the socialization of children
within families and schools will not be adequate. For the problem of
rape to be solved, men must give up their monopolization of power in
the society as a whole, and in more than token ways (Russell, 1975).

To Clark and Lewis, the social control theory is a corollary of their
structural theory. "All unequal power relationships must," they maintain, "in the end, rely on the threat or reality of violence to maintain
themselves" (1977, p. 176). William Goode, a well-known American
sociologist, developed this same argument many years ago (1971),
and Jalna Hanmer, a British sociologist, has recently come to the
same conclusion (1978).

## Male Dominance Plus a Culture of Violence

Social anthropologist Peggy Sanday's research suggests that a
combination of two theories of rape is helpful in understanding the
causes of rape: She found high rape rates in societies that were both
highly dominated by males and in which considerable violence occurred. Sanday studied a cross-cultural sample of 186 tribal societies.
In 95 of them there was sufficient information on the incidence of
rape to test her hypotheses.

Sanday defined "rape prone societies" as those in which rape was
used socially to threaten or punish women and/or where there was a
high incidence of rape. Sanday found that less than one-fifth (17 percent) of the 186 societies in her sample could be classified as "rape
prone" (1979, p. 4) Almost half (47 percent) were found to be rape
free (i.e., rape was reported as absent or as being a rare occurrence).
The remaining societies were those in which rape was reported as
occurring, but the evidence on frequency was ambiguous (1979, p. 4).

Sanday's first conclusion was that rape is not a frequent occurrence in most tribal societies. Second, she maintains that "considerable evidence suggests that rape is an expression of a social ideology
of male dominance" (1979, p. 4). By this she means that in rape prone

societies females held less power and authority; women did not participate in public decision making, and men expressed contempt for
women. In these societies, fathers were not involved with the care of
infants and young children, and relationships between fathers and
daughters were aloof and cool. In addition, male violence was glori-
fied and rewarded (1979, p. 4).

In contrast, "in rape free societies women participate in all aspects
of social life—religion, politics, and economics. Interpersonal relations ... are marked by mildness as opposed to the violence which
frequently erupts in rape prone societies" (1979, p. 4). This generalization also held for intergroup relations; these societies tended not to
engage "in a military complex where warfare is a way of life for
males" (1979, p. 4).

Sanday suggests that male dominance, including male sexual violence, evolved as a response to stress (1979, p. 8).

> When humans perceive an imbalance between resources and popula-
> tion, or when they perceive that their social identity and way of life
> must be defended, they will place men in the front line to fight for
> survival. If the struggle for survival is successful, men are rewarded
> with glory, and male violence becomes a way of life passed on from
> parent to male child. Programmed for violence and faced with sexual
> repression, some men turn to rape. (1979, p. 8)

Sanday adds that "rape is also the means by which some men show
other men that they can be fierce" (1979, p. 8).

Assuming that these results may be applied to the situation in the
United States, one wonders what stress in particular might be encouraging male violence here. Is it the role of the United States as one of
the major forces in the world power struggle? Is it a consequnce of
the daily battle many Americans wage to survive in a society with
enormous disparitites in wealth? Or, is it that males in the United
States feel threatened by females? Any and all of these factors may be
sources of stress.

Whatever the sources of stress, Sanday's finding that a culture of
violence, combined with male domination, is associated with rape
prone societies may help to explain the high rape rate in the United
States.

### Ineffectiveness of the Institutions of Social Control

[O]ver half the admitters [men who admit rape] and all of the deniers
[incarcerated sex offenders who deny rape] never expected to be pun-

ished for their sexual violence, perhaps because they were aware that reporting and conviction rates for rape are low. (Scully & Marolla, 1983, p. 42)

*Rapist:* "When I took her home to her apartment she was telling me goodnight and I raped her...."

*Interviewer:* "Did you think that she might report it?"

*Rapist:* "No. It would be very difficult because she was seen at a party hanging all over me so it would be very difficult for her to say that I raped her."

"I was charged with assault with intent to commit rape. The way I was treated by the police was incredible. It was as if I was a new recruit on the force. A captain on the sheriff's office took me into his office and gave me a cup of coffee ... and said, 'Damn women always causing trouble for everybody.' He did not treat me like a criminal at all."
(Rapists; Russell, 1975, p. 249, p. 253)

The women's movement successfully drew public attention to the issue of rape in the early 1970s. It was equally successful in its push for changes in laws pertaining to nonmarital rape. By 1980, in fact, almost every state had passed some form of rape reform legislation (Feild & Bienen, 1980, p. 171).

Typically, such reforms include the following: limiting the cross-examination of the victim about her sexual history; disallowing what used to be a routine cautionary instruction from judge to jury that rape is an easy charge to make but a difficult one to defend against; redefining rape to acknowledge that males as well as females can be victimized; and including forced oral or anal penetration as rape. These reforms, however, have not passed the state legislative bodies without a considerable grassroots lobbying effort by a coalition of feminists and law and order groups (1980, p. 186).

Feminist attorney Camille LeGrand, who has contributed significantly to the movement to reform the rape laws in California, believes that these laws are now frequently more advanced than the police and courts that administer them. Hence, LeGrand says, efforts to improve rape legislation further are often ill-conceived; they create the illusion that important changes are being made when this in fact is not the case (personal communication, 1984).

The fact that the police often unjustifiably unfound cases of reported rape was mentioned in the discussion of the prevalence of rape in Chapter 1. Thomas McCahill et al.'s research in Philadelphia yielded shocking information about the extent to which that city's rape victims' reports were totally and purposefully lost in the system (1979). The findings of this study are very relevant to this analysis of the ineffectiveness of the institutions of social control where rape is concerned. However, these findings were presented in some detail in Chapter 1 and will not be repeated here.

The failure of the prison system to rehabilitate prisoners, particularly sexual offenders, is also cause for considerable alarm. The literature on rape in prison suggests that incarceration not only provides rapists with a rape supportive subculture within which to continue raping, but also provides a training ground for men who have never raped before (Scacco, 1982). As was pointed out in Chapter 2, rape in prison is a means of obtaining status, power, as well as "manhood" and sex. As one frequent victim of gang rape in prison, Donald Tucker, has so chillingly written,

> I know from other victims of prison rape how the male seeks compensation for the trauma of the total loss of control by striking back and asserting control; as it was lost in violence so it is regained in violence. *It may be that the most serious cost of prison rape to society is that it takes nonviolent offenders and turns them into people with a high potential for violence,* full of rage and eager to take vengeance on the society which they hold responsible for their utter humiliation and loss of manhood. (in Scacco, 1982, p. 75; emphasis in the original)

Donald Tucker knows whereof he speaks. Earlier in the same article he describes himself as a rapist.

> Feeling a need to assert my own masculinity in spite of my status as a Punk, I decided, with Terry's[1] consent, to try to "turn" the boy myself.... He was very lonely, insecure, frightened, and depressed: feelings I knew well. I approached him gently, without sexual vibes, offering friendship, protection, and advice. He took the bait, spilling out all his troubles and anxieties to me, coming out of his depression and becoming dependent on me.

> The next day I told him I was horny and needed relief; it was time for him to do something for me, and that's the way jail was. He was shocked and protested that he wasn't "that way," but he was also afraid of being thrust into isolation or worse.... As a result, his will to resist was paralyzed with indecision: just what I had hoped for.

> I pried open his mouth and proceed to fuck his face while tears trickled from his eyes, while Terry watched. As a cocksucker he was terrible, but the thrill of conquest was so strong that I soon had a powerful orgasm, and felt that my manhood was vindicated. (Scacco, 1982, pp. 70–71)

Prisons are indeed appalling jungles of destruction. But the fact remains that failing to use the prison system only aggravates the rape problem. Studies have shown that many rapists feel free to rape because they have little fear of being apprehended. Some are aware that if they are acquainted with the victim, she will have little credibility in the eyes of the police and the criminal justice system (Russell, 1975; Smithyman, 1978; Benecke, 1982).

In a few dramatic cases, rapists have claimed that incarceration has stopped them from continuing to rape—for example, Eldridge Cleaver (1968), an incarcerated rapist interviewed by Timothy Benecke (1982), and one of the four rapists interviewed for Russell's study (1975).

Scully and Marolla report that an incidental effect of prison education on some of the rapists in their study was to lower their hostility toward women. This in turn was believed by these researchers to lower the likelihood of a repetition of their rape behavior (1983, p. 30). "Time in prison," according to Scully and Marolla, "without education, appears to turn out a rapist very much like the one who came in" (1983, p. 29). These authors do not comment on the impact of rape in prison on the perpetrators, the victims, and the other inmates.

The work of Neil Malamuth and his colleagues shows that approximately 35 percent of male students believe that they might rape a woman if they could get away with it. (See Chapter 1 for more information about this research.) Devastating as prisons are to prisoners, if rape is to become a less tempting crime, potential rapists must believe that rape is likely to lead to incarceration.

Prisons could, of course, be reformed so that they rehabilitate rapists and other criminals instead of merely punishing them. But as long as only a tiny minority of rapists are being apprehended, fear of incarceration cannot be utilized as a major inhibitor of rapists. Hence, we should not be surprised to learn from Smithyman's study of undetected rapists that

> many of the respondents commented upon how easy it was to plan, execute the rape(s), and avoid the possible negative consequences attendant upon detection. The failure of the rape(s) in which the respondents participated to result in either actual or perceived negative consequences combined with the experience of sexual pleasure and in some cases an enhanced sense of power and achievement suggests that the rapes described by the respondents were in a large measure low cost and relatively rewarding events. (1978, pp. 123–124)

Because the rapist's behavior so often ends up being a low-cost, high-reward event, Smithyman argues that it is "likely that he will rape again" (1978, p. 124). Indeed, 74 percent of the rapists in his sample had raped more than once already, and 36 percent had raped four or more times (1978, p. 31).

## Note

1. Tucker described himself as Terry's punk.

# 8

# FACTORS REDUCING POTENTIAL VICTIM'S ABILITY TO AVOID RAPE

## Socialization of Women as Victims

Where differences in physical strength have become immaterial through the use of arms, the female is rendered innocuous by her socialization. Before assault she is almost universally defenseless both by her physical and emotional training. (Millett, 1970, p. 44)

Women's helplessness is itself part of the psychosis that makes rape a national passtime. (Greer, 1973, p. 82)

On examining this culture's notion of femininity, we see that such "feminine" traits as submissiveness, passivity, and weakness make women more subject to rape (Russell, 1975). When these acculturated patterns are operative in a rape situation, victims are castigated for this socially-ordained behavior. Often, the incident is regarded as something other than rape (1975, p. 271). Many women behave toward their rapists as they've been trained to act—submissively. Afterward, they blame themselves for their victimization.

This is not to say that strong, assertive women are never raped. Particularly in intimate relationships, it may in fact take some assertiveness to be raped. After all, the rape victim is saying no to sex (Russell, 1975, p. 268). This statement is particularly applicable to victims of wife rape (Russell, 1982). Nevertheless, conformity to traditional notions of femininity often makes women more vulnerable to rape, at least once they are in a situation where an unarmed man intends to try to rape them (1975, p. 268).

On the other hand, women who reject traditional notions of femininity are more likely to take risks that result in their vulnerability to rape by a stranger—for example, going places without a man, hitchhiking, living alone and the like. The price of greater freedom for women is a greater risk of rape.

With armed rapists, women's socialized femininity probably has less significance than when they are unarmed. But many victims are often unduly intimidated by would-be rapists; they have received life-long conditioning to behave submissively toward men, and think of themselves as weak and men as strong (1975, p. 268). One victim who was raped in a car by a man who offered her a ride, commented,

> I hated myself for not being able to take a stand in the situation. He wielded his power with such confidence, and there I was, feeling absolutely helpless. I shouldn't have to feel that helpless even though I am small and less muscular and all that.... But it's like once you're in there, you become paralyzed with this feeling that he's a man, he's got muscles, and he knows about things like guns. (1975, pp . 268–269)

Many women, particularly those from middleclass backgrounds, have not had the opportunity to develop their strength, or even to know it. Women are not taught to fight and they are usually discouraged throughout their lives from learning how to fight. Fighting is considered unladylike. Even anger is considered unladylike (1975, p. 269).

Passivity also affects many women's feelings and actions *after* they have been raped. Having been overcome by a rapist leaves a feeling of having been conquered. Virgins are especially susceptible to this feeling, which explains why some of them consent to see their rapists again. Some women have even married their rapists (Russell, 1982, pp. 246–256). The fact that they do so does not mean that the experience was not upsetting to them. Rather, feeling conquered, they no longer act on a principle of self-determination. Many men share this view of rape as conquest (1975, p. 271).

When rape occurs within a dating relationship, particularly one in which some petting has occurred, the woman is especially likely to be seen as partially or wholly responsible. But it does not follow that because a woman engages in sexual "foreplay," she has acquiesced to intercourse, although the very notion of "foreplay" assumes it is preliminary to penetration (1975, p. 271). This assumption indicates the extent of male domination of sexuality, for it is common for women to desire sex that does not culminate in penetration, while men tend to be penetration-oriented (Hite, 1976, 1981).

Ideally, men should accept that a woman is entitled to respond only in the ways that are desirable to her. She should not be made to feel responsible for satisfying a man by his prescribed standards once he has been aroused. But in fact many women, wishing to avoid constant pressure and insults, give in and accept this responsibility, yielding to the "all-or-nothing" standard of sexuality (Russell, 1975,

p. 272). Many a woman accepts that she has "asked for it" if she has allowed herself to engage in what might be for her a preferred way of being sexual: cuddling and petting not necessarily culminating in intercourse. To avoid experiencing the unpleasantness and possible rape that might result from asserting her right not to engage in unwanted sexual acts, many a woman will accede to this implicit male rule (1975, p. 272).

Along with being submissive, passive, and weak, women are supposed to be kind, compassionate, patient, accepting, and dependent. They are also supposed to take the primary responsibility for problems in their relationships with men. As many of the case histories presented in *The Politics of Rape* (Russell, 1975) reveal, these traits make women more subject to rape. For example, several women did not want to appear rude or suspicious of the man who ended up raping them. Many women need to put more effort into protecting themselves instead of men's egos.

There are ways in which women contribute to their own vulnerability to rape. The most obvious is ambivalence about being treated as sexual objects. On the one hand women have learned that it is difficult to get what they want from men if they don't play into such sexist objectification. On the other hand, they feel depersonalized by it (1975, p. 273). Many women have also internalized male notions of attractiveness. In order to feel good about their appearance, they pile on makeup and display their breasts, legs, or buttocks. This contributes to their own objectification, which in turn contributes to the rape problem (1975, p. 273).

While it is unacceptable, indeed highly objectionable, to blame women for provoking rape, those who follow such male-defined notions of attractiveness cooperate with, rather than discourage, men's ability to separate sexual desire from desires for affection and friendship. It is men's ability to separate these feelings that is one of the factors enabling them to rape (1975, p. 273).

The solution is not for women to dress in drab, shapeless clothes and hide their faces. The changes must come in the way men view women, in the excessive value placed on female beauty, and in contemporary notions of femininity. It is paradoxical indeed that women are regarded as the beautiful sex, yet many cannot bear to be seen unmasked; much time, emotion, and money is invested in their artificial beautification (1975, pp. 273–274).

Males are brought up to be very much in touch with their sexual needs ("Boys will be boys," and if they won't be, they'd better pretend), and disconnected from their needs for love, romance, and affection. To be regarded as sexually successful, males must satisfy their sexual needs with females rather than by masturbation. Females, in contrast, are discouraged from being sexual. They are supposed to be virginal, or at least, to confine their sexual relations to males who really care about them, and about whom they really care (1975, p. 274).

At all costs, females must guard their "reputations." The same behavior that gives status to males (promiscuous sexual relations) endangers status for females. Yet females are taught that it is very important for them to be attractive and sought after by males. Females are also supposed to be submissive toward males.

With such a bundle of contradictions, it is a wonder that people talk about males and females being "made for each other." With these basic incompatibilities in socialized needs and expected behavior, it is not surprising that there is often misunderstanding, hostility, and even hatred between the sexes. And it is no wonder that there is rape. It is a logical consequence of the lack of symmetry in the way males and females are socialized in this society (1975, p. 274). Indeed, the remarkable thing is not that rape occurs, but that we have managed for so long to see it as a rare and deviant act. Rape is, in fact, embedded in our cultural norms, a direct result of the clash between the masculine and the feminine mystiques (1975, p. 274).

## Blaming the Victim: Victim-Precipitation Theories

*Rape Victim:* "The first staff member who saw me was a psychiatrist. His first words were, 'Haven't you really been rushing toward this very thing all of your life?' He knew nothing about me, nothing! I had never been to a psychiatrist." (Russell, 1975, p. 225)

"(I)t is difficult to assess the role of the child in provoking rape and to evaluate the aftereffects of this crime." (MacDonald, 1971, p. 111)

Rochelle Albin, in her excellent review of psychological studies of rape, attributes the notion of rape as a victim-precipitated phenomenon to Freud (Albin, 1977, p. 423). Freud's belief that women are masochistic by nature implies that rape can satisfy their self-destructive needs.

One of Freud's major followers, Helene Deutsch, considered masochistic traits as "part of the ideal and healthy female personality" (1977, p. 424). In her book *The Psychology of Women* she wrote, "Even the most experienced judges are misled in trials of innocent men accused of rape by hysterical women" (1944; cited in Albin, 1977, p. 424).

Albin believes that the psychiatric theory that places blame for rape on women—the victims, mothers, and wives of the sex offenders—to be a legacy of the Freudian view (1977, p. 427). The notion of victim-precipitated crime and the subfield of victimology are usually attributed to Hans Von Hentig, who, writing in 1948, argued as follows: "If there are criminals, it is evident that there are born victims, self-harming and self-destroying through the medium of a pliable outsider" (1948).

Marvin Wolfgang, Professor of Criminology at the University of Pennsylvania, found support for Von Hentig's thesis in his study of homicide. He reported that just over a quarter (26 percent) of homicide victims had "precipitated" their own murder by being the initiator of aggressive or dangerous behavior (1957). Wolfgang was the one actually to coin the phrase "victim precipitation." He believed that when two potential murderers come together, it is often a matter of chance who becomes the victim and who the offender.

Menachim Amir was the first to apply this notion of victim precipitation to rape. It was used to describe

> those rape situations in which the victim actually, or so it was deemed, agreed to sexual relations but retracted before the actual act or did not react strongly enough when the suggestion was made by the offender(s). The term applies also to cases in risky situations marred with sexuality, especially when she uses what could be interpreted as indecency of language and gestures, or constitutes what could be taken as an invitation to sexual relations. (Amir, 1971, p. 266)

Hence, Amir believed that the victim is sometimes a "complementary partner" in her own rape victimization (1971, p. 156). From these quotations it is obvious that Amir's theory of victim precipitation is but another form of victim-blaming. In spite of this, Amir's book, *Patterns in Forcible Rape* (1971), was generally seen as the definitive study prior to Brownmiller's *Against Our Will*.

John MacDonald likewise argues that some women invite rape (1971). Arthur Schiff maintains that over one-fifth of rape victims (21 percent) "may have been flirtatious and were in situations that might have involved considerable 'social foreplay' that 'whet the male's appetite'" (1973; cited in Katz & Mazur, 1979, p. 140).

During the previous decade, Seymour Halleck advised physicians that a major factor in managing rape victims was "the question as to whether rape actually did occur ... (or whether it was) brought on by the provocativeness of the victim ... (in which case) it is important to delve into (her) personality problems" (1962; cited in Albin, 1977, p. 428).

Feminists have pointed out that this form of victim blaming has been particularly readily applied to rape, and they have seen male bias and identification with the rapist as being the cause of it (The Boston Women's Health Collective, 1971; Griffin, 1971; Medea & Thompson, 1974; Greer, 1975; Russell, 1975; Brownmiller, 1975; Clark & Lewis, 1977). Feminist criticism has been fairly successful in causing male scholars to reevaluate their sexist assumptions and thinking. Hence such blaming of female victims is rarely revealed so blatantly in more contemporary literature.

If it is not the victim who is blamed, it is often the rapist's mother or wife who is blamed instead. Albin refers to these theories along with victim blaming as "women precipitation" theories. For example, R. Palm and D. Abrahamsen wrote about the wives of convicted rapists as follows:

They conveyed a fear of being alone in their apartment lest they be raped; a fear of being followed on the streets; a fear of going out at night.... One may assume that such marked fears actually represent a defense measure against an underlying wish to be attacked, raped, or sexually abused. (1954; cited in Albin, 1977, p. 428)

These authors proceed to describe these wives as frigid, adding that in some cases, a prolonged period of sexual frustration preceded the rape (Albin, 1977, p. 428). R. J. McCaldon, on the other hand, maintained that rape has "its roots in maternal frustration, commencing at the pre-Oedipal stage" (Albin, 1977, p. 429). Albin concludes her analysis of the theories of women-blaming thus:

This perspective was the inevitable outcome of a derogatory societal view of women, of a psychology dominated by men who shared and promulgated this view, and of research designs that reflected this male culture and male psychology. The culture thus spawned a science that affirmed and then exaggerated it. (1977, p. 429)

One of the most important contributions of the feminist analysis of rape has been its strong denunciation of the long tradition of blaming the victim. This denunciation has made an impact on the field, but even after a decade of such efforts, victim blaming still occurs in cases of both rape and child sexual abuse.

## Women's Resistance to Rape
## Undermined by Fear of Murder

"I have never felt that much anger before. If she had resisted, I would have killed her ... The rape was for revenge. I didn't have an orgasm. She was there to get my hostile feelings off on." (Rapist; Scully & Marolla, 1983, p. 55)

Out of every 10 female murder victims in the United States one is killed during rape or other sexual offenses. In *Against Our Will*, Susan Brownmiller estimated that four hundred rape-murders are committed by men every year in this country (1975, p. 198). Fear of death in the course of a rape attack is actually much greater than this figure indicates. It is unknown how many of the women who report being raped, or how many of the larger number who never report their experiences, submit because of their fear of being killed. There are likely many.

Rape-murder has consequences far beyond Brownmiller's estimate of approximately four hundred victims a year. It terrorizes many women whether or not they become rape victims. For those who are attacked, it often serves to seriously undermine their resistance efforts (Russell & Van de Ven, 1976, p. 145).

## Other Factors

Many other factors contribute to reducing a potential victim's ability to resist or avoid rape. Too often, however, the burden of trying to prevent rape has been placed on women—the actual and potential victims. Out of a desire to discourage the placement of responsibility for the rape problem on women, only four more factors will be cited here.

### VICTIM KNOWS AND TRUSTS THE ASSAILANT

Women often feel unable to resist to their maximum ability when they are raped by someone they know or trust; for example, a friend, date, lover or husband; and/or when the person has authority or power over them, such as an employer, doctor, teacher, or priest.

### VICTIM IS ISOLATED

Single women are far more frequently victimized by stranger rape than are married women. This is not merely a function of age, but is also a function of increased vulnerability to attack.

When women live in areas where there is no sense of community or concern for the welfare of neighbors, they are obviously more vulnerable to rape. Kitty Genovese, who was stabbed to death in full view of many neighbors who watched in the safety of their own homes without bothering to call the police, is but one scandalous example of this phenomenon.

## VICTIM DRINKING, DRUNK, OR AN ALCOHOLIC

The National Commission on the Causes and Prevention of Violence reported that the victim, the offender, or both are likely to be drinking prior to homicide, assault, and rape (Eisenhower, 1969, p. 25). Women alcoholics are particularly vulnerable to rape, both by strangers and intimates, since they are often in no condition to defend themselves. In addition, they may be perceived by men to be "asking for it" by being available, vulnerable, "bad" women.

## VICTIM HAS ACCESS TO FEW RESOURCES

Both male and female runaways are particularly vulnerable to rape because of their outlaw status, their lack of resources or means of making money outside of prostitution, as well as their naiveté.

As mentioned in Chapter 3, low income women who cannot afford to own a car and/or who have to live in high crime areas, are particularly subject to rape.

## CONCLUSION

Many other factors contribute to reducing women's ability to resist or avoid rape. However, rape prevention efforts must be focused on the factors that create a predisposition in men to rape, the factors that reduce their internal inhibitions to rape, and the factors that reduce their social inhibitions to rape.

# PART III

# CHILD SEXUAL ABUSE: PREVALENCE AND THE LAW

## 9

## CHILD SEXUAL ABUSE AND THE LAW

### *Current Legal Statutes Concerning the Sexual Abuse of Children*

Sexual activity between children and adults is a crime in every state. The law also requires that doctors, psychologists, teachers, child protective service workers, and others who work closely with children report all suspected cases of child sexual abuse to law enforcement agencies or to the district attorney's office (Kocen & Bulkley, 1981, p. 2) Police are required to investigate each case reported to them; prosecutors are obligated to prosecute those who commit these crimes (Kocen & Bulkley, 1981, p. 2).

According to an American Bar Association Report, reported cases of child sexual abuse frequently result in legal intervention of some kind:

> the legal action taken may be criminal prosecution of the perpetrator; or, where the offender is a parent or caretaker, a juvenile court proceeding to protect the child may be brought against the offender as well as the "passive" parent....
>
> Both proceedings may be, and often are, initiated. (Bulkley, 1981, p. iii)

This description of the legal response to child sexual abuse is contained in a Report of the National Legal Resource Center for Child Advocacy and Protection for the American Bar Association, edited by Josephine Bulkley (1981). It is an accurate description of the way child sexual abuse is *supposed to be handled*. It is also a highly misleading description of reality. In fact, many of those who are supposed to report child sexual abuse do not do so. And many cases investigated by the child protective services or the police are not "substantiated," just as reported rape cases are often unfounded. It would be foolish to presume that every reported sexual abuse case is a valid, prosecutable offense. It is equally foolish—and much more dangerous—to deny that many valid cases are erroneously discounted because of entrenched myths about the sexual victimization of children, and/or because children are manipulated or threatened into retracting their disclosures.

When legal intervention *does* occur, it is rarely as benign as the American Bar Association's description would indicate. In cases of father-daughter incest, for example, it is often the sexually abused child who is removed from her home, not the perpetrator of the crime. In more than one appalling case, daughters unwilling to testify against their fathers have been incarcerated or subjected to some other legal sanction.

## History of Legal Statutes

Until the late eighteenth century, most states prohibited "carnal knowledge," "carnal abuse," or sexual intercourse with female children 10 years old or younger (Kocen & Bulkley, 1981, p. 2). Female children of this age were considered too immature to consent knowledgably to sexual activity with another person. Those older than 10 were only protected by criminal statutes from forcible rape (Kocen & Bulkley, 1981, p. 2). In the 1950s and 1960s, in an effort to protect young females, most states raised the statutory age to 16 or 18, regardless of whether or not consent had been given (Kocen & Bulkley, 1981, p. 2). These statutes are usually referred to as statutory rape laws.

In addition to these statutory rape laws, most states have enacted legislation that protects children "from 'indecent liberties,' 'lewd and lascivious acts,' or 'molestation.' These provisons cover sexual behavior other than sexual intercourse, such as the touching of the young child's private parts or genitals" (Kocen & Bulkley, 1981, p. 3). The term "sexual intercourse" has also been redefined to include oral or anal intercourse as well as vaginal intercourse (Kocen & Bulkley, 1981, p. 2).

In the mid-1960s and continuing into the 1970s, substantial reforms in rape laws were initiated. Under most earlier statutes, only one degree of statutory rape was recognized, resulting in the sentencing of all offenders to one uniformly severe penalty. The newer statutes prohibit a range of sexual acts, and consider factors including the victim's age; the perpetrator's age; the relationship between them; and whether or not violence was used. The severity of the penalties depends on which of these factors characterized the crime (Kocen & Bulkley, 1981, p. 3).

Although most state statutes protect minors up to the age of 16 or 18, three states protect only minors below age 14 (Colorado, Hawaii, and Georgia); two protect them only below age 15 (South Dakota and Virginia); and one (North Carolina) only prohibits intercourse with minors above the age of 12 if the perpetrator is a parent or caretaker (Kocen & Bulkley, 1981, p. 4). According to Lynne Kocen and Josephine Bulkley's review, with the exception of these states,

> the laws protecting teenagers from older perpetrators demonstrate legislative interest in providing protection of the teenage child, while not punishing sexual activities between adolescents close in age. Thus, unlike the original statutory rape laws, the new statutes do not seek to establish a moral standard of preserving the virginity or chastity of the adolescent girl or of condemning premarital sex. (1981, p. 11)

Kocen and Bulkley suggest that the penalty structures constitute the most significant variation in the reform statutes. They point out, for example, that some states impose sentences of up to life imprisonment or death for sexual intercourse with a young girl, while others give only one to five years' imprisonment. Penalties for intercourse with teenagers vary from 1 year to 20 years in prison (1981, p. 12).

## Legal Statutes Concerning Incest

Every state except New Jersey[1] has incest statutes that prohibit sexual intercourse and marriage between close relatives (Wulkan & Bulkley, 1981, p. 52). These statutes punish consenting sexual intercourse as well as intercourse by force; most ignore the ages of the parties involved. However, almost all states "limit the criminal act of incest to sexual intercourse" (Wulkan & Bulkley, 1981, p. 52). This means that sexual contact involving oral or anal intercourse, or other sex acts not including vaginal intercourse, cannot be prosecuted under the incest laws in most states.

In their analysis of the incest statutes in the United States, Donna Wulkan and Josephine Bulkley comment on the recent trends in law reform:

> There appear to be mixed trends in the reform of incest laws in the United States. On the one hand, some incest statutes are moving

toward greater protection of the minor child. Others, however, are decriminalizing all incestuous sexual activity between relatives, which would include minors; one state decriminalizes incest only where it involves minors. These states presumably believe minor children are adquately protected by the criminal sexual offense statutes. At least half of the states seem to have expanded the purpose of their incest laws to include preserving the sanctity of the family by adding stepparents and adoptive parents. (1981, p. 60)

The Russell survey data on the percentage of child sexual abuse cases reported to the police will be presented next, along with information about the outcome of these cases. The experiences of these children reveal the gross mishandling of this problem by law enforcement institutions.

## The Russell Survey:
### Reported Cases of Child Sexual Abuse

"They put my stepfather in jail, then released him on bail. He and my mom came to X [the youth authority where the victim was incarcerated] and they said that if I wanted to come home, I must say I was lying. So I did." (Respondent who was molested by her stepfather when she was 12 years old; the Russell survey)

In the Russell random sample survey of 930 women, 647 cases of child sexual abuse were disclosed. Of these, only 30 cases—or 5 percent—were ever reported to the police. Only 4 cases (2 percent) of the incidents of incestuous abuse, and 26 cases (6 percent) of the incidents of extrafamilial child sexual abuse were ever reported.

Of the 30 reported cases, all of which involved male perpetrators, only 7 were known to result in convictions. In 2 additional cases, the respondents knew that the perpetrators were arrested, but did not know if convictions were obtained. It seems unlikely that successful convictions would not be known to the victim.

If the conviction rates are calculated on the basis of reported cases only, the rates for incestuous abuse and extrafamilial child sexual abuse are very similar: 25 percent and 23 percent, respectively.

If the conviction rates are calculated on the basis of the total number of experiences disclosed to the interviewers, they are .5 percent for incestuous abuse, and 1.3 percent for extrafamilial child sexual abuse.

If the conviction rate for the total number of both forms of child sexual abuse are combined, it is 1 percent.

These figures are shockingly low. However, Russell's data on child sexual abuse predates the legislation that has made the reporting of such cases mandatory. It also predates increased public awareness of the problem. Hence, it is safe to assume that the reporting rate for child sexual abuse has increased in the last few years. Whether or not conviction rates have also increased is unknown.

Of the 30 cases reported to the police in the Russell survey, 16 perpetrators were white, 10 were black, 2 were Latin, and 2 were categorized as "Other." Of the 7 cases that ended in convictions, 3 perpetrators were black, 2 were Latin, and 2 were white. This means that the conviction rate for reported cases of child sexual abuse was 100 percent for Latin perpetrators, 30 percent for black perpetrators, and only 13 percent for white perpetrators.

The numbers involved are small, and therefore do not justify generalization of these rates to the population at large. It nevertheless seems clear that perpetrators' race/ethnicity is a major determinant of who is convicted of child sexual abuse. It is also clear how extremely unrepresentative incarcerated sex offenders are of sex offenders in general in terms of race/ethnicity. It is reasonable to assume that they are equally unrepresentative by other criteria such as social class, mental health, and so forth.

The two cases involving white perpetrators in the Russell study will now be examined to see what might explain why these men were singled out for conviction.

Jennifer was 16 years old when the 35-year-old father of the child she was babysitting tried to get her to touch his penis.

He was the janitor in a big apartment house who worked at night. His wife had me take care of her baby when she went to town. I was wheeling the baby around and I got a little too close to his door. He opened it and he was in his robe. He wanted me to come in. He said, "Touch my thing and I'll give you candy," or something like that. He pointed to his genitals. I pushed the baby carriage through the door at him and took off running. [Did anything else sexual occur with him?] No, nothing because I pushed the carriage at him. My mother heard me telling what happened to another little girl and asked me about it. She then called my father and he came home with detectives who quizzed me about it. He was arrested and we took him to court. His wife testified that he'd violated all of their daughters, and he had done it to another little girl in the building too. He was arrested and run out of town. Although he was convicted, because he hadn't actually touched me, he was told to leave the city. It never happened to me again, ever. [Upset?] Extremely upset. [Effect on your life?] Some effect, though until you brought it up, I hadn't thought about it in a long time. I wasn't actually touched, although it felt like I had been at the time. My mind was touched by it, that's for sure. I was told by the judge to forget it, but how can you forget things like that? I imagine if a person is really raped they probably couldn't bear to be touched by a nice, gentle man again.

Jennifer's would-be perpetrator was somewhat of an extreme case because he was known to have sexually abused all of his daughters, as well as at least one other girl. Another unusual aspect of this case was the fact that his wife testified against him. The fact that Jennifer was white was also probably an important factor. Had she been black, Latina, or from some other Third World group, a conviction might have been more difficult to obtain.

The approach of Jennifer's perpetrator fits the stereotype of the pedophile as a dirty old man who offers a young girl candy—a stereotype which when met, likely makes judges and juries more willing to convict. It seems most unlikely that Jennifer's perpetrator would have been convicted for propositioning her if the criminal justice system hadn't wanted to get him for all his other offenses too.

Ronnie, who was also white, was 7 years old when she was attacked by a stranger who she estimated to be in his 30s.

> When I was 7 years old I was lost and a man professed to know where I lived. He said he was going to take me home and he started taking me across the park. He dragged me bodily into the bushes and beat the shit out of me. [Exactly?] He threw me down and started hitting me in the face and I started screaming and passed out. The next thing I remember was waking up in the hospital. [Did he assault you sexually?] No. [Was he attempting to?] I suppose so; he was a mental case. [Do you remember him doing anything sexual?] No. Fortunately somebody heard and the cops came right away. My memory about it is blurry. [If the cops hadn't come, do you think you would have been sexually assaulted?] Yeah, and he'd try to kill me or something. Later I saw him eying girls at Golden Gate Park.

Ronnie specifically described her attacker as "a mental case" who, after his conviction, was sent to "a mental place" for six months. Since she only supposed that he was trying to sexually assault her, it is debatable whether this case should even be considered sexual abuse. Because Ronnie mentioned this experience in answer to a question on child sexual abuse, the decision was made to count it as such. Indeed, Jennifer's case is also somewhat borderline in terms of the Russell study's definitions (to be discussed in Chapter 10) since no sexual contact occurred. However it was considered an attempt at contact that was interrupted by Jennifer's pushing the baby carriage at the man in question. Hence it qualified as a case of sexual abuse. It seems clear that the white men in these two cases have little in common with the vast majority of perpetrators of child sexual abuse who never get convicted.

As already mentioned, only 2 percent of the incidents of incestuous abuse of females in Russell's study were ever reported to the police, compared with 6 percent of the cases of extrafamilial child sexual abuse of females. The fact that incestuous abuse is even less likely to be reported than child sexual abuse outside of the family is hardly surprising, given what is known about power relationships within the family and the secrecy that commonly surrounds the breaking of the incest taboo.

Not a single case of child sexual abuse by a female perpetrator was reported to the police in the Russell survey. Does this indicate a greater reluctance to report sexual abuse when the perpetrator is a female, or is there some other explanation? When the 26 female perpetrators of child sexual abuse are compared with the 621 male perpetrators, it emerges that girls reported much less upset when the perpetrator was female (only 27 percent reported being very or extremely upset compared to 58 percent of those abused by male perpetrators), and much fewer long-term effects (22 percent said the abuse had no long-term effects when the perpetrator was female compared with 46 percent when the perpetrator was male).

These findings are probably due to the fact that female perpetrators were significantly less likely to use physical force or violence (46 percent compared with 83 percent), or to abuse the child at the most serious level (intercourse, anal or oral sex, and/or attempts at these acts versus manual fondling of genitals or breasts, or other sexual touching—8 percent versus 46 percent). In addition, the age difference between the victim and perpetrator was considerably and significantly greater when the abuser was male. (In only 27 percent of the cases involving a female perpetrator was the age difference greater than five years, compared with 61 percent of the cases involving male perpetrators.) In general, the mean age of female perpetrators was considerably younger: 18 years compared with 30 years for male perpetrators. However, there was no significant difference in the age of the victim when attacked (11.7 years for those abused by female perpetrators versus 12.4 years for those abused by males).

What we see here is that sexual abuse by females not only occurs much less frequently than does sexual abuse by males, but it is much less traumatic when it does occur: Female perpetrators less often use violence, force, or verbal threats, and they are less likely to molest children much younger than themselves. Not surprisingly, then, victims of female perpetrators are less likely to report the sexual abuse to the police. It seems likely that a similar comparison of male and female perpetrators of boy children would yield the same results.

The extremely low rates of reporting found by the Russell survey for cases of child sexual abuse show that reported cases represent only the tiny tip of a massive iceberg. This finding is all the more alarming in light of the fact that almost one third (32 percent) of the victims of incestuous child abuse reported that their perpetrators had also sexually abused one or more other relatives.[2]

Given the enormous secrecy that usually surrounds cases of incest, often permanently, it is quite remarkable that such a large percentage of victims knew that at least one other relative had been sexually abused by the same perpetrator. Moreover, the 53 percent who said that their perpetrator had *not* sexually abused another relative may of course be wrong. It is common for victims to think that they alone have been abused, even when this is not the case (see MacFarlane & Korbin, 1983, for an astounding example of this phenomenon).

## Notes

1. Although New Jersey has repealed its incest statute, according to the American Bar Association Report it has "one of the most comprehensive criminal sexual offense laws protecting children, including age differentials between victims and perpetrators, specifically defined relationships between victims and perpetrators, and graduated penalties" (Wulkan & Bulkley, 1981, p. 56).

2. Sixteen percent of the respondents said they did not know if their perpetrators had sexually abused another relative, and 53 percent said that another relative had *not* been sexually abused by their perpetrator. These figures add to 101 percent because of rounding to the nearest whole number.

# 10

# THE INCIDENCE AND PREVALENCE OF CHILD SEXUAL ABUSE

Researchers and practitioners have reached no consensus on the sex acts that constitute sexual abuse, nor on the age that defines a child. Nor do they agree about which is the most appropriate concept: child sexual abuse; sexual victimization; sexual exploitation; sexual assault; sexual misuse; child molestation; sexual maltreatment; child rape.

To confuse the matter further, these terms frequently have been limited to describing sexual behavior that occurs between adults and children (e.g., Finkelhor, 1979; Mrazek & Kempe, 1981, p. 12; NCCAN, 1981, pp. 4–5). Cases in which children are raped or otherwise sexually abused by their peers, younger children, or children less than five years older than themselves are often discounted as instances of child sexual abuse. In this book, the terms child sexual exploitation, child sexual abuse, and child sexual victimization will be used interchangeably; they include sexual abuse by peers or younger children.

The term *incidence* will refer to cases of child sexual abuse that occurred within a specified period of time, and *prevalence* will refer to the percentage of children victimized by such an experience, whether once or many times.

## The Incidence and Prevalence of Incest and Extrafamilial Sexual Abuse of Children

Both the incidence and prevalence of child sexual abuse, in the family and outside of it, are unknown. Kirson Weinberg, in his classic study originally published in 1955, estimated that there was one case of incest per million persons per year in the United States (1976, p. 34). Franco Ferracuti estimated that between one and five cases of incest per million persons occurs every year throughout the world (1972). Many other estimates have been made, but none of them is based on representative samples.

Meiselman attempted to list all studies of incest with samples larger than five published in this country (1978, pp. 45–49). Many of the studies were based on cases obtained by referrals from therapists, psychiatric hospitals, courts or social agencies, and private practices; some of the studies had been conducted on incarcerated offenders. The samples used in all 36 studies were highly selected and nonrepresentative. Studies of extrafamilial child sexual abuse are equally unrepresentative.

The National Incidence Study includes cases known to investigatory bodies such as child protective service agencies, as well as professionals in schools, hospitals, and other major agencies. This study estimated a rate of 0.7 cases of child sexual exploitation per 1,000 children per year, as compared with 3.4 cases of other physical assault, 2.2 cases of emotional abuse, 1.7 cases of physical neglect, 2.9 cases of educational neglect, and 1.0 case of emotional neglect per 1,000 children per year. The number of substantiated cases of sexual exploitation was 44,700 (NCCAN, 1981, p. 18).

The finding that there were proportionately more serious injuries (including but not limited to physical injuries) associated with sexual exploitation than with physical assault suggests that only the most serious cases of sexual abuse were recognized as deserving inclusion (NCCAN, 1981, p. 22). Just as many cases of reported rapes are unfounded each year by the police, many legitimate cases of child sexual abuse are unsubstantiated by the professionals who investigate them.

Most other estimates have focused on the *prevalence* of incest and/or other child sexual abuse, rather than on incidence. Psychiatrist and author Judith Herman presents data from five surveys, undertaken by various researchers, on the prevalence of sexual abuse of female children since 1940. She points out that cumulatively, these studies have recorded information from over 5,000 women from many different regions of the United States, and primarily from the more privileged strata (1981, p. 12). According to Herman,

> The results of these five surveys were remarkably consistent. One-fifth to one-third of all women reported that they had had some sort of childhood sexual encounter with an adult male. Between four and twelve percent of all women reported a sexual experience with a relative, and one woman in one hundred reported a sexual experience with her father or stepfather. (1981, p. 12)

**TABLE 10.1**

**The Prevalence of the Sexual Abuse of**
**Female Children: A Comparison of Five Studies**

| Study | Date | Number of Female Subjects | Population | Percentage Sexually Abused by Adult | Percentage Abused Before Puberty | Mean Age of Child | Percentage Abused by Family Member | Percentage Abused by Father or Stepfather | Sex of Adult Aggressor Male (in percentages) | Female |
|---|---|---|---|---|---|---|---|---|---|---|
| C. Landis | 1940 | 295 | Middle class hospital patients and controls | — | 23.7 | — | 12.5 | — | — | — |
| Kinsey | 1953 | 4441 | White middle class | — | 24 | 9.5 | 5.5 | 1.0 | 100 | 0 |
| J. Landis | 1956 | 1028 | College students | 35 | 24 | 11.7 | — | — | 100 | 0 |
| Gagnon | 1965 | 1200 | White middle class | — | 28 | 9.9 | 4.0 | 0.6 | 98.5 | 1.5 |
| Finkelhor | 1978 | 530 | College students | 19.2 | 17.0 | 10.2 | 8.4 | 1.3 | 94 | 6 |

SOURCE: This table was compiled and presented by Judith Herman, *Father-Daughter Incest* (1981), p. 13. Reprinted by permission.

Herman points out that the results of these five studies are even more consistent than they may at first appear; much of the variation that exists results from differences in the kinds of sexual incidents reported (1981, p. 12). For example, in Judson Landis's study, over half of the encounters reported by women occurred with exhibitionists with whom no physical contact was involved. In contrast, only 20 percent of the incidents reported by David Finkelhor in his study were encounters of this kind, while 75 percent were incidents involving physical contact (1981, pp. 12, 14).

If experiences with exhibitionists are excluded, the data from these two surveys become very similar: 15.8 percent of the women in Landis's study reported a childhood sexual experience involving physical contact with an adult, as compared with 14.4 percent of the women in Finkelhor's study (Herman, 1981, p. 14).

Estimates based on prevalence surveys of sexual abuse in nonclinical populations are generally more valid than those based on clinical, prison, or other highly selected populations. However, since none of the surveys cited above were based on random samples of the population (or even random samples of students), it is not valid to generalize from them to the population at large. Russell's study is the only one undertaken to date that was specifically designed to assess the prevalence of sexual abuse on the basis of a random sample. Although limited to the city of San Francisco, Russell's findings about the incidence and prevalence of sexual abuse of children are the most valid available at this time. (The methodology of Russell's study was described in Chapter 1.)

## The Russell San Francisco Survey

**THE DEFINITIONS**

The Russell survey defined *extrafamilial child sexual abuse* as

One or more unwanted sexual experiences with persons unrelated by blood or marriage, ranging from attempted petting (touching of breasts or genitals or attempts at such touching) to rape, before the victim turned 14 years, and completed or attempted forcible rape experiences from the ages of 14 to 17 years (inclusive).

Since incestuous abuse was expected to be generally more traumatic than extrafamilial child sexual abuse; and since the issue of whether or not the sexual experience was wanted or not is so much more complex in intimate relationships, Russell used a broader definition for *incestuous child abuse:*

> Any kind of exploitive sexual contact or attempted sexual contact, that occurred between relatives, no matter how distant the relationship, before the victim turned 18 years old.

Experiences involving sexual contact with a relative that were both wanted *and* with a peer were regarded as nonexploitive. (For example, sex play between cousins or siblings of proximate ages.) A peer relationship was defined as one in which the respondent was less than five years younger than her partner. The 40 cases of exploitive sexual contact between relatives where the respondent was 18 years or older when it started are excluded from this analysis.

Russell's definitions of these two forms of child sexual abuse are narrower than those used by some other researchers, some of whom include exhibitionism and/or other experiences such as verbal propositions that involve no actual sexual contact or attempt at contact (for example, Finkelhor, 1979; Gagnon, 1965; Landis, 1956).

In 1978, when the interviews for the Russell survey were conducted, California law defined child molestation as "all sex acts upon children under the age of fourteen, when the intent of sexually stimulating either party is involved" (Beserra et al., 1973, p. 160). Since the Russell research was conducted in California, the study used the age of 13 and younger as its criterion for child sexual abuse. Other researchers have used other ages. Finkelhor, for instance, defined a child as a person under 17 years of age (1979); the National Child Abuse and Neglect publications use 18 years as their criterion (1981, pp. 4–5).

In many states 18 is the age of consent; it is also the age specified in the Child Abuse and Neglect reporting statute. So prevalence rates will be reported here for the age groups of 13 and under, and 17 and under.

THE INTERVIEW SCHEDULE

The Russell interviewers found in pretesting that memories stored in many different categories were most readily tapped by asking a number of different questions in a wide variety of ways. The questions used to elicit memories of child sexual abuse experiences follow. (The sections in parentheses were read by the interviewer only if the respondent had already mentioned a childhood sexual experience.)

(1) Before you turned 14, were you ever upset by anyone exposing their genitals?

(2) Did anyone ever try or succeed in having any kind of sexual intercourse with you against your wishes before you turned 14?

(3) In those years, did anyone ever try or succeed in getting you to touch their genitals against your wishes (besides anyone you've already mentioned)?

(4) Did anyone ever try or succeed in touching your breasts or genitals against your wishes before you turned 14 (besides anyone you've already mentioned)?

(5) Before you turned 14, did anyone ever feel you, grab you, or kiss you in a way you felt was sexually threatening (besides anyone you've already mentioned)?

(6) Before you turned 14, did you have any (other) upsetting sexual experiences that you haven't mentioned yet?

The following questions, including the two questions on incestuous sexual abuse, did not stipulate an age limit. They nevertheless yielded many experiences of child sexual abuse.

(7) At *any* time in your life, have you ever had an unwanted sexual experience with a girl or a woman?

(8) At any time in your life, have you ever been the victim of a rape or attempted rape?

(9) Some people have experienced unwanted sexual advances by someone who had authority over them, such as a doctor, teacher, employer, minister, therapist, policeman, or much older person. Did *you ever* have *any* kind of unwanted sexual experience with someone who had authority over you, at *any* time in your life?

(10) People often don't think about their relatives when thinking about sexual experiences, so the next two questions are about relatives. At *any* time in your life, has an uncle, brother, father, grandfather, or female relative ever had *any kind* of sexual contact with you?

(11) At any time in your life, has anyone less closely related to you such as a stepparent, stepbrother, or stepsister, in-law or first cousin had *any* kind of sexual contact with you?

(12) In general, have you *narrowly missed* being sexually assaulted by someone at any time in your life (*other* than what you have already mentioned)?

(13) And have you *ever* been in any situation where there was violence or threat of violence, where you were also afraid of being *sexually* assaulted—again, *other* than what you (might) have already mentioned?

(14) Can you think of any (other) unwanted sexual experiences (that you haven't mentioned yet)?

Separate questionnaires were completed for every case of sexual contact or attempted contact that met Russell's definitions of incestuous or extrafamilial child sexual abuse. Interviewers were instructed to obtain sufficiently detailed descriptions of the sexual contact(s) to ensure that the level of intimacy violated could be precisely coded.

### PREVALENCE FIGURES

Table 10.2 shows that *16% of the sample of 930 women reported at least one experience of incestuous abuse before the age of 18 years.* These 152 women reported a total of 186 experiences with different perpetrators. *Of these women 12 percent (108) had been sexually abused by a relative before reaching 14 years of age.*

These prevalence figures exclude eight cases of incestuous abuse in which the respondent's age at the time it occurred was missing. The figures also exclude two cases in which the interviewer failed to determine whether actual sexual contact had occurred or had been attempted between the respondent and her relative. Hence, even in the unlikely event that all respondents were willing to disclose their experiences of incestuous abuse, these figures err on the side of underestimation.

Using the more stringent definition of extrafamilial sexual abuse, *31 percent of the sample of 930 women reported at least one experience of sexual abuse by a nonrelative before reaching the age of 18 years.* These 290 women reported a total of 461 experiences with different perpetrators. *Twenty percent (189) of these women had been sexually abused by a nonrelative before reaching 14 years of age* (see Table 10.2).

It is not surprising that there is some overlap between the respondents who have experienced incestuous child abuse, and those who have experienced extrafamilial child sexual abuse. When these two categories of child sexual abuse are combined, *38 percent (357) of the 930 women reported at least one experience of incestuous and/or extrafamilial sexual abuse before reaching the age of 18 years; 28 percent (258) reported at least one such experience before reaching 14 years of age* (see Table 10.3).

The Russell study uncovered shockingly high prevalence figures for child sexual abuse. These figures would undoubtedly be even higher had Russell used definitions of both incestuous and extrafamilial child sexual abuse as broad as those used in some other studies. Some respondents, for instance, replied to the two questions on incest—

**TABLE 10.2**

**Different Measures of the Prevalence and Incidence
of Incestuous and Extrafamilial Child Sexual Abuse (separated)**

| | Women Who Had at Least One Experience (Prevalence; N = 930) | | Number of Experiences of Sexual Abuse with Different Perpetrators* (Incidence) |
|---|---|---|---|
| | Sample Percentage | Number | Number |
| Incestuous abuse of females involving sexual contact (17 years and under)** | 16 | 152 | 186 |
| Incestuous abuse of females involving sexual contact (13 years and under)** | 12 | 108 | 134 |
| Extrafamilial sexual abuse of females involving petting or genital sex (17 years and under) | 31 | 290 | 461 |
| Extrafamilial sexual abuse of females involving petting or genital sex (13 years and under) | 20 | 189 | 255 |

*Multiple attacks by the same perpetrators are only counted once; abuse involving multiple perpetrators are also counted as only one experience.
**8 cases of incestuous abuse are excluded because of missing data on the age of the respondent.

which specifically asked about incidents involving sexual contact—by describing experiences that did not involve actual or attempted physical contact. It is probable that many other respondents would also have revealed such experiences had they been asked about them.

Despite their incompleteness, these inadvertently obtained data are of considerable interest. Similar quantitative data were also obtained about other noncontact experiences in childhood, such as being upset by witnessing someone exposing their genitals. In response to questions about extrafamilial child sexual abuse, additional quantitative

## TABLE 10.3

### Different Measures of the Prevalence of Incestuous and Extrafamilial Child Sexual Abuse of Females (combined)

| | Women Who Had at Least One Experience (N = 930) | |
| --- | --- | --- |
| | Sample Percentage | Number |
| Incestuous and/or extrafamilial sexual abuse of females under 18 years | 38 | 357 |
| Incestuous and/or extrafamilial sexual abuse of females under 14 years | 28 | 258 |
| Incestuous and/or extrafamilial sexual abuse of females under 18 years—broad definition (includes noncontact experiences, e.g., exhibitionism, sexual advances not acted upon, etc.) | 54 | 504 |
| Incestuous and/or extrafamilial sexual abuse of females under 14 years—broad definition (as above) | 48 | 450 |

data that did not meet Russell's definition of sexual abuse were also recorded, for example: unwanted kisses, hugs, and other nongenital touching.

Russell then applied these broader definitions of incestuous and extrafamilial child sexual abuse (including experiences with exhibitionists as well as other unwanted non-contact sexual experiences). *Of the 930 women 54 percent (504) reported at least one experience of incestuous and/or extrafamilial sexual abuse before they reached 18 years of age, and 48 percent (450) reported at least one such experience before they reached 14 years of age* (see Table 10.3).

For various reasons, including the fact that detailed information was only obtained on child sexual abuse involving physical contact or attempted contact, the narrower definitions of incestuous and extrafamilial child sexual abuse will be used throughout the remainder of this book.

### THE PERPETRATORS OF INCESTUOUS CHILD ABUSE

In the Russell survey, 40 percent (74 cases) of incestuous child abuse occurred within the nuclear family (i.e., the perpetrators were

**TABLE 10.4**

**Incestuous Abuse by Type of Perpetrator**
**Before Victim 18 Years of Age**

| Perpetrator | Number of Women* | Percentage of Women in Sample (N = 930) | Number of Incidents with Different Perpetrators |
|---|---|---|---|
| Father (biological, step, foster or adoptive) | 42 | 4.5 | 44 |
| Mother (biological, step, foster or adoptive) | 1 | 0.1 | 1 |
| Grandfather | 8 | 0.9 | 8 |
| Grandmother | 0 | 0 | 0 |
| Brother | 20 | 2.2 | 26 |
| Sister | 3 | 0.3 | 3 |
| Uncle | 46 | 4.9 | 48 |
| Aunt | 0 | 0 | 0 |
| In-law (male only) | 8 | 0.9 | 9 |
| First cousin (male or female) | 28 | 3.0 | 28 |
| Other relative (male or female) | 18 | 1.8 | 19 |

*If a woman was sexually abused by more than one category of relative, she is included in each.

parents or siblings). Forty-two women reported an incestuous relationship with their fathers before the age of 18 (including 27 biological fathers, 15 step, 1 foster, and 1 adoptive father. Since two women were sexually abused by both their biological and stepfathers, the count includes two more perpetrators [44] than victims [42]). This constitutes *4.5 percent of the random sample of 930 women* (see Table 10.4).

Sexual abuse by uncles is very slightly more prevalent than father-daughter incestuous abuse: 4.9 percent of the women in the sample reported at least one such experience before the age of 18. Three percent (3 percent) of the women surveyed reported a sexually abusive experience with a first cousin (all but two of whom were male) before they turned 18. Just over 2 percent of the women reported at least one incestuous experience with a brother, 0.9 percent with a male in-law, 0.9 percent with a grandfather, 0.3 percent with a sister, 0.1 percent with a mother, and 1.8 percent with some other male or female relative. Not a single case of sexual abuse by grandmothers or aunts was reported.

The percentage of female perpetrators would likely have been higher had males as well as females been interviewed. But this random sample of women reported only 8 female perpetrators of incestuous sexual abuse (only 4 percent of all incest perpetrators).

## THE PERPETRATORS OF EXTRAFAMILIAL CHILD SEXUAL ABUSE

Table 10.5 reveals that only 15 percent of the perpetrators of extrafamilial child sexual abuse were strangers to their victims; 42 percent were acquaintances and 41 percent were more intimately related to their victims (friends of the respondent; friends of the family; dates; boyfriends; lovers). Of these perpetrators 40 percent were also classified as authority figures. Two-thirds of them were so classified because they were much older adults (stranger; acquaintances; friends of the family; parents' lovers; household employees; neighbors).[1]

Perpetrators of extrafamilial sexual abuse of female children were overwhelmingly male: Table 10.5 shows that only 4 percent were females. This is exactly the same percentage of female perpetrators as was found for incestuous abuse.

## THE PERPETRATORS OF ALL CHILD SEXUAL ABUSE COMBINED

It is becoming more widely recognized that most perpetrators of child sexual abuse are known to their victims. Yet, the Russell survey reveals that when all cases of incestuous and extrafamilial child sexual abuse are combined, the majority of the perpetrators are not relatives: 11 percent were total strangers, 29 percent were relatives, and *60 percent were known but unrelated to their victims.*

## SERIOUSNESS OF INCESTUOUS CHILD ABUSE

The Russell survey obtained data on incestuous abuse that ranged from unwanted but nonforceful kissing by a cousin to forcible rape by a biological father. A total of 18 different categories of sexual abuse were distinguished by whether or not force was used, as well as the degree of sexual violation involved. For simplifcation, this 18-category typology was collapsed into the following 3 categories:

> *(1) very serious sexual abuse,* ranging from forced penil-vaginal penetration to attempted fellatio, cunnilingus, analingus, and intercourse— *not* by force;

### TABLE 10.5

**Perpetrators of Extrafamilial Sexual
Abuse of Females Under 18 Years**

| Perpetrator | Male Perpetrators | | Female Perpetrators | |
|---|---|---|---|---|
| | Percentage | Number | Percentage | Number |
| Stranger | 15 | (71) | 0 | (0) |
| Acquaintance | 40 | (185) | 2 | (8) |
| Friend of family | 14 | (64) | 0 | (2) |
| Friend of respondent | 9 | (43) | 2 | (7) |
| Date | 9 | (40) | 0 | (0) |
| Boyfriend, lover, husband* | 7 | (33) | 0 | (0) |
| Authority figure (not classifiable | 2 | (8) | 0 | (0) |
| Total | 96 | (444) | 4 | (17) |

*Five women who were raped by their husbands before they turned 18 are included here, since, although they are relatives, clearly sexual abuse by husbands cannot be regarded as incestuous.

> *(2) serious sexual abuse,* ranging from forced digital penetration of the vagina to nonforceful attempted breast contact (unclothed) or simulated intercourse;
> *(3) least serious sexual abuse,* ranging from forced kissing, intentional sexual touching of the respondent's buttocks, thigh, leg, or other body part, including contact with clothed breasts or genitals, to attempts at any of the same acts without the use of force.

Table 10.6 summarizes the frequency with which these different degrees of incestuous child abuse occurred in the survey. Also included there is the relationship between the victim and the perpetrator, and the sex of the latter.

This table reveals that 23 percent of all incidents of incestuous child abuse were classified as *very serious,* 41 percent as *serious,* and 36 percent as *least serious.* Forty-one percent (77) of the cases reported involved force; 59 percent (109) involved no force. Note that force includes threat of force as well as the inability to consent due to being unconscious, drugged, asleep, or in some other way, totally helpless.

Only one of the eight female perpetrators, a distant female relative, used force. No female was reported to have perpetrated a sexual violation in the *very serious* category.

TABLE 10.6
## Seriousness of Incestuous Abuse Before 18 Years of Age by Relationship with Perpetrator*

| | Male Perpetrator** | | | | | | | | Female Perpetrator** | | | | |
|---|---|---|---|---|---|---|---|---|---|---|---|---|---|
| | Biological Father | Step, Adoptive Foster Father | Grand-father | Biological and Half Brother | Uncle | In-law | First Cousin | Other Male Relative | Biological Mother | Sister | First Cousin | Other Female Relative | Total |
| **(1) Very serious sexual abuse:** Completed and attempted vaginal, | 7 | 8 | 0 | 7 | 8 | 2 | 6 | 5 | 0 | 0 | 0 | 0 | 43 |
| oral, anal intercourse, cunnilingus, analingus, forced and unforced*** | 26% | 47% | | 27% | 17% | 22% | 23% | 29% | | | | | 23% |
| **(2) Serious sexual abuse:** Completed and attempted genital | 9 | 5 | 2 | 16 | 14 | 1 | 15 | 7 | 1 | 3 | 1 | 2 | 76 |
| fondling, simulated intercourse, digital penetration, forced and unforced*** | 33% | 29% | 25% | 62% | 29% | 11% | 58% | 41% | | | | | 41% |
| **(3) Least serious sexual abuse:** Completed and attempted acts of | 11 | 4 | 6 | 3 | 26 | 6 | 5 | 5 | 0 | 0 | 1 | 0 | 67 |
| intentional sexual touching of buttocks, thigh, leg, or other body part, clothed breasts or genitals, kissing, forced and unforced*** | 41% | 24% | 75% | 12% | 54% | 67% | 19% | 29% | | | | | 36% |
| Total | 27 | 17 | 8 | 26 | 48 | 9 | 26 | 17 | 1 | 3 | 2 | 2 | 186 |

*Eight cases of incestuous abuse are excluded because of missing information on the respondent at the time of the abuse.
**Categories of relatives where there were no incidents of sexual abuse are omitted.
***The term force includes physical force, threat of physical force, or inability force or inability to consent because of being unconscious, Drugged asleep, or in some other way totally helpless.

Table 10.6 reveals that stepfathers were much more likely than any other relative to sexually abuse their daughters at the most serious level.[2] In almost half of the cases of sexual abuse by stepfathers (47 percent), *very serious* abuse was reported, as compared with 26 percent by biological fathers and a range of from 17 percent to 29 percent by other male relatives. Since many more females have biological fathers than stepfathers, the fact that as many as 15 stepfathers (8 percent of all incest perpetrators) were reported by these women compared with 27 biological fathers (15 percent of all incest perpetrators) confirms the widespread belief that stepfathers are more likely to abuse their daughters than are biological fathers.

Table 10.6 also reveals that when incestuous abuse occurs within the same generation, the *least serious* incidents are much less likely to be reported. Only 12 percent of the incidents with brothers and 19 percent with first cousins involved abuse at this level, as compared with 75 percent of the incidents with grandfathers and 54 percent with uncles. It may be that even relatively mild experiences are remembered because they are more distrubing when they are cross-generational than when they are not. Another possible explanation is that the incest taboo is weaker for brothers and cousins, so, like stepfathers, they may permit themselves to be more seriously abusive if they so desire.

### SERIOUSNESS OF EXTRAFAMILIAL CHILD SEXUAL ABUSE

When the same differentiation is made between the *very serious, serious,* and *least serious* incidents of extrafamilial child sexual abuse, 53 percent (243) were classified as *very serious,* 27 percent (125) as *serious,* and 20 percent (93) as *least serious* (see Table 10.7). A comparison of these percentages to those reported for incestuous child abuse reveals that sexual abuse of children outside the family is of a significantly more serious nature. The incest taboo, although frequently violated, may serve to restrain those who abuse their relatives. Or it may be a consequence of Russell's methodology, which included only incidents of rape and attempted rape for extrafamilial child sexual abuse of 14- to 17-year olds. Because incestuous abuse was defined more broadly than extrafamilial sexual abuse even prior to 14 years of age, more minor episodes of sexual contact with relatives qualified for inclusion.

Table 10.7 reveals that authority figures were by far the most likely perpetrators to engage in the less serious types of sexual abuse. Only 25 percent of them were involved in *very serious* sexual abuse, as compared with 90 percent of dates, 88 percent of boyfriends/lovers, 73 percent of strangers, 72 percent of acquaintances, 70 percent of friends of the respondent, and 50 percent of friends of the family.

### COMPARISONS WITH OTHER STUDIES

David Finkelhor's research on the sexual abuse of children was also based on survey data—albeit a population of students who were not randomly selected. This makes his findings regarding perpetrators of child sexual abuse the most comparable with Russell's (1979).

Of the students surveyed by Finkelhor 26 percent reported a sexual experience with a relative, as compared with only 16 percent who reported a childhood sexual experience with an older person (1979, p. 86). The latter experiences included both incestuous and extrafamilial

TABLE 10.7
## Seriousness of Extrafamilial Child Sexual Abuse Before 18 Years of Age by Relationship with the Perpetrator

| | Male Perpetrator* | | | | | | | Female Perpetrator* | | | |
| | Stranger | Acquaintance | Friend of Family | Friend of Respondent | Date | Boyfriend, Lover | Authority Figure | Acquaintance | Friend of Respondent | Authority Figure | Total |
|---|---|---|---|---|---|---|---|---|---|---|---|
| (1) *Very serious sexual abuse:* Completed and attempted vaginal, oral, anal, intercourse, cunnilingus, analingus, forced and unforced** | 37 / 73% | 54 / 72% | 10 / 50% | 30 / 70% | 36 / 90% | 29 / 88% | 45 / 25% | 0 | 2 | 0 | 243 / 53% |
| (2) *Serious sexual abuse:* Completed and attempted genital fondling, simulated intercourse, digital penetration, forced and unforced** | 7 / 14% | 7 / 9% | 7 / 35% | 7 / 16% | 3 / 7% | 3 / 9% | 80 / 44% | 1 | 4 | 6 | 125 / 27% |
| (3) *Least serious sexual abuse:* Completed and attempted acts of intentional sexual touching of clothed breasts or genitals, forced and unforced** | 7 / 14% | 14 / 19% | 3 / 15% | 6 / 14% | 1 / 3% | 1 / 3% | 57 / 31% | 3 | 1 | 0 | 93 / 20% |
| Total | 51 | 75 | 20 | 43 | 40 | 33 | 182 | 4 | 7 | 6 | 461 |

*Categories of relatives where there were no incidents of sexual abuse are omitted.
**The term force includes physical force, threat of physical force, or inability to consent because of being unconscious, drugged, asleep or in some other way totally helpless.

child sexual abuse. The Russell prevalence rate of 16 percent for the incestuous abuse of females 17 years and under is substantially lower than Finkelhor's 26 percent. This difference is due in part to the fact that Finkelhor applied no age limit to cases of incest.

Far more cross-generational incestuous child abuse was reported in Russell's survey than in Finkelhor's. If the categories of "other" male and female relatives are excluded (since it is not self-evident whether or not these involve cross-generational incestuous abuse), then 60 percent of the incestuous child abuse in Russell's survey was cross-generational, as compared with only 14 percent in Finkelhor's study. More specifically, 24 percent of the perpetrators of incestuous abuse in Russell's San Francisco survey were fathers (including stepfathers, one adoptive and one foster father) and 26 percent were uncles. This compares with only 4 percent fathers and 9 percent uncles in Finkelhor's sample (1979, p. 87).

One striking similarity between the two studies is the absence of a single sexually abusive aunt in either of them. Only one incestuous mother was reported in each of the studies. Both studies found a minority of female perpetrators. Russell's survey, however, found only 8 cases of female perpetrators (4 percent of all perpetrators)—compared with 35 cases (19 percent) reported by Finkelhor (1979). The subject of female perpetrators of child sexual abuse will be discussed more thoroughly in Chapter 11.

One reason for the large disparities between Russell's findings and Finkelhor's is that his definition of incest is much broader than Russell's. For example, he included "an invitation to do something sexual"; "other people showing his/her sexual organs to you"; and "you showing your sex organs to other person" (1979, p. 178). Russell included as incestuous abuse only those experiences that involved some direct physical contact or attempted contact.

Also, Finkelhor did not differentiate between abusive and nonabusive experiences (1979, p. 84). Experiences that do not involve actual sexual contact are much more likely to be nonabusive, particularly when they occur between peers.

Finally, some differences in the findings of these two surveys may have occurred because of their different methodologies. Women may be more reticent to disclose the more taboo experiences of father-daughter (and other cross-generational) incestuous abuse on a self-administered questionnaire in a classroom situation, as was required by Finkelhor's methodology. Russell, on the other hand, conducted face-to-face interviews with well-trained interviewers who first spent time building rapport with respondents.

Another dramatic difference between the findings of Russell's representative survey and those of other nonrepresentative surveys is on the question of sexual abuse by strangers. Only 11 percent of the perpetrators of child sexual abuse in Russell's sample were total strangers. This figure is much lower than the 24 percent reported by Finkelhor (1979), the 58 percent reported by Gagnon (1965), and the 65 percent reported by Landis (1956). Similarly, 60 percent of the perpetrators in Russell's sample were neither total strangers nor related, compared with 26 percent in Gagnon's study, and 33 percent in Finkelhor's.

These differences may be explained by the fact that Russell's survey uncovered more of the types of experiences that are rarely detected or divulged, including those withheld from agencies and researchers.

## SUMMARY, CONCLUSION, AND IMPLICATIONS

It is safe to assume that some of Russell's random sample of 930 women were unwilling to disclose experiences of child sexual abuse to the interviewers. It is equally certain that a significant number of them had repressed such experiences from their conscious memories. Despite all of this, as well as the fact that the definitions used by Russell's study were narrower than those used in other major studies, astonishingly high rates of child sexual abuse were disclosed to Russell's interviewers. Why?

Once again, the methodology employed is probably responsible for the uncommonly high disclosure. Russell used female interviewers only; selected interviewers meticulously; conducted training sessions to sensitize interviewers to the issue of child sexual abuse; created an interview schedule that facilitated the development of effective rapport before the topic was broached; and asked a multiplicity of questions.

Finkelhor commented on his estimate of a 1 percent prevalence rate of father-daughter incest:

> One percent may seem to be a small figure, but if it is an accurate estimate, it means that approximately three-quarters of a million women eighteen and over in the general population have had such an experience, and that another 16,000 cases are added each year from among the group of girls aged five to seventeen. (1979, p. 88)

Judith Herman concurred with Finkelhor's 1 percent estimate (1981). The rate of father-daughter incestuous abuse reported in Russell's survey is four and one-half times higher than this 1 percent estimate. The rate of other incestuous and extrafamilial child sexual abuse is similarly much higher than any prior study had indicated. More specifically:

(1) 16 percent of the sample of 930 women reported at least one experience of incestuous abuse before the age of 18 years; 12 percent reported at least one such experience before the age of 14 years;

(2) 31 percent reported at least one experience of extrafamilial sexual abuse before the age of 18 years, and 20 percent reported at least one such experience before the age of 14 years;

(3) When both categories of sexual abuse are combined, 38 percent reported at least one experience before the age of 18 years, and 28 percent reported at least one such experience before the age of 14 years.

These alarming prevalence rates are based on the first random sample survey ever conducted on this subject. There is reason to believe that the sexual abuse of female children in San Francisco, where the study was conducted, is no more prevalent there than in other cities of comparable size. It may be assumed, therefore, that these findings are indicative of the prevalence of child sexual abuse in other areas.

This means that *over one-quarter of the population of female children have experienced sexual abuse before the age of 14, and well over one-third have had such an experience by the age of 18 years.* Furthermore, the Russell study confirms the fact that only a minute percentage of cases are ever reported to the police: 2 percent of incestuous and 6 percent of extrafamilial child sexual abuse cases.

## Sexual Abuse of Boys

The fact that many boys are sexually abused has been denied or ignored until very recently by both experts and the public at large. The neglect of this problem has been part of the more general neglect of all sexual victimization of males (Groth & Gary, 1982, p. 144). Consequently, as Nicholas Groth and Thomas Gary point out, "Dependable information in regard to the sexual molestation of male children ... is very limited, and much more research needs to be directed toward this issue" (1982, p. 144).

Despite the paucity of research, Groth and Gary conclude their review of the literature on the prevalence of the sexual abuse of boys by stating that boys "are the targets of reported victimization in almost a third of the offenses committed by male adults" (1982, p. 146). This figure is consistent with David Finkelhor's figures. In his survey of 796 college students, Finkelhor was surprised to find that as many as 8.6 percent of the male students had been sexually victimized as boys. This figure compared with 19.2 percent of the women students who had been sexually abused as girls (1979, p. 55).

Finkelhor's definition of sexual victimization included sexual experiences between (1) a child twelve or under with an adult 18 or over, or (2) a child twelve or under with a person under 18 but at least five or more years older than the child, or (3) a young adolescent between 13 and 16 years with a partner at least 10 years older (1979, pp. 55–56).

Finkelhor's survey data led him to conclude that a great deal of sexual abuse of boys is simply not being reported (1979, p. 68). He and Groth both maintain that boys are less likely to report experiences of sexual abuse than girls, and that this form of abuse is, in general, less likely to come to public attention. Finkelhor offered the following reasons in his analysis of his student survey:

(1) Boys reported fewer negative experiences than girls (1979, p. 79); "boys' experiences occur at an older age with generally younger

partners. They less frequently involve family members and are felt to be less frightening and shocking" (1979, p. 71).

(2) Boys may feel greater shame and/or "have been indoctrinated into an ethic of greater self-reliance" (1979, p. 138).

(3) "Professionals in the field may be less prepared for the possibility of sexual victimization of boys and thus less likely to identify it" (1979, p. 138).

(4) "Sexual victimization of girls may arouse a more protective response and thus be promoted to case status by various public and family authorities" (1979, p. 138).

Finkelhor's view that boys may feel greater shame than girls is supported by the fact that many males who are sexually abused suffer the additional trauma of feeling that their masculinity has been undermined. Being victimized places boys in a passive role, which they consider female; when the perpetrator is a male, the taboo against homosexuality is violated, causing the victim to feel like a "sissy."

There are, however, other plausible arguments that suggest that girls may be less likely to report than boys. Finkelhor himself suggests that "The cultural conception of girls as sexual merchandise that can be ruined or devalued means that far more is at stake when they are victimized" (1979, p. 71). All the arguments for why each sex might be less likely to report than the other have merit, and perhaps serve to balance each other.

In a more recent article, Finkelhor presents a table summarizing several studies on the ratio of boy to girl victims in child sexual abuse cases (1981; see Table 10.8).

On the basis of these studies, as well as estimates drawn from surveys in the general population, Finkelhor speculates that from 2.5 percent to 8.7 percent of men are sexually abused as children (1979, p. 30). On the basis of similar estimates, he suggests that two to three times as many girls are victimized than are boys. Like girls, boys are most commonly victimized by men (1979, p. 30).

Additional data on the incidence and prevalence of sexual abuse of boys is included in Chapter 11.

Finkelhor reported the following four findings from his review of the literature on the sexual abuse of boys on matters other than prevalence or incidence:

Boys appear to be more likely than girls to be victimized by nonfamily members;

**TABLE 10.8**

**Ratio of Boy to Girl Victims in Child Sexual
Abuse Cases According to Various Studies**

| Study | Year | Number of Boys per 100 Girls | N |
|---|---|---|---|
| *Child protective agencies* | | | |
| DeFrancis | 1969 | 11 | 250 |
| National Reporting | 1978 | 15 | 6096 |
| *Hospitals* | | | |
| Jaffe et. al. | 1975 | 13 | 291 |
| Rogers | 1979 | 33 | 114 |
| Ellerstein & Canavan | 1980 | 12 | 145 |
| *Police* | | | |
| Queen's Bench | 1976 | 47 | 131 |
| Swift | 1978 | ~50 | ? |
| *Mixed agency* | | | |
| National Incidence | 1980 | 20 | 3124 |
| *General surveys* | | | |
| Bell & Weinberg | | | |
| Heterosexual | 1978 | 32 | 385** |
| Homosexual | 1978 | 47 | 804** |
| Finkelhor | 1979 | 48 | 796** |

SOURCE: This table was compiled and presented by Finkelhor in "Sexual Abuse of Boys: The Available Data," Unpublished paper, 1981, p.11. Reprinted by permission.
**Ns of whole survey, not Ns of victims.

boys are more likely to be victimized in conjunction with other children; boy victims are more likely to come from impoverished and single-parent families, and to be physically as well as sexually abused;

sexual abuse of boys is more likely to be reported to the police than to a hospital or child protective agency (1979).

A more thorough comprehension of these and other findings concerning the sexual abuse of boys awaits further research.

### PERPETRATORS OF THE SEXUAL ABUSE OF BOYS

The extent to which boys are sexually abused by men and women is extensively discussed in Chapter 11. Regarding the sexual orientation of the men who sexually abuse boys, Groth and Gary point out that "It is commonly presumed that when an adult becomes involved with a child of the same sex, that adult is *ipso facto* homosexual" (1982, p. 144). According to Groth and Gary, this presumption is incorrect. They argue that

> The error here lies in equating the behavior (a sex act) with a personality attribute (a sexual orientation) and mistaking sex as the primary or essential criterion for identifying the attraction when in fact it is age. (1982, p. 144)

Groth and Gary maintain that perpetrators have individual preferences in regard to both age and sex, "but the term 'homosexual' identifies only the sexual determinant and leads to the faulty supposition that sex is the only and exclusive component of attraction" (1982, p. 144). These researchers therefore use the term homosexual to refer only to "physically mature persons who sexually prefer other physically mature agemates of the same sex" (1982, p. 145). Indeed, they conclude, "Pedophilia, the sexual attraction to children, in fact appears to be more a variant of heterosexuality than of homosexuality" (1982, p. 15).

### MOTHER-SON INCEST

There has been a strong fascination about mother-son incest in the literature—particularly the psychoanalytic literature—as well as in films. This fascination persists despite the fact that "incest between mother and son is so extraordinary that a single case is considered worthy of publication" (Herman, 1981, p. 18).

Judith Herman mentions that she was only able to find a total of 30 documented cases of mother-son incest in the entire literature. These included 8 cases that "might more accurately be described as rape, since they involve situations in which an adolescent or adult son subjected his mother to forced intercourse" (1981, p. 18).

The attention given to mother-son incest appears to be way out of proportion to its significance.

### FATHER-SON INCEST

Herman was able to locate 32 cases of father-son incest in the literature (1981, p. 20). However, she cited a clinical report in which 10 cases of father-son incest were identified within the population of *one* child-guidance clinic. Herman pointed out that

The authors were not looking for incest and were astonished by the large number of cases they encountered.... The authors were led to the conclusion that father-son incest may be significantly under-reported. (1981, p. 20)

Certainly, there has been very much less attention in the literature or the media to father-son incest than to mother-son incest. Mother-daughter incest has likewise been almost totally neglected.

In his review of the research on parent-child incest, Finkelhor reported as follows:

If we can take the National Reporting sample as indicative of the actual distribution of abuse—admittedly a big leap—we would have to conclude that women when they abuse at all, are more likely to abuse daughters than sons, and that mother-son incest is the rarest from of parent-child sex abuse. (1981, p. 18)

A discussion of the relationship between boys' experiences of sexual abuse and their becoming sexual offenders or nonsexual offenders in their adult years will be reviewed in Chapter 12 on the causes of child sexual abuse.

## Is Sexual Abuse of Girls Increasing in the United States?

According to the *National Study of the Incidence and Severity of Child Abuse and Neglect,* the incidence of child sexual abuse reported to Child Protective Service Agencies, the police, and other social service or treatment facilities is increasing each year (1981).

Parents United in Santa Clara County, California, was one of the first, and is perhaps the best-known, facility for the treatment of incest in the country. Parents United reports that since its inception in 1971, each year has been marked by a dramatic increase in the number of cases of incest brought to its attention (Giarretto, 1982). Other facilities, such as the Sexual Assault Center at the Harborview Medical Center in Seattle, Washington, report similar increases (Lucy Berliner, personal communication, 1983).

Most child protective service workers at these and other treatment centers attribute the escalating use of their services to the growing public awareness of their existence, not to an increase in the occurrence of child sexual abuse (Finkelhor, 1979, pp. 131–132). According to David Finkelhor, most observers believe that "what we are witnessing is a revolution in consciousness, a situation where, because of changed mores, professionals are more sensitive to identifying instances of sexual abuse and victims and their families are more willing than before to seek help" (1979, p. 132).

In 1979 Finkelhor addressed the question, Is child sexual abuse, both incestuous and extrafamilial, increasing, decreasing, or remaining roughly the same? After a detailed comparison of data gathered in three studies—Alfred Kinsey et al. (analyzed by John Gagnon, 1965), Judson Landis (1956), and himself (1979)—he concluded that the incidence of adults physically molesting girls has probably stayed about the same in the last thirty years, and the incidence of exhibitionism toward girls has probably declined (1979, p. 134). Finkelhor notes that since his survey was undertaken in 1978, his conclusion "does not apply to the experiences of children within the last five years or so, since it has been at least five years since even our most recent interviewees were children" (1979, p. 134).

Russell's survey makes possible a comparison of the experiences of different groups of women of different ages. In doing so, it provides a unique opportunity to evaluate whether incestuous and extrafamilial sexual abuse of girls is increasing or decreasing. Of particular importance is the comparison between the incidence of child sexual abuse among different cohorts of women; that is, subgroups of women who were born around the same period of time and who are currently about the same age. Also compared will be the rates of child sexual abuse experiences reported to have occurred in different decades.

### PROBABILITIES OF THREE TYPES OF SEXUAL ABUSE BY AGE

It is useful to compare the patterns in incestuous abuse over time with the patterns in the other kinds of sexual assault studied. Figure 10.1 plots the probability (in five-year periods) of experiencing for the first time each of three types of sexual exploitation: (1) incestuous abuse (at any age); (2) extrafamilial child sexual abuse (before 14 years); and (3) forcible rape and attempted rape—combined (at any age).

Combining the first experiences of each type of assault for all 930 women in the survey reveals the age patterns for the probabilities of these three types of sexual exploitation. Extrafamilial sexual abuse of girls increases steadily from birth to age 10–14 (the oldest age group measured for this form of abuse[3]) and is the most common form of sexual abuse reported in childhood. Incestuous abuse is also concentrated in childhood, but more incestuous abuse than extrafamilial sexual abuse happens to girls under the age of 5.

The highest percentage of first incestuous abuse experiences also occur in the 10–14 year age period. This percentage declines during the later teenage years. However, it is important to remember that some of the girls who were incestuously abused for the first time at a young age may have continued to be abused into their later teen years, and even into their 20s. By age 20, incestuous abuse rarely occurs for the first time.

Forcible rape and attempted rape become the more common forms of sexual assault in the late teenage years. A first experience of rape remains high in probability during each of the five-year age periods preceding the late 20s. Probabilities of a first experience of forcible rape or attempted rape decline evenly through the later portions of the mature years.

### COHORT RATES FOR INCESTUOUS ABUSE

Figure 10.2 shows the cumulative proportion of women who disclosed one or more experiences of incestuous abuse before the age of 18 for five cohorts of women:

*Cohort 1:* those born in 1918 and earlier who were 60 and older at the time of the interviews;
*Cohort 2:* those born 1919-1928 who were in their 50s;
*Cohort 3:* those born 1929-1938 who were in their 40s;
*Cohort 4:* those born 1939-1948 who were in their 30s;
*Cohort 5:* the youngest group, women born 1949-1960 who were from 18 to 29 years of age when interviewed.

Only the first experience of those women who disclosed more than one experience of incestuous abuse are tabulated here; and only those experiences that occurred before the victim turned 18 years of age are included from this point on.

Figure 10.2 shows some relationship between the cohort's current age and the percentage of the cohort reporting a first experience of incestuous abuse. This relationship, however, is not a totally linear one: Cohorts 1 and 2 reported the lowest cumulative incidence of incestuous abuse by age 18 (7.9 percent and 11.7 percent, respectively). However, women in Cohort 5, the youngest group of women, reported a lower incidence of incestuous abuse by the age of 18 (17.8 percent) than did Cohort 3 women (21.3 percent). Cohort 4 women (now in their 30s) reported the highest incidence (24 percent).

In cases of incestuous abuse that occurred before the child turned 10 years old, the relationship is also not *completely* linear; for

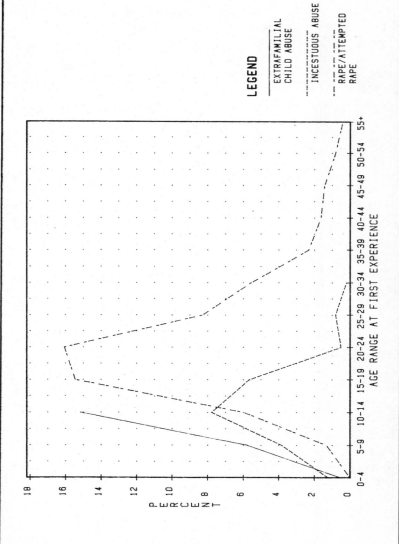

**Figure 10.1 Incidence of Different Types of Sexual Assault. Probability of First Occurrence in Five-Year Age Groups**

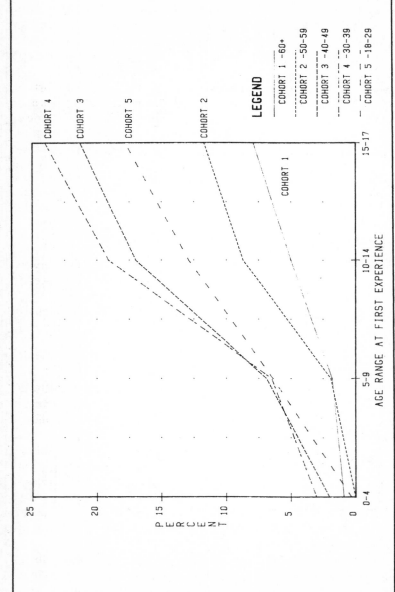

Figure 10.2  Cumulative Proportion of Women Experiencing Incestuous Abuse for Five Cohorts of San Francisco Women

example, there is virtually no difference between Cohorts 1 and 2, both of whom reported the least incestuous abuse before they were 10 years old (1.8 percent and 1.9 percent, respectively). There is also very little difference in the rates of incestuous abuse before the age of 10 for Cohorts 3, 4, and 5 (6.9 percent, 6.5 percent, and 6.4 percent respectively).

Although the relationship between the ages of the five cohorts of women and the amount of incestuous abuse reported at various ages is not perfectly linear, the increase in the incidence of incestuous abuse reported by the women in the first four cohorts is substantial. Also, despite the decline in the percentage of incestuous abuse reported by the fifth and youngest cohort, the 17.8 percent incidence figure for those women is still more than twice as high as the 7.9 percent reported by the oldest cohort.

### COHORT RATES FOR EXTRAFAMILIAL CHILD SEXUAL ABUSE

Figure 10.3 reveals little evidence of a linear relationship between the age of the cohort and the percentage reporting experiences of extrafamilial sexual abuse of girls before the age of 14 years.

Cohort 4, the 30–39-year-old women, reported the highest rates of this form of abuse (23.8 percent).

Cohort 3, the 40–49 year olds, come a close second (23.0 percent).

Cohort 5, the youngest women aged 18–29, are a very close third (22.3 percent).

Cohorts 1 and 2, the two older cohorts, reported significantly less extrafamilial child sexual abuse than did the other three: Women in Cohort 1 reported slightly more abuse than did women in Cohort 2 (17.9 percent and 16.4 percent, respectively).

In cases of extrafamilial child sexual abuse prior to 10 years of age, there is extremely little difference between four of the cohorts, with from 5 percent to 6 percent of all of them reporting this type of abuse.

Cohort 4 is the exceptional cohort here, reporting a significantly higher rate of extrafamilial child sexual abuse before 10 years of age than did the other cohorts (9.6 percent).

Figure 10.3 makes it clear that the younger age groups do not report significantly more extrafamilial child sexual abuse than do the older ones. Thus, it is unlikely that the increases in incestuous abuse over time are due to a greater willingness on the part of the younger

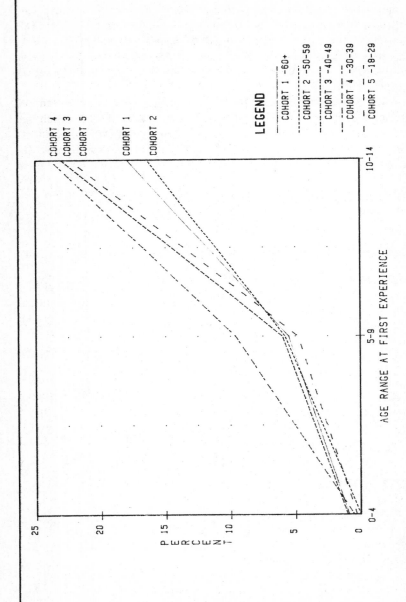

**Figure 10.3  Cumulative Proportion of Women Experiencing Extrafamilial Child Sexual Abuse for Five Cohorts of San Francisco Women**

women to disclose such experiences. The same argument was made regarding the increases in forcible rape and attempted rape (see Chapter 1 for a discussion of the trends in forcible rape). There is no reason to believe that these women would be willing to disclose forcible rape and incestuous abuse, but unwilling to disclose extrafamilial child sexual abuse.

Another demographic technique is applied to Russell's data on incestuous abuse in Figure 10.4. By presenting the data on which the cohort analysis was based in another way, the plotted lines emphasize the changes over time in the occurrence of incestuous abuse by the age of 5, 10, 15, and 18. Figure 10.4 portrays more visually what may also be observed in Figure 10.2: Incestuous abuse before the age of 5 years decreased from .9 percent for Cohort 1 to 0 percent for Cohort 2. It subsequently increased slightly to 2 percent for Cohort 3, 3 percent for Cohort 4, followed by a decline to .3 percent for the youngest Cohort 5. This decline for Cohort 5 was what broke the otherwise quite linear pattern of increasing incestuous abuse for the younger cohorts revealed in Figure 10.2.

For incestuous abuse before the age of 10, the percentages of Cohorts 1 and 2 that were victimized by incest were almost identical (1.8 and 1.9, respectively). This was followed by a considerable increase in incestuous abuse for Cohort 3 (6.9 percent), after which there was practically no change for Cohorts 4 and 5 (6.5 percent and 6.4 percent, repectively).

Incestuous abuse before the age of 15 shows an even greater increase from the oldest Cohort 1 (5 percent) to Cohort 3 (17 percent). This increase is followed by a decline from 19.1 percent for Cohort 4 to 12.9 percent for Cohort 5. The pattern for incestuous abuse occurring by age 18 is very similar to that just described for incestuous abuse by age 15, including the decline for the youngest Cohort 5.

In summary: Figure 10.4 shows an increase in incestuous abuse of girls by age 10; for older girls a substantial increase was interrupted by a considerable decrease for the youngest cohort.

Figure 10.1 reveals that more incestuous abuse than extrafamilial child sexual abuse was reported for girls under the age of 5. This pattern is again evident when comparing Figures 10.4 and 10.5. This difference, however, may be one of methodology and not one of the ages at which these two forms of sexual abuse occur. For example, there was a somewhat more stringent definition of extrafamilial child sexual abuse than of incestuous child abuse. (See Chapter 1 for more information on these methodological differences as well as the rationale for using them.)

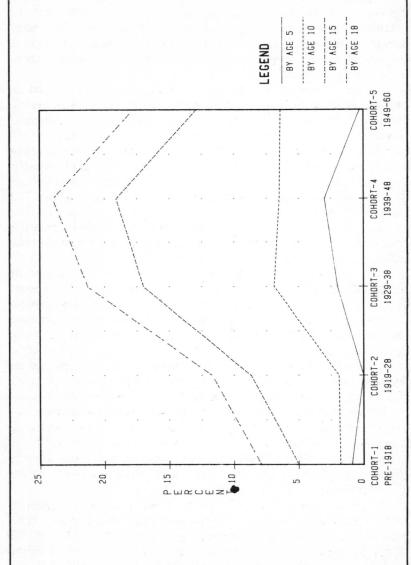

Figure 10.4 Cumulative Proportion of Women Experiencing Incestuous Abuse by a Specified Age for Five Cohorts of San Francisco Women

Figure 10.5 reveals that there is virtually no change in the reported incidence of extrafamilial sexual abuse of children younger than 5 years old.

The trend for girls under 10 years old is also remarkably constant at about 5 percent or 6 percent (except for a sudden increase to 9.6 percent for Cohort 4).

With regard to girls under the age of 14, Cohort 2 reported the lowest percentage of extrafamilial child sexual abuse. However the difference between Cohort 2 and Cohort 1 is very small (16.4 percent and 17.9 percent, respectively).

Figure 10.5 also reveals a significant increase in the percentage of women in Cohort 3 reporting extrafamilial sexual abuse before 14 years (23.0 percent). The percentage changes little for Cohorts 4 and 5, although there is a very slight decline for Cohort 5 (from 23.8 percent to 22.3 percent).

In summary: A comparison of Figures 10.4 and 10.5 reveals that the increase in incestuous abuse for girls by age 10 is not evident for extrafamilial sexual abuse. The most significant difference in the plotted graphs for incestuous abuse of girls under 15 years, and for extrafamilial sexual abuse of girls under 14 years, is that there was a much greater increase from Cohorts 1 through 4 for incestuous abuse than for extrafamilial sexual abuse. The decline in incestuous abuse for Cohort 5 was also much more substantial. Finally, Cohort 1 reported the lowest percentage of incestuous abuse by 15 years of age, while Cohort 2 reported the lowest percentage of extrafamilial sexual abuse by age 14.

### PERIOD RATES FOR INCESTUOUS ABUSE BY SPECIFIED AGES

The analysis will now focus on how the incidence of incestuous abuse has fluctuated over time, specifically from 1916 to 1961. This analysis cannot proceed beyond 1961 because there were no women in the sample who were four years old or younger in the next five-year period between 1964 and 1968; hence these women were not at risk of incestuous abuse in their first four years. Since the probabilities are calculated cumulatively, the lack of data for this age group lowers the probabilities for all the other age groups as well.[4]

Figure 10.6 presents data on what are known as *period rates*. The same data as were plotted in Figure 10.2 are here reorganized by combining first experiences of incestuous abuse reported by different

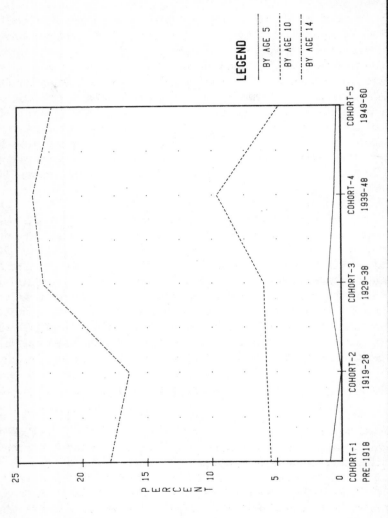

Figure 10.5  Cumulative Proportion of Women Experiencing Extrafamilial Child Sexual Abuse by a Specified Age for Five Cohorts of San Francisco Women

groups of women, then focusing on the years in which the abuse occurred. For example, these period rates combine the experiences of the women who were aged 0–4 years in 1949–1953, with those of women who were 10–14 in 1949–1953, and so on. The years falling at the midpoint of each 5-year period are used in the graphic presentation of the period rates. Although it is customary to use equal interval age groups in this kind of analysis, the definition of child abuse employed in the Russell survey requires limiting the analysis here to girls under 18 years of age.

Figure 10.6 shows that the period rates for incestuous abuse by ages 15 and 18 years of age are very similar. For incestuous abuse by age 18 there was a steady increase (despite fluctuations) from 8.7 percent in 1916—the date when the analysis begins—until 1956, by which date 28.1 percent of the women at risk had been incestuously abused. In 1961 there was a decline in the incidence of incestuous abuse to 19.8 percent, almost the same as the 1951 rate of 19.5 percent. There is no way of knowing whether this decline was a temporary fluctuation or the beginning of a trend.

The period rates for incestuous abuse before the age of 10 have also fluctuated considerably. Nevertheless the rates have increased fairly steadily since 1916 (when the incidence of incestuous abuse was 1.9 percent of the women at risk), to 6.5 percent in 1961. The greatest peak occurred in 1936 (9.0 percent). The dramatic decline evident between 1956 and 1961 for incestuous abuse by 15 and 18 years of age did not occur for girls under 10 years old; the fluctuations in the rates of incestuous abuse were greater for the two older age groups. Although the rates for the latter two groups have declined quite sharply since the 1956 peak, it is significant that the most recent 1961 rates are still among the highest.

### PERIOD RATES FOR EXTRAFAMILIAL CHILD SEXUAL ABUSE BY SPECIFIED AGES

The rates of extrafamilial child sexual abuse plotted in Figure 10.7 reveal great fluctuations for girls under 10 and under 14 years of age. First to be evaluated will be the changes over time from 1916 to 1961 for girls under 14.

The incidence of extrafamilial sexual abuse was 22.9 percent in 1916. By 1926 the figure had declined considerably to 14.7 percent. This was followed by a very slight increase in 1931 (to 15 percent), then a fairly marked increase in 1936 (22.4 percent), with the largest peak occurring in 1946. After 1946, the rate of extrafamilial sexual abuse before 14 declined as dramatically as it had increased—to 16.9

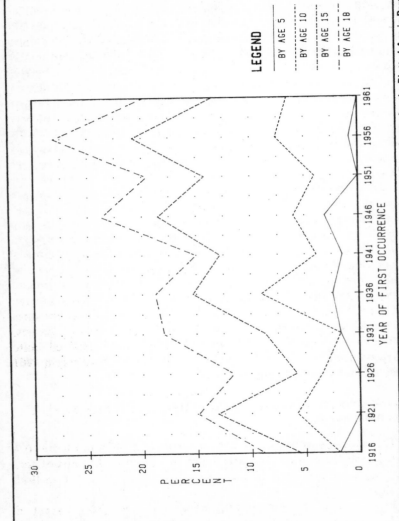

**Figure 10.6    Period Rates of Incestuous Abuse by Specified Ages. Percent Reporting First Experiences by the Plotted Age in Particular Years.**

percent in 1956. This decline was followed by another increase in 1961 to 20.3 percent. This rate is, however, lower than that which occurred in 1916.

The period rates for extrafamilial sexual abuse of girls under 10 are very similar to those just described for girls under 14. Starting at a rate of 7.4 percent in 1916, the incidence decreased to 4.6 percent in 1921. After 1921 the rate then increased to 8.3 percent in 1931, followed by another decline to 3.8 percent in 1941. In 1946 a dramatic increase occurred in the rate of extrafamilial sexual abuse of girls under 10 (14.5 percent), as well as in the rate of extrafamilial sexual abuse before 14 years. By 1956 the rate had declined to an all time low of 3.1 percent; then it increased again in 1961 to a rate of 6.4 percent.

In summary, there has been no significant increase over time up until 1961 in extrafamilial sexual abuse before 10 years of age, except for a marked but temporary peak in 1946.

Figure 10.8 presents the period rates for both incestuous and extrafamilial child sexual abuse. Viewed together, they provide a visual comparison of the changes over time for these two types of sexual abuse.

### INTERPRETATION OF PERIOD RATES

The picture that emerges from this period rate analysis of child sexual abuse is both complex and confusing. It indicates that incestuous abuse was at a low point during World War I (1914–1918), the period when this measurement began, and that it also declined during World War II (1939–1943). Then, in the periods following both World Wars, there was an increase in incestuous abuse. There were other periods of decline that cannot be related to war: 1926, 1951, and 1961 for incestuous abuse before 15 years of age; and 1931 for incestuous abuse before 10 years of age. Although the occurrence of war appears to coincide with a decline in incestuous abuse, we cannot be sure that the war played a causative role.

Extrafamilial child sexual abuse showed a marked decline during World War II, followed by a tremendous peak afterward. Unlike incestuous abuse, there was also a peak in the rate of extrafamilial child sexual abuse during World War I (1916), followed by a decline after it ended.

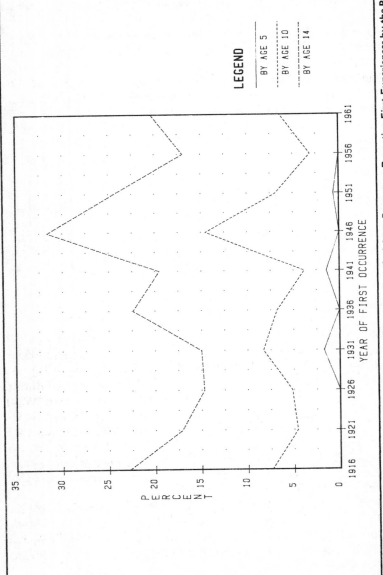

**Figure 10.7   Period Rates of Extrafamilial Child Sexual Abuse by Specified Ages. Percentage Reporting First Experiences by the Plotted Age in Particular Years**

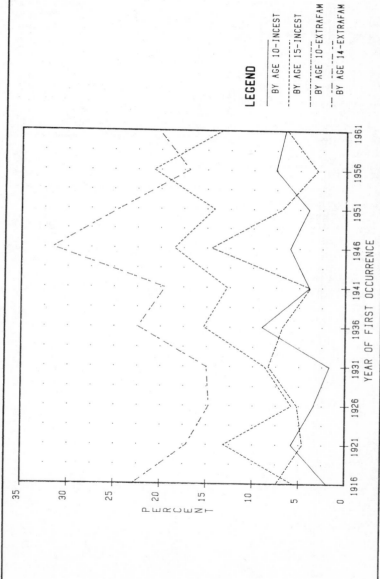

Figure 10.8 Period Rates of Incestuous and Extrafamilial Child Sexual Abuse by Specified Ages. Percent Reporting First Experiences by the Plotted Age in Particular Years

What factors, aside from war, explain the fluctuations in these rates over time? Perhaps social historians will offer some answers. What is clear now is that despite fluctuations, incestuous abuse increased over the years from 1916 to 1961, while extrafamilial child sexual abuse merely fluctuated without significantly decreasing or increasing during this period.

## Notes

1. Authority figures such as medical physicians, employers, and professors are almost always much older than the children they molest, as well as having authority by virtue of their profession. The criterion for qualifying someone as a "much older adult" was not strictly based on the age of the perpetrator, nor on the age difference between this person and the victim. Instead, an attempt was made to ascertain from what respondents said, what had determined the perpetrators' status as an authority figure in their eyes. While this method is somewhat subjective on both the coders and the respondents' parts, it seemed more accurate than applying "objective" age criteria that are arbitrary and of dubious meaning.

2. The category "stepfathers" includes one foster father and one adoptive father.

3. After 14 years of age, the definition changes to include only cases of forcible rape or attempted rape.

4. In addition, the number of women who had been at risk between the ages of 5 and 9 years during 1964 and 1968 was very low (only 25 women). This category only included women whose age at the time of the interview was 18 or 19 (i.e. only two years rather than the five years applicable to all the other categories for age when interviewed).

# 11

# THE GENDER GAP AMONG PERPETRATORS OF CHILD SEXUAL ABUSE

## Coauthored with DAVID FINKELHOR

Just as it has been assumed until recently that boys were rarely victims of sexual abuse, it has also been commonly assumed that very few women commit sexual abuse against children. Past studies that collected data on the gender of perpetrators confirmed the latter assumption. Recently, however, some researchers and scholars of child sexual abuse have begun to question that this is the case.

Nicholas Groth, a prison psychologist, is one example. Although he encountered only 3 women out of 253 adult offenders against children (1 percent) in his professional work prior to 1979 (1979, p. 189), he concluded his discussion of the female offender by arguing that sexual victimization of children by women "may not be as infrequent an event as might be supposed from the small number of identified cases" (1979, p. 192).

Groth offered the following explanation of his view: (1) Women may "mask sexually inappropriate contact with a child through the guise of bathing or dressing the victim" (1979, p. 192); (2) the sexual offenses of females are "more incestuous in nature, and the children are more reluctant to report such contact when the offender is a parent (i.e., their mother) and someone they are dependent upon" (1979, p. 192); (3) it may be that boys are more frequently the targets of female offenders than girls, and that "boys are less likely to report or disclose sexual victimization than girls" (1979, p. 192).

Kenneth Plummer, a sociologist of sexual behavior, believes that the notion of pedophiles as men only is an inaccurate "stereotype" (1981, p. 227). He maintains that there is a "considerable degree of adult female-child sexuality" (1981, p. 228). Like Groth, Plummer argues that such "activity" (he appears to deliberately avoid using the word abuse) is hidden "because of the expectations of the female role which simultaneously expect a degree of bodily contact between woman and child and deny the existence of sexuality in women" (1981, p. 228). He maintains that the physical affection that is socially prescribed for women may result in prison sentences for men.

Psychologists Blair and Rita Justice suggest that so few cases of mother-son incest are reported in the literature because this form of incest is the least likely to come to light. "In our experience," they write, "mothers engage more frequently in sexual activity that does not get reported: fondling, sleeping with a son, caressing in a sexual way, exposing her body to him, and keeping him tied to her emotionally with implied promises of a sexual payoff" (1979, p. 179).

In the last year or two, experts in the field have increasingly expressed the view that the extent of abuse by females has been seriously underestimated. The popularity of this opinion demands a review and interpretation of the data available on this subject.

## The Evidence: Studies Based on Reported Cases

Most early studies of sexual abuse consistently reported a very small number of cases of abuse by females (see Table 11.1). For example, De Francis's study, based on cases reported to the Brooklyn Humane Society, found only 3 percent of perpetrators to be women (1969). Another early study based on reports to the San Francisco Police Department similarly found few women perpetrators (Queen's Bench Foundation, 1976). These and other early studies also found very low rates of abuse against boys. Many observers wondered whether many more cases of abuse committed by women would surface as abuse of boys became more evident.

Later, more comprehensive studies did reveal more abuse of boys— but not much more abuse by women. The two most systematic studies of reported cases of sexual abuse of both boys and girls were done by the American Humane Association (1978) and the National Center on Child Abuse and Neglect (NCCAN; 1981). Of particular relevance here are their findings in regard to women perpetrators.

The National Incidence Study, conducted by NCCAN, was a congressionally sponsored multimillion dollar effort. Its goal was to estimate the extent and nature of child abuse. The study chose 26 counties to be representative of the entire United States, and developed procedures for data collection on both reported and unreported cases from professionals in these counties (NCCAN, 1981). The study concluded that 44,700 cases of sexual abuse were known to professionals in 1979. Of these victims 17 percent were boys.

## TABLE 11.1

### Percentage of Perpetrators Who Are Women:
### Case Report Studies

| Study | Percentage of Women Perpetrators | Total Perpetrators (N) |
|---|---|---|
| **Male Children** | | |
| National Incidence Study | 24* | (91) |
| American Humane Association | 14 | (757) |
| Griffith et al. | 6 | (245) |
| Ellerstein and Canavan | 0 | (16) |
| De Jong et al. | 4 | (103) |
| **Female children** | | |
| National Incidence Study | 13** | (664) |
| American Humane Association | 6 | (5052) |
| **Male and female children** | | |
| Queen's Bench | 4 | (123) |
| De Francis | 3 | (250) |
| Jaffe et al. | 0 | (291) |

*This includes 10 female only, and 12 female *and* male perpetrator cases.
**This includes 27 female only, and 60 female *and* male perpetrator cases.

SOURCES OF CASES: National Incidence Study (1981): Cases known to professionals in 26 countries (chosen to represent U.S.) and reported anonymously to study in year starting April 1979. American Humane Association (1979): Cases reported to mandated reporting agency in 31 states for 1978. Griffith et al. (1981): Cases coming to attention of hospital-based sexual assault unit. Ellerstein & Canavan (1980): Cases coming to attention of hospital-based based sexual assault unit. Queen's Bench (1976): Cases coming to attention of San Francisco Police Department July 1, 1975 to June 30, 1976. De Francis (1969): Cases coming to attention of Society for Protection Against Cruelty to Children. Jaffe (1975): Cases coming to attention of hospital-based sexual assault unit.

Unfortunately, the study provided misleading information about the sex of perpetrators. Table 55 of the study's main report indicates that 46 percent of the sexual experiences encountered by children included a female perpetrator. Reanalysis of the data from the report (summarized below) provides a more accurate breakdown (Finkelhor & Hotaling, 1983).

The National Incidence Study defines a caretaker as a perpetrator not only if he or she had sexual contact with a child, but also if he or she "permitted acts of sexual abuse to occur." In many cases of incestuous abuse, mothers (or some other female caretakers) are believed to know that abuse is occurring but fail to stop it. By including these women as perpetrators, the National Incidence Study makes its figures on perpetrators difficult to interpret. If the data are reanalyzed using only those who actually *committed abuse* as perpetrators, the percentage of female perpetrators drops dramatically to 13 percent in the case of female victims and 24 percent in the case of males.

But even these percentages of female perpetrators are inflated for two reasons. First, the study did not clearly link perpetrators with the type of maltreatment they were guilty of. Thus, if in one family a mother neglected a child while a father sexually abused the child, both mother and father were listed as perpetrators. Since sexual abuse is listed as one of the abuses that occurred, it is impossible to determine who did what. Thus, some of the women included as perpetrators of sexual abuse were really perpetrators only of some other kind of neglect or maltreatment.

Second, the study considered an adult caretaker to be an active perpetrator of sexual abuse if the adult provided "inadequate or inappropriate supervision ... of the child's voluntary sexual activities," if the child was involved with a person at least two years older, and where negative consequences ensued for the child. So here also, some mothers listed as active perpetrators may very well not have been engaged in sexual contact with the child.

There was a final problem: Many of the women listed as perpetrators in the figures noted above (and in Table 11.1) were perpetrators of abuse in which a male was also listed as a perpetrator. Twelve of the 22 cases involving male children, and 60 of the 87 cases involving female children, involved both male and female perpetrators. Even if these were situations in which the female was committing a sexual form of abuse, most clinical accounts involving both male and female perpetrators identify the male as inititiator of the sexual abuse. Frequently the female partner is participating under duress. It is certainly not justified to consider these situations as straightforward instances of sexual abuse of children by females.

For all of these reasons, it seems likely that the figures for female perpetrators from the National Incidence Study—24 percent in the case of boys and 13 percent in the case of girls—are too high.

The American Humane Association study is another large-scale effort to collect and analyze data on child abuse (1978). This organization collects data annually from the official child abuse and neglect reporting agencies in all 50 states. The portion of these data available for analysis consisted of 6,096 reports of sexual abuse from 31 states for the year 1978. Of these reports 803 involved boys.

The American Humane Association study also listed many women as perpetrators because they simply "allowed" sexual abuse to occur. This made determining the exact number of female perpetrators quite complicated. Unlike the National Incidence Study, the American Humane Association study made it impossible to distinguish between perpetrators who committed abuse and those who simply allowed it. At best, it was possible to isolate situations in which only one perpetrator was listed and that perpetrator was a female. Using this method, it emerges that females acting alone represented 14 percent of the perpetrators against boys, and 6 percent of the perpetrators against girls. These figures are similar to the equivalent figures derived from the National Incidence Study if only cases of sole female perpetrator are counted.

Both of these studies indicate that *female perpetrators more frequently sexually abuse girl children than boy children.* The percentage of female perpetrators who sexually abuse boys is higher (14 percent versus 6 percent in the American Humane Association study), but there are a great many more girl victims than boy victims: 6 percent of 5,052 girls, in contrast to 14 percent of 803 boys. The stereotype that women are more likely to sexually abuse boys than girls is not supported by the data from these studies.

## The Evidence: Studies Based on Self-Reports

The shortcomings of data based on reported cases are well-recognized. Those who believe that there is much unreported sexual abuse by females argue that such abuse only rarely comes to public attention, and thus fails to show up in statistics on reported cases (such as those cited above).

Fortunately, there are now a number of studies that have collected data on sexual abuse of children by adults from the self-reports of the victims. All of these studies (listed in Table 11.2) are based on interviews with adults recalling their childhood experiences. Such studies reveal that only a small minority of cases located in this manner were ever reported to public agencies as cases of sexual abuse or child molestation (Finkelhor, 1981; Russell, 1983a). As already mentioned, Russell found that only 2 percent of all cases of incestuous abuse, and 6 percent of all cases of extrafamilial sexual abuse of females under 18 years of age, had ever been reported to the police.

Information about each of the studies listed in Table 11.2 will now be provided, except for Russell's which has already been described (see Chapter 1).

**TABLE 11.2**

**Percentage of Perpetrators Who Are Women:**
**Self-Report Studies**

| Study | | Percentage of Women Perpetrators | Total Perpetrators (N) |
|---|---|---|---|
| **Male children** | | | |
| Bell & Weinberg: | Heterosexual sample | 27 | (11) |
| | Homosexual sample | 14 | (84) |
| Finkelhor: | Student sample | 16 | (23) |
| | Boston sample | 15 | (13) |
| Fritz et al. | | 60 | (20) |
| Gebhard et al. | | 27 | (30) |
| **Female children** | | | |
| Bell & Weinberg: | Heterosexual sample | 7 | (15) |
| | Homosexual sample | 22 | (62) |
| Finkelhor: | Student sample | 6 | (119) |
| | Boston sample | 0 | (65) |
| Fritz et al. | | 10 | (42) |
| Fromuth | | 5 | (139) |
| Russell | | 4 | (651) |

SAMPLE SOURCES: Bell & Weinberg (1981) Heterosexual: Random sample of 336 male and 150 female San Francisco residents. Bell & Weinberg (1981) Homosexual: Volunteer sample of 684 male and 292 female San Francisco homosexuals. Finkelhor (1979) Student: 796 students in Social Science courses in seven New England colleges. Finkelhor (1982) Boston: Random sample of 187 male and 334 female residents of Boston. Fritz et al. (1981): 412 male and 540 female psychology students. Gebhard et al. (1965): Volunteer sample of 477 men who had never been convicted of any offense more serious than traffic violations. Information on women perpetrators was only known in 269 cases (i.e., 56%). Fromouth (1983): 482 female psychology students. Russell (1983a): Random sample of 930 San Francisco females.

The Bell and Weinberg data cited in Table 11.2 are from a study about homosexuality, not child sexual abuse. However, two distinct samples in the study were asked questions about childhood sexual experiences with adults. One was a sample of homosexual men and women obtained by paid recruiters from a variety of sources in the gay community in San Francisco. The second was an area probability sample of heterosexual adults in San Francisco, which was used as a control group to compare with the large homosexual sample. Both samples were asked questions about first homosexual and heterosexual experiences prior to puberty, if any, and the sex and age of the partners in these relationships. The Bell and Weinberg figures on the first prepubertal contacts these respondents had with persons 16 years of age or older have been recalculated from the statistical appendix to *Sexual Preference* (Bell et al., 1981, pp. 97, 118).

Finkelhor's student survey (1979) consisted of a sample of 796 college students recruited from seven New England colleges and universities. They were given self-administered questionnaires to fill out during class time. The figures refer to sexual experiences prior to age 12 with a person at least 5 years older, and experiences that occurred between 12 and 16 years with a person 10 or more years older.

Finkelhor's Boston survey (1982) consisted of an area probability sample of 521 adult residents of that city who had a child between the ages of 6 and 14. The experiences of the adults that were tallied included any sexual experience with someone at least 5 years older that occurred before the age of 16, and were considered by the victims to be abusive.

Fritz et al. collected self-report data from a sample of psychology students at the University of Washington (1981). Their question asked about a "sexual interaction with a post-pubescent person at least 5 years older than you before you reached puberty (excluding those cases in which exposure of male genitals was the only form of interaction)."

Gebhard et al. (1965) interviewed 1,356 men who had been convicted for at least one sex offense (their sex-offender group); 888 men who had been convicted for a misdemeanor or felony that did not include a sex offense (their prison group); and 477 men who had never been convicted for anything more serious than traffic violations (their control group). The large majority of the sex offenders and almost all the prison group were interviewed while incarcerated.

Fromuth (1983) studied psychology students at Auburn University using a definition exactly the same as that used in the Finkelhor (1979) student survey.

Kinsey and his colleagues also collected data on this subject. Since they were missing some important information, their report did not name the sex of the perpetrators. Nonetheless, they wrote of the male sample: "The record includes some cases of pre-adolescent boys involved with adult males" (1948).

The bulk of evidence from these self-report studies indicates that sexual abuse of children by older women represents a distinct minority of child sexual abuse cases. *Twenty-seven percent or less of boys were sexually abused by women,* with one exception. *Ten percent or less of girls were abused by women,* again with one exception (explained below).

The first exception is found in the 1981 study by Fritz et al., which surveyed the undergraduate psychology students at the University of Washington. Close to 5 percent (4.8 percent) of the boys in that sample reported having had a "sexual interaction with a post-pubescent person at least five years older than (themselves) before they reached puberty" (1981). Fritz et al. reported that *60 percent* of these experiences were with females, mostly older female adolescents.

This 60 percent figure is dramatically higher than that obtained in Finkelhor's student sample (1979) despite its use of a similar type of population, a similar definition of molestation, and a similar questionnaire methodology. Unfortunately, the principle investigator of the Fritz et al. study (Nathaniel Wagner) has since died. Many of the questionnaires have been lost, and it is no longer possible to reanalyze the findings to try to find the source of the discrepancy (K. Stoll, personal communication, 1981). Given the consensus of the other studies shown in Table 11.2, it seems likely that the Fritz et al. findings resulted from an unusual sample or an error in tabulation.

The second exception is the figure in Table 11.2 for female children in the Bell and Weinberg homosexual sample (1978). Of the 62 lesbians who reported a childhood experience with a person over 16, 22 percent of them reported that these occurred with older women. One possible explanation of the discrepancy is that lesbians may have different patterns of childhood sexual abuse than heterosexual women. It is not known whether sexual contact with the older women influenced them to become lesbians, or whether their early sexual orientation made them more vulnerable to experiences with adult women rather than adult men, or a combination of both. Whatever the explanation, this finding cannot be taken to confirm high rates of sexual abuse by females in the general population.

There are other reports of higher rates of victimization of children by older females from less representative populations, for example, studies of childhood experiences of incarcerated sex offenders. Groth reported that 51 percent of a sample of sex offenders had been victimized when they were young; of these, 25 percent had been victimized by a female (1983). MacFarlane also found that 51 percent of a sample of attendees at a Parents United National Conference (an organization for incest offenders and their families) had been victimized; of these, 33 percent had been victimized by females (1983). Both of these are unusual groups, for whom victimization (and perhaps victimization by females) may have played a role in their becoming sex offenders. They are not samples that can be used to estimate how widespread sexual victimization is—nor how widespread sexual victimization by females is—in the general population.

Because figures from sources similar to Groth's and MacFarlane's are often quoted, it is important to emphasize just how unrepresentative such samples of sex offenders in jail or treatment are.

Such samples are not representative of sex offenders in general because most sex offenders are never reported, let alone caught or persuaded to get help. As already mentioned, in the Russell survey only 2 percent of the perpetrators of incestuous abuse, and 6 percent of the perpetrators of extrafamilial child sexual abuse, were ever reported to the police. The percentage of all child sexual abuse cases that resulted in conviction was even smaller: 1 percent.

In order to get caught or end up in treatment, a sex offender has likely behaved atypically, even for sex offenders: He or she may have been unusually repetitive or conspicuous; his or her guilt or remorse may have been so great that he or she sought treatment or self-reported, or his or her behavior may have been so flagrantly bizarre that any denial of sexual abuse had no credibility. In addition, because of racial and class prejudices, apprehended offenders are more likely to be lower class or members of minority groups, a conclusion supported by Russell's data on convictions (see Chapter 9).

Not only are apprehended offenders unrepresentative of perpetrators in general, but incarcerated or in-treatment sex offenders who were themselves sexually abused in their childhood are not representative of sexual abuse victims either. Available data do suggest that those with a history of victimization are at greater risk of becoming perpetrators than those who were never sexually abused in childhood. But not all victims become perpetrators. It is likely that those who do become perpetrators had victimization experiences that were different in some way from those who do not become perpetrators—more severe, more unusual, or more disturbing. So the victimization experiences of a group of incarcerated offenders are almost certainly atypical of the victimization experiences of other people.

### Rationale for Questioning the Magnitude of the Gender Gap

The data collated from a variety of studies confirm that most sexual offenses against children are perpetrated by males. It also seems true that some early studies presented unrealistically low estimates of the numbers of female perpetrators. Current studies based on reported cases may still be underestimating such offenses.

The most accurate estimate of sexual abuse by older females is about 5 percent for female children (ranging from 0 percent to 10 percent) and about 20 percent for male children (ranging from 14 percent to 27 percent). Especially since contacts with female children occur at least twice or three times as frequently as do contacts with male children, the theory that perpetrators of sexual abuse are primarily men seems clearly supported (Finkelhor, 1979, 1982).

Despite the apparent accuracy of this conclusion, various objections have been raised against using the available data to resolve the issue of male preponderance. These objections will now be addressed.

(1) Sexual abuse by adult female perpetrators is less often perceived as abusive than is abuse by men.

Some observers speculate that much contact between children and older or adult women goes unnoticed in surveys, because the children do not feel abused or victimized, or even upset. Some children, in fact, may consider it pleasurable.

By not using terms like sexual abuse or victimization, several of the studies in Table 11.2 contradict these speculations. Bell and Weinberg (1981), for example, asked only about sexual contacts that respondents had had before puberty, and then asked for the age of the partner (as distinct from perpetrator). The Bell and Weinberg figures listed in Table 11.2 are based on contacts with "partners" older than age 16, regardless of whether they were positive or negative experiences.

Similarly, students in the Finkelhor student sample were asked simply to note experiences that they had had before the age of 12 with a person over 16, and experiences they had had before age 12 with any other persons (1979). Experiences were included in the tally because they met certain age difference criteria, not because they were considered either positive or negative, upsetting or pleasurable. Thus the figures in both the Bell and Weinberg and Finkelhor samples were not limited to experiences perceived as abusive by the respondents. Positive experiences with older females would have been included in these figures.

Some experts question whether it makes a difference if the experiences examined are considered abusive by the respondent or not. The Finkelhor Boston survey data (1982) are useful for examining this issue, too. In that survey, adult respondents were asked to list any experiences they had had before the age of 16 with a person 5 years older than themselves (irrespective of whether it was considered abusive). The males listed 24 such experiences, 5 of which (or 21 percent) were with older females. Later the respondents were asked whether they considered the experience to be abusive. Thirteen of the experiences were considered abusive including 2 (or 15 percent) of the experiences with females.

So, asking only about abusive experiences *was* found to make some difference (though it was insignificant statistically). But it is not accurate to say that a much larger percentage of experiences with older women is disclosed when respondents are asked about both positive and negative experiences.

(2) Women can mask sexually inappropriate behavior more easily than can men.

Both Groth and Plummer believe that since women have more socially prescribed and acceptable physical intimacy with children, their sexual contacts with children might go unnoticed. A woman could, for instance, have a 3-or 4-year-old child suck on her breast as a way of gaining sexual gratification, without having this behavior identified as abuse.

There are indeed some caretaking activities that could mask abuse by a woman. Breast-feeding and bathing young children are two of these. It seems unlikely, however, that women could mask the activities that comprise the vast majority of abuse engaged in by men: having the child fondle the adult's genitals, putting the penis on or in the vagina, performing oral sex. A woman engaging in comparable activities would have a hard time disguising them as normal mothering. And even if the mother-child relationship is secluded from the scrutiny of other adults, the mother is still left with the difficult task of masking the sexual activity from the children themselves.

Professionals who work with children believe that for the most part children are very good at distinguishing touch that is affectionate from touch that is sexual and intended for the adult's gratification. It is especially hard to imagine that preadolescent boys, who are particularly inclined by their peer culture to see sexual content in behavior, could fail to notice an older woman being sexual with them.

Like men, women may try to disguise the sexual nature of their activities with children by telling them that it is just a game or just a way of expressing affection. Children may believe these deceptions for a short time, but later come to realize their true nature. It is possible that women can deceive children more easily than men can at the time of sexual contact. But any consistent sexual activity would surely show up in reports of older children who look back on their younger years and recognize the sexual content of the contact. In fact, few such reports occur.

What this discussion actually reveals is that despite the ample opportunities for sexual abuse that mothers have, remarkably few seem to take advantage of them. An activity such as breast-sucking has the dual characteristics of being both a typical act of sexual lovemaking and a basic nurturant interaction between mother and child. It seems fraught with possibilities for abuse. Yet, reports from clinical populations or general surveys reveal extremely few cases of inappropriate breast-sucking between mothers and older children.

By contrast, if a basic part of the early nurturing of children included fondling their father's penis, would most fathers allow this activity to remain dedicated to the child's needs? Given the nature of male sexuality in this culture, it seems more likely that many children would be encouraged to repeat this act long after they had outgrown their need for it. The contrast revealed by this comparison illustrates the apparent restraint that is the norm in relations between women and children. Although some sexual activity may be masked, the amount would seem to be small.

   (3) Women commit special kinds of sexual abuse that go unnoticed and
   unmeasured.

In discussions of sexual abuse by women, certain activities are mentioned that are not considered in discussions of sexual abuse by men. Justice and Justice for example referred to "sleeping with a son, ... exposing her body to him, and keeping him tied to her emotionally with implied promises of a sexual payoff," as forms of sexual abuse by women that go unrecorded (1979). The giving of frequent enemas by mothers is also sometimes mentioned.

Studies of sexual abuse of children by adults have not usually asked about such behaviors, which are generally judged to be in a different category. In their extreme forms, these activities constitute psychological, rather than sexual abuse (in which children are used for the direct physical gratification of an adult's sexual needs).

It is not at all clear that women engage in more of this psychological abuse than men do. Judith Herman points out that a large number of fathers have "seductive" relationships with daughters that border on overt sexual abuse but never quite cross the line (1981). There are also forms of psychological abusiveness often used by men: making sexual references to their daughter's breasts or body, or exposing children inappropriately to pornography. Women seem to engage in such behavior far less frequently.

The point about male preponderance is not that women never do harmful things to children's sexuality. It is that women do not seem to use children as often as men do for their direct physical sexual gratification. If the question of sexual abuse is to be broadened to include a wider range of psychological sexual abuses, then the behavior of both men *and* women must be submitted to this kind of larger scrutiny.

(4) Sexual offenses by females are less likely to be reported because they are primarily incestuous.

There is some speculation that the quantity of abuse by females is obscured because it so often occurs within the family. The assumption here is that incestuous child abuse is less subject to public reporting than is extrafamilial child sexual abuse.

However, no evidence substantiates the idea that sexual abuse by females is preponderantly incestuous. In the surveys conducted by both Finkelhor (1979) and Russell (1983a), the ratio of female perpetrators involved in incestuous abuse was not significantly different from that of extrafamilial child sexual abuse. Moreover, this speculation does not explain why sexual abuse by females is so rarely evident in these self-report studies.

(5) Sexual abuse by females is obscured because women more often abuse boys, who are more reluctant to report the abuse than girls are.

Some believe that sexual abuse by females appears infrequently because it happens predominantly to boys, and boys are less likely to report. While prior research does indicate that boys are less likely to report abuse either to parents or to public agencies (Finkelhor, 1979), data have already been presented showing that in studies of both reported cases and self-reports, a greater absolute number of cases involved females sexually abusing girls, not boys.

Moreover, this explanation would only apply to underreporting of sexual abuse in public records, not self-report studies. In fact, since sexual contacts between young boys and older women would seem to be among the least stigmatized of the cross-generational contacts, candor about such experiences in self-report studies would be expected to be even higher (Finkelhor & Redfield, 1982).

## Theories to Explain the Low Rate
## of Sexual Abuse by Women

All evidence cited supports the conclusion that the traditional view of child molestation as a primarily male deviation is essentially correct. Women rarely use children for their own direct sexual gratification.

In spite of the fact that child molestation has traditionally been accepted as a male deviation, this was rarely the subject of theoretical interest until feminist theorists entered the field. This well-established truth about molestation was not examined by nonfeminists for the insights it could offer about the causes of the problem.

The explanation of male preponderance is significant to virtually every theory of child sexual abuse. Gender, as a variable, interacts with virtually every other variable proposed by every theory. Every theory of child molestation must explain not just why adults become sexually interested in children, but why that explanation applies primarily to males and not females.

For example, one popular theory invoked to explain child sexual abuse by adults is that a victimized child becomes a victimizer in an attempt to master the trauma and take on the power of the adult perpetrator. This theory ignores the fact that many more girls than boys are the victims of sexual abuse. If being the victim of sexual abuse increases the risk of becoming a perpetrator, there should be many more women perpetrators than men.

In fact, it is mainly boy victims of sexual abuse who grow up to be child molesters. There is no reason implicit in the theory to explain why girls should not master their trauma through an identification with the perpetrator, just as boys do. Perhaps this is because girls do not readily identify with perpetrators, who are usually males. The sex of the perpetrator, however, has not been cited as an important contingency when this theory is applied to boys. Sexual victimization by both women and men is considered likely to contribute to a boy's becoming a perpetrator (de Young, 1982).

In response to this dilemma, it has been said that while girl victims don't often grow up to be perpetrators, they do often seem to grow up to be the mothers of victims. The victimization rates among victims' mothers do seem to be very high (Goodwin, 1982). While this phenomenon may be parallel to sexually abused males becoming perpetrators in adulthood, a different kind of theory must be invoked to explain it. Every theory of child sexual abuse, just like this one, must have a way of accounting for the different operation of its dynamics in males and females.

The question of why men abuse so much more than women should indeed be the subject of theoretical inquiry. Perhaps the most popular theory to account for low rates of female perpetrators is what we will call the "limp penis" theory. Many people assume that an erection cannot be forced, and therefore that potential women perpetrators cannot gain satisfaction from sexual aggression in the way that men can. This is believed to discourage sexual abuse by women.

There are many problems with this theory. Erections *can* be forced, as accounts of sexually abused boys and homosexual rape clearly show. Moreover, much abuse by women occurs, as we have indicated, against female children. Most importantly, the limp penis theory simply does not take into account that most perpetrators of sexual abuse do not get their satisfaction from intercourse but from either manipulating the child's genitals or having the child manipulate their own. Women can do this too, getting satisfaction from touching the child, or having the child manually stimulate them. The child does not need to be aroused. So the limp penis is not a valid explanation of why women are less likely to abuse children sexually.

Several other factors deserve consideration in the formulation of a satisfactory theory to explain the gender gap among perpetrators of child sexual abuse. These include the following:

(1) Women are socialized to prefer partners who are older, larger, and more powerful than themselves. Being in a position of dominance or authority is antagonistic to the role relationship which most women find sexually arousing. Men, on the contrary, are socialized to prefer partners who are younger, smaller, innocent, vulnerable, and power-less. Clearly, children would be more sexually attractive to men than to women.

(2) Heterosexual women do not generally act as initiators of the first sexual encounter in sexual relationships. Since women are rarely invited by children to engage in sex, such contacts are thus less likely to occur. Males, on the other hand, are not only expected to take the initiative, but also to overcome resistance—and sometimes even to perceive resistance as a cover for sexual desire.

(3) Men appear to be more promiscuous than women. This observation has been ascribed by some to biological factors (Symons, 1979). Whatever its source, if women are less motivated to have multiple sexual partners, they may be less likely to sexualize relationships with children.

(4) Men seem able to be aroused more easily by sexual stimuli divorced from any relationship context (by pornography, for example). Women on the other hand, rely more on a totality of cues, including the nature of the relationship with the sexual partner. The fact of a partner being a child may interfere with women's ability to experience sexual arousal.

(5) Men appear to sexualize the expression of emotions more than women do. Women seem better able to distinguish situations of affection and intimacy that do not involve sex (such as family relationships) from those that do. Men are more likely to define all affectional contacts as sexual, and thus to become aroused by them.

(6) Men and women appear to react in different ways to the unavailability of sexual opportunities. Having sexual opportunities seems more important to the maintenance of self-esteem in men than it is to women (Person, 1980). When other alternatives are blocked, men may more readily turn to children (or other sexual outlets) to maintain their sense of self-esteem.

(7) The role for which women are socialized includes maternal responsibilities. Women, therefore, may be more sensitive to the well-being of children, and more inhibited from sexual contact by knowledge that such contact would be harmful to the child (Herman, 1981). Because women interact much more with children (including their own children) than men do, a kind of bonding may occur between women and children that fosters protectiveness and responsibility which develops more seldom between men and children.

(8) Since women are more often victims of sexual exploitation of various kinds, they may be better able to empathize with the potential for harm that results from such contact, and may therefore be more likely to control whatever sexual impulses they have toward children.

(9) Sexual contact with children may be more condoned by the male subculture than by the female subculture (Finkelhor & Redfield, 1982). Rush (1980a) has documented how sexual involvement by men with children has been accepted and encouraged throughout Western history. Without equivalent encouragement, women may be less likely to develop sexual interest in children.

**CONCLUSION**

This review of both evidence and arguments supports the belief that the extent of sexual abuse by adult female perpetrators is small. There is every reason to believe that child sexual abuse is primarily perpetrated by males. Furthermore, the Russell data on sexual abuse of females indicates that male perpetrators may be responsible for more serious and traumatic levels of sexual abuse than are female perpetrators (see Chapter 9). The question is, Why are so many experts in the field arguing that the number of female perpetrators has been seriously underestimated?

At least two factors account for this wave of speculation about hidden sexual abuse by females. On the one hand, clinicians are seeing (and also noticing) more cases of sexual abuse by females than ever before. The number of such cases may even have jumped dramatically. But in fact, the number of cases of sexual abuse *of all types* coming to light has increased dramatically. The types of cases coming to attention are therefore more varied. Because very few or no cases of female perpetrators came to light in the past, as they now come to light in proportion to their actual prevalence, it may seem at first like a dramatic new development. Certainly the absence of such cases in the past awards them particular notice when they arrive. This increase (or sudden appearance) has led to questioning of the traditional beliefs about female perpetrators.

Some people assumed in the past that sexual abuse by females *never* occurred. This assumption was wrong and requires correction. Sexual abuse by women *does* occur in some fraction of cases: probably about 5 percent in the case of girls and 20 percent in the case of boys. But to take the appearance of some cases of sexual abuse by women to mean that sexual abuse is not primarily committed by men is also wrong, and is not supported by the data.

There is another important reason for the current questioning of the long-held presumption of a male preponderance. Because some social workers and researchers are ideologically uncomfortable with the idea of a male preponderance, they have been quick to rush to the possiblity that it might not be true.

The fact that it is primarily men who commit sexual abuse does have discomforting ideological implications. In a cultural climate where feminists have called upon men to relinquish certain traditional modes of behavior, such facts bolster feminists' arguments, and may thus create defensiveness in those who oppose feminist thinking. Some people find the problem of sexual abuse an easier cause to promote when it is not entangled in "gender politics." Political support for issues of general "human" concern is easier to mobilize than support for issues that appear to benefit one social group more than others—particularly when that group is a stigmatized one of lower status.

Reality can not be twisted to suit this particular ideological or political need. The solution to the widespread and destructive problem of child sexual abuse can only occur if we face the truth about it. This truth is well documented by the evidence, as well as by the current understanding of sex roles and male and female sexuality.

# PART IV

# THE CAUSES OF
# CHILD SEXUAL ABUSE

## 12

## FACTORS CREATING SEXUAL FEELINGS TOWARD CHILDREN

David Finkelhor developed a model for his analysis of the sexual abuse of children upon which this book's presentation of the causes of sexual exploitation is based. This model suggests four preconditions that must be fulfilled for sexual abuse of children by an adult to occur (1981):

(1) The adult must have sexual feelings for a child, or for children in general.
(2) The adult must overcome his or her internal inhibitions against acting out the sexual feeling(s).
(3) The adult must overcome the external obstacles to acting out the sexual feeling(s).
(4) The adult must overcome the resistance or attempts at avoidance by the child, if these occur (1981, p. 2).

According to Finkelhor's theory, the presence of only one, two, or three conditions is not enough in itself to explain sexual abuse. "To explain abuse requires an explanation of the presence of all four prior conditions" (1981, p. 9).

Finkelhor also suggests that there is a logical sequence to these four preconditions.

Only some individuals have sexual feelings about children. Of those that do, only some overcome their internal inhibitions to act on these feelings. Of those who overcome their internal inhibitions, only some overcome external inhibitions—the surveillance of other family members or the lack of opportunity—and act on the feelings. (1981, p. 8)

When the first three preconditions are met, the child at risk may resist directly (by running away, for example), or indirectly (by being assertive in such a way as to avoid the sexual abuse). The child may not resist and hence become the victim of abuse. Or, the child may resist but be overcome by force (1981, pp. 8–9).

This model makes a valuable contribution to the understanding of sexual abuse of children by adults. Even more useful for the task undertaken here is the framework it provides for categorizing and integrating many of the theories of causation developed by researchers and clinicians. Since sexual abuse appears to be a phenomenon caused by a multiplicity of factors, the theories to be reviewed here will be organized within Finkelhor's framework, as were the theories about rape.

First, Finkelhor's own attempt to integrate the many factors causing the sexual abuse of children will be presented in Table 12.1.

Finkelhor points out that much of the prior theorizing about the sexual abuse of children has emphasized one or two factors: the psychodynamics of pedophilia (the condition of being sexually attracted to children), or a family systems model of father-daughter incest, in which the roles of all members of the family are seen as contributing to the victimization (1981, p. 9). Much sexual abuse of children falls into neither category, and some falls into both.

Many children are abused by relatives other than fathers or members of the nuclear family, and by adults who would not be diagnosed as pedophiles (1981, p. 9). Finkelhor's model is at a sufficiently general level "that all kinds of abuse can be integrated within it. It suggests that abuse by fathers and abuse by pedophiles both require an explanation of how the sexual feelings toward the child arose, why there were no effective inhibitors and why a child's resistance was either absent, impossible, or insufficient" (1981, p. 9).

Many of the theories described in the section on the causes of rape are relevant both to the sexual abuse of children and to the rape of adults. They will not be repeated here.

### Adults' Biological Desire to Relate Sexually to Children

David Finkelhor raises the question of whether there are any adults who have no sexual interest in children; he regards this as an unresolved question (1981, p. 3). He mentions the traditional Freudian theory that human beings are potentially naturally polymorphous perverse and therefore capable of sexual arousal from a wide variety of stimuli, including children. According to Freud, early

## TABLE 12.1

### Finkelhor's List of Factors
### Predisposing Adults Toward Sexual Abuse of Children*

*Sexual Feelings about Child*

Male sex-role socialization
Exposure to child pornography
Exposure to advertising that sexualizes children
Childhood sexual experiences
Sexual experiences with other children

*Overcoming Internal Inhibitors*

Socialization in cultural values that do not inhibit
  sexual interest in children
Low impulse control
Alcohol
Setback to ego
Stress
Frustration in other marital/sexual relationship

*Overcoming External Inhibitors*

Mother who is absent, sick, powerless
Poor protection by mother
Domineering father
Crowding or sleeping together
Opportunities to be alone together
Social isolation
Geographical isolation

*Overcoming Resistance by Child*

Child is emotionally deprived
Child is socially isolated
Child knows the adult
Child has special fondness for adult
Child is vulnerable to incentives offered by adult
Child feels helpless and powerless
Child is ignorant of what is happening
Child is sexually repressed and has sexual curiosity
Coercion

*Reprinted by permission.

socialization and cultural taboos repress people's capacities to respond sexually to many possible sources. "The implication from this
viewpoint," Finkelhor maintains, "is that all adults have a potential
sexual interest in children, but that it is to a greater or lesser degree
repressed" (1981, p. 3).

In contrast to the Freudian theory, John Gagnon and others
believe that social learning plays an important role in the development of sexual interest and expression. By implication, adult sexual

feelings for children are not universal, but "may emerge in the course of certain developmental conditions" (Finkelhor, 1981, p. 3).

Paul Gebhard and his associates at the Institute for Sex Research in Indiana offer yet another perspective on this question. They consider that "it is easy to envision how a person under stress and starved for affection might find in the uninhibited responses of a child a strong sexual stimulation" (1965, p. 55). The authors point out that the tendency to express affection and love through physical contact is universal, but that it conflicts with taboos against incest, homosexuality, and large age disparities between sexual partners. This dilemma is solved in our culture "by assuming that physical contact is not sexually motivated in certain areas. For example," Gebhard et al. continue,

> We see a sexual element when an unrelated male and female embrace, but when a mother and adult son embrace we automatically reject the idea of there being any sexuality involved. In the same way a certain amount of physical contact, which would be construed as sexual under other circumstances, is socially permitted between children and adults. If the child and adult are related, it is not only permitted but expected. (1965, p. 55)

However, these authors maintain, the psychological and physical constitution of human beings is such that the sexuality or asexuality of a particular act can not always be regulated by the demands of the social situation. Our physiology reacts to warmth and body contact. Thus "a grandfather bouncing his grandchild on his lap may be aghast to discover he is developing an erection, a brother embracing his sister upon his return from a long absence may guiltily recognize a sexual response in himself" (1965, p. 55).

These researchers appear to have difficulty differentiating between physical contact that is affectionate and that which is sexual. This difficulty seems more typical of males than females. Gebhard et al. reveal this gender bias when they disparage the idea that some physical contact is not sexually motivated.

Gebhard et al. also argue that the culturally constructed mental barriers against acting on such desires can be weakened by stress, hunger for affection, intoxication, and senility. Hence, they conclude, "it is not hard to see how an initially asexual relationship can readily become sexual" (1965, p. 55).

While these authors concede that not all sexual offenders against children "are innocent victims of the conflict between biology and society," this theory fails to explain why relatively few women seem to be torn by the same conflict—or at least why relatively few act out their desires. Their answer to this question is once again, biological: "The average female has a much weaker 'sex drive' than the average male" (1965, pp. 9–10). Consequently, "females rarely resort to violence in their sexual behavior (1965, p. 10). Gebhard et al. make no attempt to substantiate this theory, but instead proceed to elaborate on the different types of sex offenders against both children and adults.

The issue of biological versus social causes for differences between male and female sexuality has not yet been resolved by social scientists. But even if we assume that biological factors play some role, we cannot discard the social factors which mold and transform biological needs—particularly those not necessary for an individual's survival (for example, the need for sex, as opposed to the need for food).

## Male Sex-Role Socialization

This factor has already been discussed at length in the section on the causes of rape. The "masculinity" and "virility mystiques" described in Chapter 5 also play a significant role in some men becoming sexually attracted to children.

Finkelhor points out that "not much is known about people who have sexual feelings for children independent of acting on those feelings," but one good guess is that "these feelings occur much more frequently among men than among women" (1981, p. 4). Pedophilia, a term used to describe "a persistent and long-term sexual interest in children, is virtually unknown among women" (Mohr et al., 1964). Indeed, as was emphasized in Chapter 11 on the gender gap among perpetrators, women are much less likely than men to engage in any kind of sexual abuse. In addition, child pornography appears to be consumed almost entirely by men (Finkelhor, 1981, p. 4).

Finkelhor argues that differences between the socialization of males and females are primarily responsible for the sex differences mentioned; he cites the following relevant examples:

(1) Men are not as well socialized (as women) to distinguish between sexual and nonsexual forms of affection;

(2) Men are socialized to become more easily aroused by sexual activities and sexual fantasies divorced from the content of the relationships in which they occur; and

(3) The attraction gradient: the fact that men are socialized to be attracted to partners who are smaller, younger and less powerful than themselves—in other words, more childlike—whereas the opposite is true for women (1981, pp. 4–5).

As a consequence of these factors, Finkelhor concludes that "being male is one powerful predisposing factor to having sexual feelings toward children" (1981, p. 5).

Males are socialized to be initiators, aggressors, and seducers of women and adolescent female partners, whether or not they are willing (Russell, 1975; Hite, 1981). Females, on the contrary, are socialized to be passive and to wait for male initiative. This results in the development in many women of a "responsive sexuality."

"Responsive sexuality" means that many women learn to be sexually attracted or excited in response to being desired, rather than for their own internal reasons. This is totally the opposite of males, many of whom can be sexually attracted to, and excited by, women or girls who are not only disinterested, but even repulsed and disgusted (as in rape). This attitude difference increases both the likelihood that males will sexually abuse children, and that females will not.

Judith Herman concurs with Finkelhor's conclusion that being male is in itself a powerful predisposing factor to the sexual abuse of children. Herman points out that "the power relations in the family do not suffice to explain why fathers frequently take advantage of their superior position to make sexual use of their children while mothers do not" (1981, p. 55). She offers the following explanation for this key difference between the behaviors of mothers and fathers:

> It is the sexual division of labor, with its resultant profound differences in male and female socialization, which determines in mothers a greater capacity for self-restraint, and in fathers a greater propensity for sexually exploitive behavior. (1981, p. 55)

Herman specifies further that

> The rearing of children by subordinate females ensures that boys and girls will differ in almost every aspect of personality development, including the formation of gender identity, the acquisition of conscience, the growth of the capacity to nurture, and the internalization of the incest taboo. The result is the reproduction of a male psychology of domination and a female psychology of victimization. (1981, p. 55)

Herman notes that several other feminist scholars who have revised psychoanalytic theory have, as she has, "called attention to the profound sex differences created by the fact that mothers, not fathers, nurture children" (1981, p. 55). Examples include Juliet Mitchell, Helen Block Lewis, and Nancy Chodorow. Other writers and researchers on incest have also emphasized this point, for example, Kee MacFarlane (personal communication, 1982), and Louise Armstrong (1978).

## Childhood Sexual Trauma and/or Experiences of Sexual Abuse by Adults

Some researchers believe that an experience of sexual trauma or sexual abuse in childhood can cause an adult to be sexually interested in children.

In their classic work, *Sex Offenders,* Gebhard et al. investigated the frequency of "prepubertal sexual relationships with adults" reported by their sample of incarcerated sex offenders (1965, p. 456). These researchers consistently avoid the term "sexual abuse" in this context, presumably because they do not consider adult-child sexual relationships as necessarily abusive. Nevertheless, their study provides relevant data on this issue.

Gebhard et al. compared the responses of the incarcerated sex offenders with those of incarcerated male prisoners who had not been convicted of sex offenses, and with those of male volunteers outside of prison who were interviewed for Kinsey et al.'s study of male sexuality (1948). Gebhard et al. referred to the male volunteers as a control group. However, this group was not selected by any random sampling process, as would be necessary for a scientifically selected control group.

Gebhard et al. defined an adult as "anyone fifteen or over who, in addition, was at least five years older than the interviewee at the time of the relationship" (1965, p. 456). They differentiated between three types of prepubertal experiences involving "exhibition or approach," "masturbation, mouth-genital, or anal sex," and "coitus." For simplicity, these three categories are collapsed here into one.

Table 12.2 indicates that most of the sex offender groups reported more prepubertal experiences of sexual abuse by adults than was the case for the control group (3 percent of the control group reported sexual experiences with adult females, and 8 percent with adult males). This finding offers some confirmation of the theory that experiences of child sexual abuse by both male and female adults may play a causative role in creating a desire in men to have sex with children. The tentative note here is based on the fact that correlation cannot prove causation.

The prison group of men who had not been incarcerated for sex offenses also reported very high rates of prepubertal sexual abuse. This finding suggests that these childhood sexual traumas may be a causative factor in general antisocial—not solely *sexual* antisocial—behavior by males in later life. The mean percentages for the different groups of sex offenders reporting prepubertal sexual experiences with adults are as follows: 8 percent for those reporting experiences with

**TABLE 12.2**

**Prepubertal Sexual Experiences with Adults by
Sex of Adult for Control, Prison, and Sex-Offender Groups**

| Groups | Percentage Reporting Sexual Experiences with Adult Females | Percentage Reporting Sexual Experiences with Adult Males | N for Whom Information Available |
|---|---|---|---|
| (1) Control | 3 | 8 | (269) |
| (2) Prison | 10 | 31 | (359) |
| (3) Sex offenders | | | |
| (a) Heterosexual offenders against: | | | |
|     Children | 10 | 24 | (135) |
|     Minors | 16 | 14 | (57) |
|     Adults | 9 | 21 | (43) |
| (b) Heterosexual aggressors against: | | | |
|     Children | 10 | 16 | (19) |
|     Minors | 4 | 30 | (23) |
|     Adults | 10 | 22 | (111) |
| (c) Incest offenders against: | | | |
|     Children | 8 | 19 | (52) |
|     Minors | 6 | 13 | (53) |
|     Adults | 0 | 12 | (16) |
| (d) Homosexual offenders against: | | | |
|     Children | 8 | 32 | (78) |
|     Minors | 6 | 35 | (110) |
|     Adults | 4 | 33 | (165) |
| (e) Peepers | 3 | 24 | (29) |
| (f) Exhibitionists | 12 | 17 | (76) |

SOURCE: Adapted from Gebhard et. al., 1965, Table 26, p. 466. Reprinted by permission.

adult females, and 22 percent of those reporting experiences with adult males. Both these means are lower than the percentages reported by the prison group who had not been incarcerated for sex offenses (10 percent and 31 percent, respectively).

In summary: The findings reported by Gebhard et al. confirm the conclusions of Nicholas Groth, Theoharis Seghorn, and Richard Boucher. As reported in the section on the causes of rape, these conclusions state that childhood sexual trauma (including sexual experiences of any kind with adults) may result in later development in the victims of a sexual interest in children.

The findings of these researchers do not explain why this only happens in some instances. Nor do they explain why females rarely respond to their childhood sexual victimization by becoming perpetrators of child sexual abuse. (This is not to say that no women respond to such experiences by becoming perpetrators.)

A common explanation for why some male child sexual abuse victims become sex offenders is that these men, by repeating the conditions of their own victimization, are trying to control or master the hurt (Finkelhor, 1981, p. 5). This same theory is sometimes used to explain why females who were victimized as children are more apt to become *victims* of sexual assault in later life (Summit & Kryso, 1978, Herman, 1981). This opposite response by males and females may be due to the greater tendency of males to act out their anger and pain on others, versus the greater tendency of females to internalize their anger and pain and to take responsibility for their own victimization. Neither response is, of course, a healthy one.

## Childhood Sexual Experiences with Other Children

In *Lolita,* Vladimir Nabokov's fictionalized portrayal of a pedophile, the character Humbert explained the origin of his sexual interest in young girls as a powerful and erotic, but frustrated childhood romance. Some researchers believe that an intense erotic childhood experience can permanently imprint children on a person's sexual orientation (e.g., Rossman, 1976; Finkelhor, 1981, p. 5). Why this happens with males so much more frequently than with females is rarely addressed, let alone explained.

In their comparison of incarcerated sexual offenders and nonsexual offenders, Gebhard et al. report that "prepubertal sex play, like prepubertal masturbation, seems to be associated with subsequent adult sexual activity with female children or with males of any age. One wonders," they speculate,

whether sexual acts of any sort before puberty may not weaken age and sex distinctions in adult life. The man who somewhere in his mind harbors the recollection of the pleasures he had as a child with other children, female or male, may be more prone to repeat these acts. At any rate he is more aware than is the male without prepubertal sexual activity that children can experience sexual pleasure. (1965, p. 446)

Further research is needed to evaluate whether or not Gebhard et al.'s speculations on this matter are correct. However, it seems unlikely that healthy sex play between children would lead to the development of desires in adulthood that require the exploitation of children for satisfaction. As already mentioned, Gebhard et al. fail to distinguish between nonexploitive and exploitive sex; this applies to their analysis of child-child sexual contacts as well as adult-child sexual relationships.

If a distinction is made between child-child sexual experiences that are abusive, and those that are not abusive the hypothesis that there is a connection between childhood sexual abuse and adult sexual interest in children becomes more compelling—even if more limited to men. Once again, if this hypothesis were applied to women it would predict that most adult perpetrators of child sexual abuse would be female. As pointed out in Chapter 11, this is decidedly not the case.

## Effects of Exposure to Child Pornography

The earlier section on the relationship between pornography and rape offered evidence that pornography can actually eroticize rape for men previously unstimulated by this fantasy or practice. Similarly, although much child pornography is probably consumed by pedophiles who are already stimulated by children, exposure to it may create new converts. It seems equally likely that child pornography can reinforce a partially developed interest and rationalize acting it out (Finkelhor, 1981, p. 5).

By the simple laws of classical and instrumental conditioning, stimuli portraying adult sexual behavior in repeated association with portrayals of children enjoying or accepting this behavior can make sex with children an exciting idea. Such portrayals likely feed the self-serving belief—common among child sexual abusers—that the children aren't hurt by such experiences, and that the experiences are enjoyable to both adult and child. Those who work with these men are accustomed to the incredulity they often express when told that their behavior is (or was) damaging to the children involved. As Judith Herman wrote of father-daughter incest:

> Boiled down to their essentials, the excuses of the father are these: first, he did no harm, and second, he is not to blame. With monotonous

regularity, these arguments appear in every sort of literature on the subject, from the scholarly to the pornographic, showing how widespread is the tendency to defend male sexual prerogatives. (1981, p. 22)

Very little research has focused specifically on child pornography. Ironically, the Commission on Obscenity and Pornography did not permit research using children to be conducted, because they were concerned about protecting human subjects (1970).[1] Yet they were willing to conclude that pornography causes no harm, and a few members of the commission specifically included children in this generalization (1970).

## Note

1. Because of a similarly misdirected concern for the protection of children, the federally funded evaluation of child sexual abuse treatment programs did not permit the researchers to ask the children treated what kind of sexual abuse they had suffered. In another federally funded study of runaways, the researchers could not ask whether these youngsters had been sexually abused, although there was reason to believe that many had been (Kee MacFarlane, personal communication, 1982).

# 13

# FACTORS REDUCING INTERNAL INHIBITIONS AGAINST CHILD SEXUAL ABUSE

## *Internalization of Cultural Values Sanctioning Sex with Children*

### MINIMIZATION OR ADVOCACY OF ADULT-CHILD SEX

"Millions of people who are now refraining from touching, holding, and genitally caressing their children, when that is really part of a caring, loving expression, are repressing the sexuality of a lot of children and themselves." (Warren Farrell, quoted by Nobile in *Penthouse,* 1977)

"Sex by age eight or else it's too late." (Motto of the Rene Guyon Society; Rush, 1980a, p. 187)

In her excellent book *Father-Daughter Incest,* Judith Herman points out that Alfred Kinsey, "though he never denied the reality of child sexual abuse, did as much as he could to minimize its importance" (1981, p. 16). With regard to sexual contacts between adults and female children within and outside of the family, Kinsey et al. acknowledged that 80 percent reported being "emotionally upset or frightened" (Kinsey et al., 1953, p. 121). However, they considered this to be due to adverse conditioning rather than a sign of having been sexually abused. This is how he and his colleagues put it:

It is difficult to understand why a child, except for its cultural conditioning, should be disturbed at having its genitalia touched, or disturbed at seeing the genitalia of other persons, or disturbed at even more specific sexual contacts. When children are constantly warned by parents and teachers against contacts with adults, and when they receive no explanation of the exact nature of the forbidden contacts, they are ready to become hysterical as soon as any older person approaches, or stops and speaks to them in the street, or fondles them, or proposes to do something for them, even though the adult may have had no sexual objective in mind. Some of the more experienced students of juvenile problems have come to believe that the emotional reactions of the parents, police officers, and other adults who discover that the child has had such a contact, may disturb the child more seriously than the sexual contacts themselves. The current hysteria over sex offenders may very well have serious effects on the ability of many of these children to work out sexual adjustments some years later in their marriages. (1953, p. 121)

Kinsey and his colleagues failed to distinguish between what Herman refers to as "nuisance' acts such as exhibitionism, and frankly exploitive acts such as the prostitution of women and the molestation of children. Ignoring issues of dominance and power," Herman continues, "they took a position that amounted to little more than advocacy of greater sexual license for men" (1981, p. 17).

Extrapolating from Kinsey's statistics, Herman estimates that interviews were obtained by these researchers with over 40 women who reported sexual relations with their fathers, and 200 women who reported sexual contact with grandfathers, uncles, and older brothers. These interviews were not analyzed, in spite of the fact that "to date, this remains the largest number of incest cases ever collected from the population at large" (1981, p. 17). Kinsey and his colleagues had the courage and honesty to inform the scientific community and the public at large about the prevalence of homosexuality, masturbation, premarital and extramarital sexual relations, sexual contacts with animals, and some women's capacity for multiple orgasms, but they were not willing or perhaps able, for reasons unknown, to deal with incestuous and nonincestuous child sexual abuse.

Later statements by two of the authors of the Kinsey Reports on males and females indicate that their relative silence on the subject in 1948 and 1953, when these volumes were published, may have been no accident. Judith Herman has speculated that these men may have thought the public was not yet ready to hear about incest (1981, p. 18). In 1976 Wardell Pomeroy, one of the authors of the Kinsey Reports, wrote the following two paragraphs in *Forum,* a skin magazine affiliated with *Penthouse:*

When we examine a cross-section of the population, as we did in the Kinsey Report, rather than a selection of those in prison for incest or those who seek therapy because they are disturbed by incest, we find many beautiful and mutually satisfying relationships between fathers and daughters. These may be transient or ongoing, but they have no harmful effects. (1976, p. 101)

Incest between adults and younger children can also prove to be a satisfying and enriching experience, although difficulties can certainly arise. (In any case, I want to emphasize that in no case would I condone incest—be it between adults or between children and adults—when force, violence, or coercion are involved). (1976, p. 10)

To point out that parentheses are rarely used for emphasis is a rather trivial point. Far more serious is Pomeroy's euphemistic understatement that "difficulties can certainly arise" in incestuous relations between adults and children. He completely overlooks the larger issue of whether children are ever in a position to consent to sex with an adult.

In a 1977 article, Philip Nobile quotes another member of the Kinsey team, Paul Gebhard, as saying that only a tiny percentage of the incest cases disclosed to the Kinsey researchers were ever reported to police or psychologists, and "in the ones that were not reported, I'm having a hard time recalling any traumatic effects at all. I certainly can't recall any from among the brother-sister participants, and I can't put my finger on any among the parent-child participants" (1977, p. 118).

These comments by Pomeroy and Gebhard suggest that their relative silence about incest may not have been due to a belief that the public wasn't ready to hear about it when the Kinsey Reports were published; rather, the silence may have resulted from the researchers' unwillingness to reveal their own benign attitudes toward it.

In 1979, sociologist James Ramey equated the incest taboo with other irrational and harmful sexual prohibitions. Accordingly he argued that "we are roughly in the same position today regarding incest as we were a hundred years ago with respect to our fear of masturbation" (1979, pp. 1–2, 6–7). Ramey went on to assert that

we may be doing considerable damage to those who have been or are currently involved in incest. The blatant sensationalism of television, added to congressional hearings which equate incest with rape, child abuse, violence, child slavery, and child pornography combine to scapegoat many people.... It is easy to blame one's problems on the latest scapegoat. It is also easy to set up guilt reflexes where no guilt existed before. (1979)

In her excellent critique of Ramey and other members of what she calls the pro-incest lobby, Herman points out that Ramey's statement implies that most incest victims would not be distressed by the experience but for being manipulated by the media (1981, p. 24).

Herman emphasizes that these pro-incest proponents ignore the question of power. Their argument, she states, avoids coming to grips with the reality that, in relation with adults, there is no way that a child can be in control or exercise free choice.... Adults have more power than children. This is an immutable biological fact. Children are essentially a captive population, totally dependent upon their parents or other adults for their basic needs. Thus they will do whatever they perceive to be necessary to preserve a relationship with their caretakers. If an adult insists upon a sexual relationship with a dependent child, the child will comply. (1981, p. 27)

Hence the issue of whether or not the child consents to sexual behavior becomes irrelevant.

The research of Judith Herman (1981), David Finkelhor (1979), Florence Rush (1980a), and many others, as well as several painful but powerful first person accounts (e.g., Armstrong, 1978; Brady, 1979; Allen, 1980; McNaron & Morgan, 1982; Bass & Thornton, 1983), all suggest that incest involving adults and children causes considerable distress and/or trauma. The researchers, journalists, and self-interested participants (or would-be participants) in adult-child sexual relations who advocate such behavior, or who simply discount the negative effects (as Kinsey did), must surely be seen as contributing to the reduction of internal inhibitions against acting out sexual desires toward children by those who are so inclined.

### VIEW OF FEMALE SEXUALITY
### AS A COMMODITY AND CHILDREN AS PROPERTY

"From the time I was, I guess, 14 till almost 17, whenever my mother was gone, I'd find my stepfather by my bed at night. He would make advances, and when I ended up in tears sometimes, he'd say, 'Well, what difference does it make? You've had all this before. Why should it bother you?'" (Victim raped at 4 years old; Russell, 1975, p. 117)

"I've been your father since you were three. I've been a good father. You owe it to me." (Stepfather to his 14-year-old stepdaughter; the Russell survey)

Just as females are viewed as the property of males, children are almost universally seen as the property of their parents. Some fathers assume that this includes the right of sexual access, particularly to their daughters. Louise Armstrong, author of *Kiss Daddy Goodnight: A Speakout on Incest,* maintains that an incestuous father must have "a sense of paternalistic prerogative in order to even begin to rationalize what he's doing.... He must have a perception of his children as possessions, as *objects"* (1978, pp. 234–235).

Roland Summit and JoAnn Kryso have differentiated nine types of incest. This is how they describe the men involved in the type they refer to as "imperious incest":

> These men set themselves up as emperors in their household domain. They play out an incredible caricature of the male chauvinistic role, requiring wife and daughter to perform acts of sexual fealty. The man, who initiated three daughters into his service, even constructed a throne for himself. (1978, p. 245)

Another type of abuse, also involving fathers viewing their daughters as possessions, is described by Summit and Kryso as "misogynous incest." These researchers believe that for these types of fathers, possessing their daughters sexually is an assertion of their invulnerability to the control of women, as well as an act of "punitive defiance" toward their wives (1978, p. 245).

Judith Herman's theory about incestuous fathers and their feeling of being entitled to sexual access to their daughers is less complicated than Summit and Kryso's, and not confined to one or two types of abusive fathers. Herman maintains that

> Implicitly the incestuous father assumes that it is his prerogative to be waited upon at home, and that if his wife fails to provide satisfaction, he is entitled to use his daughter as a substitute. It is this attitude of entitlement—to love, to service, and to sex—that finally characterizes the incestuous father and his apologists. (1981, p. 49)

More detailed information about the widely held view in this culture of female sexuality as a commodity is available in Chapter 6.

## PREDATORY MALE SEXUALITY

> "The oldest girl I raped was only fifteen, which couldn't be called a woman. The feeling that I finally had a young girl with whom I could do anything I wanted to, was almost enough to make me ejaculate by itself. Touching their bodies, making them perform fellatio, looking at them; these things were all very good, as far as feeling."

> "This took place when I was in ninth and tenth grade in high school. We were very attracted to two thirteen-year-old neighbors. We all knew these girls well. Over a period of a year, starting one summer, my friends and I would catch and hold the girls down, then strip her (sic) of her clothing. We would then fondle their breasts and insert fingers into their vaginas. They would struggle and sometimes scream, but we would not physically harm them. I think they secretly very much enjoyed being taken, but didn't want us to know." (Male respondents; Hite, 1981, p. 728, 729)

Feminist theorists Lorenne Clark and Debra Lewis view the long patriarchal history and continuing male power over women, as well as the tradition that sees women as the property of men, as the basis for the often predatory expression of male sexuality (1977). The very notion of what constitutes masculinity encourages predatory behavior (see the earlier discussion of the masculinity mystique). Although the culture strongly supports predatory male behavior toward adolescent and adult females, it is more ambiguous when it comes to children.

On the one hand the law criminalizes sexual relations with underage females or males (the definition of "underage" varies from state to state). Such activity is called statutory rape. Social mores, as well as laws, have ruled as unacceptable sex between adults and children of the same family. Child-adult sexual relations outside the family have also been regarded as perverse and pathological, as well as illegal.

On the other hand, males are presented with the ambiguous message that it is acceptable to try to seduce females who are 18 years and older in California (or 12 years and older in Georgia), but that same act is criminal with younger females. This message has become increasingly confusing as younger and younger females are being held up as ideal sex objects for men of all ages. Gloria Steinem is one of many feminist theorists to suggest that this model of sexual objectification meets the needs of the growing number of men who are terrified of dealing with women close to their own ages, because they cannot as easily find the power disparity they desire with them (Steinem, 1977).

## PERPETRATORS' INTERNAL INHIBITIONS LESSENED
## WHEN VICTIM AND PERPETRATOR ARE NOT BLOOD RELATIVES

"I kept crying and saying no. He kept saying, 'Relax,' and that there was no danger of pregnancy because he was sterile. He wasn't sensitive to anything but his own horniness." (Respondent who was raped by her stepfather when she was 14; the Russell survey)

"He called me up into the bedroom and said I was old enough to know about these things and he handed me a dirty magazine to read.... Every time I rejected him he would have me beaten." (Respondent who was molested by her stepfather when she was 9; the Russell survey)

Incest is frequently still defined legally as "the crime of marrying, and/or having coitus with a person or persons who are biologically closely related (consanguineous)" (Beserra et al., 1973, p. 145). Because this definition of incest emphasizes what are popularly known as blood ties, it has been common to consider sex between those who are not consanguineally related as nonincestuous or, at the very least, as a less serious breach of the incest taboo.

If it is correct that the incest taboo is most rigidly applied to those who are consanguineally related, one would anticipate that non-blood relatives would be overrepresented among incest offenders. This appears to be the case.

In David Finkelhor's survey of 796 students, he found the rate of father-daughter incest to be almost five times greater in the families with stepdaughters than in any other subgroup in the survey (1979, p. 122).

In the Russell random sample survey 17 percent, or 1 out of approximately every 6 women who had a stepfather as a principal figure in her childhood years, was sexually abused by him. The comparable figures for biological fathers were 2 percent, or 1 out of approximately every 40 women. In addition, when a distinction was made between very serious sexual abuse (including experiences ranging from forced penile-vaginal penetration to nonforceful attempted fellatio, cunnilingus, and anal intercourse) and other less serious forms, 47 percent of the cases of sexual abuse by stepfathers were at the *very serious* level of violation compared with 26 percent by biological fathers (1984).

One possible explanation for these findings discussed by Russell is that stepfathers, because of their nonconsanguineal relationships to their daughters, may feel less bound by the normative disapproval of incest (1984). Many stepfathers who feel desire for their stepdaughters likely do not act on their feelings because they recognize that it would involve a violation of their stepdaughter's trust, a betrayal of their wives, a breach of the norms and laws against relating sexually to a child, and so on. Biological fathers have all these factors to consider *plus* the incest taboo.

Louise Armstrong has argued that it is not incest that is taboo; it is talking about it that is not acceptable (1978). Since Armstrong wrote this in 1978, it has become a commonly accepted idea among those concerned with the problem of incestuous abuse. While the widespread prevalence of incestuous abuse may seem to provide support for this conclusion, Russell's comparison of biological and stepfathers who sexually abuse their daughters suggests that it may be a somewhat misleading notion, if not seriously erroneous. Weak as the incest taboo may appear to be, it may nevertheless explain at least partially why, compared to stepfathers, relatively few biological fathers sexually abuse their daughters (see Russell, 1984, for a more extensive discussion of this issue).

## PERPETRATORS' INTERNAL INHIBITIONS LESSENED
## BY LACK OF OPPORTUNITY FOR BONDING

There is another possible explanation for the greater prevalence and seriousness of sexual abuse by stepfathers found by Russell: the bonding that commonly occurs between biological fathers and their daughters may be absent between stepfathers and stepdaughters. This difference in bonding may be due to the stepfathers' absence in the early years of their stepdaughters' lives, rather than because they view them as related to them in a different and less meaningful way (Russell, 1984).

Herman argues persuasively that if fathers (presumably biological *or* stepfathers) shared with their wives the task of nurturing their children, they would be much less likely to sexually abuse their daughters (1981, p. 206). Indeed, she considers this the key explanation for the enormous discrepancy between the extent of sexual abuse by mothers and that perpetrated by fathers (1981, p. 63). Although Herman does not discuss stepfathers in this context, it follows from her argument that stepfathers who enter the lives of their daughters when they are already past babyhood may be more likely to sexually abuse them.

### SEXUAL ABUSE OF CHILDREN
### AS A CONSEQUENCE OF SUBCULTURAL NORMS

There may be certain subcultures in which inhibitions against incest and other sexual abuse of children are unusually low. Roland Summit and JoAnn Kryso, for example, refer to the folklore that isolated mountain settings promote incest, and mention encountering "an occasional migrant family that seems to accept as natural the practice of intrasibling and intergenerational incest" (1978).

In their study of incarcerated sex offenders, Gebhard et al. attributed the occurrence of incestuous abuse of minors (between 12 and 15 years) to "a cultural tolerance of incest" in some cases (1965, p. 248). In reference to the incestuous abuse of adult women (i.e., 16 years and older), these researchers maintained that "the subculture variety" is the commonest type of offender (1965, p. 268). "Such an offender" they wrote, "was a member of a Tobacco Road type milieu wherein incest was regarded as unfortunate but not unexpected.... The general rule seems to be that in the eyes of these offenders puberty renders a female eligible for sexual exploitation" (1965, pp. 268, 270).

Finkelhor suggests caution in accepting such reports "since the subcultures which are described as lacking in these restraints—such as rural Appalachia—are highly stigmatized, subject to many stereotypes and prejudices, and not easily studied" (1981, p. 6). However, there are a fair amount of data suggesting that incest occurs more frequently in rural families than among urban ones (Riemer, 1940; Lukianowicz, 1972; Lustig et al., 1966; NCCAN, 1981, p. 31).

In the national study of the incidence and severity of child abuse and neglect, for example, 46 percent of the sexual abuse cases were identified in rural counties, although only 31 percent of the children in the United States live in such counties (1981, p. 31). Because this study suffers from so many serious methodological problems, Finkelhor and Hotaling suggest that its findings be accepted with a great deal of caution (1983). In addition, other researchers have reported that incest is not predominantly a rural phenomenon (Cormier et al., 1962; Maisch, 1972, p. 228; Weinberg, 1955).

According to Weinberg, families in which incest occurs are more often black and foreign-born than the proportion of these minorities in the population at large (Weinberg, 1976, pp. 43–44). However, a more thorough national survey concluded that black children are underrepresented in all abuse categories, including sexual abuse (NCCAN, 1981, p. 29). This was particularly true when the researchers controlled for the family's total household income (1981, p. 29).

In Russell's random sample survey, the prevalence of incestuous abuse of females under 18 years among whites, blacks, and Latinas was very similar. However, significantly less incestuous abuse was reported by Asian women. Incestuous abuse was also equally distributed across social classes.

## Poor Impulse Control or Inability to Defer Gratification

Some experts believe that sexual offenders against children share an inability to defer gratification of their desires (Gebhard, 1965, p. 81). Gebhard et al. arrived at this theory after interviewing heterosexual offenders who did not use force or violence when they sexually abused children.

This inability to defer gratification is seen as a personality defect in otherwise normal men in some cases, and the result of mental deficiency in others. Its manifestations in offenders include

> rushing into marriage with brief previous acquaintance; devoting little time to precoital play; turning to children as sexual partners rather than waiting to work out the adult relationships they preferred; high masturbation frequencies by married men; a relatively heavy reliance

on prostitutes; and a large ratio of child victims who were strangers rather than acquaintances or friends. (1965, p. 81)

Roland Summit and JoAnn Kryso maintain that a lack of impulse control is one of "two general characteristics common to those who sexually abuse their children" (1978). They believe that this lack of control may be a persistent quality of the individual, or a result of transient stress.

## Disease or Psychopathology

The common stereotype of sex offenders is that they are sick degenerate monsters. But research indicates that only a small proportion of these men are mentally retarded, senile, or psychotic (Finkelhor, 1979, p. 21; Cohen & Boucher, 1972; Glueck, 1954; Gebhard et al., 1965). Most of them are not sadistic; use of force or violence occurs in a minority of cases. Many of these men prefer to use their resources, authority or charm to gain the child's cooperation or at least her or his obedient submission.

It is also not common for intercourse to be perpetrated or even attempted with prepubescent children. Some theorists attribute this to the presumed preference of some perpetrators for noncoital sex with children, rather than their desire not to hurt the child (Finkelhor, 1979, p. 21).

Other explanations include the likelihood that some perpetrators are deterred from having intercourse because of the physical pain and damage to the victim that may result from this act. Also, in a culture that defines virginity in females as not having experienced vaginal penetration by a penis, some perpetrators believe that they have not been guilty of the "ultimate" act, and hence have not done any (or as much) damage to the child. The incest laws, with their focus on vaginal intercourse, reinforce this view.

The evidence against the theory that all sexual offenders are mentally ill is overwhelming. Yet, as with theories of rape, many theorists of child sexual abuse focus on the personalities of the sexual offenders. Some also focus on the personalities of their wives and/or their victims.

Most theorists recognize differences between sexual offenders; different theories of causation are usually offered for each type of perpetrator. Nicholas Groth's typology of sexual offenders is by far the best known and most widely used in the field at this time. According to Groth, there are two basic types of sexual offenders against children: the *fixated* and the *regressed* (1982).

*(1) Fixated sex offenders.* Groth believes that fixated sex offenders suffer from arrested sociosexual development. He lists the following eleven characteristics as distinguishing them from regressed offenders (1982, p. 217):

(1) Their primary sexual orientation is to children.
(2) Their sexual interest in children emerges at the onset of adolescence.
(3) Their sexual attraction to children is not precipitated by stress.
(4) Their sexual orientation to children is persistent and involves compulsive behavior.
(5) Their sexual offenses tend to be premeditated.
(6) They identify closely with the victim and may behave on the same level as children, or they may play a parental role toward the child.
(7) Their primary sexual interest is in boys.
(8) They rarely have sexual contacts with agemates, and tend to be "single or in a marriage of 'convenience.'"
(9) They usually have no history of alcohol or other drug abuse.
(10) They are immature characterologically, and suffer from "poor sociosexual peer relationships."
(11) Their sexual offenses constitute a "maladaptive resolution of life issues."

According to Groth, fixated offenders who are sexually attracted to preadolescent children are technically described as *pedophiles,* while those who are sexually attracted to adolescent children are *hebephiles* (1982, p. 216).

*(2) Regressed sex offenders.* In contrast to fixated sex offenders, Groth describes the profile of regressed sex offenders as follows (1982, p. 217):

(1) Their primary sexual orientation is to their own agemates.
(2) They become sexually interested in children only in adulthood.
(3) Their sexual attraction to children is usually precipitated by stress.
(4) Their involvement with children is frequently on an occasional basis.
(5) Their first sexual offense is more likely to be impulsive than premeditated.
(6) They regress to involvements with children as a result of conflicts in their adult relationships; they treat the child as a substitute for an adult, and in incest situations, they totally abandon their parental role.
(7) Their primary sexual interest is in girls.

(8) Their sexual contact with children co-occurs with their sexual relationships with adults, and they are usually married or in long-term cohabiting relationships with women.

(9) The consumption of alcohol is quite often associated with their sexual offenses.

(10) They have more traditional lifestyles than the fixated offenders, although their peer relationships are often undeveloped.

(11) Their sexual offenses constitute a "maladaptive attempt to cope with specific life stresses."

In short, regressed offenders' sexual interst in children, according to Groth, "appears to be a departure from their more customary and conventional orientation" (1982, p. 216). Groth stresses the importance of determining whether a sex offender is fixated or regressed "since this will have important implications with regard to the meaning of his offense, what risk he represents to the community, the treatment of choice, and prognosis for recovery or rehabilitation" (1982, p. 217). For example, regressed offenders have a much more optimistic prognosis than do fixated offenders.

Groth points out "the wide variety of individual differences" between sex offenders. This observation in turn suggests that his typology of two is oversimplistic. He maintains, for example, that

Some are attracted only to girls; others, only to boys; some to both. Some are interested only in prepubertal children; others, in young adolescents; some in both. Some are drawn only to their own children; others, only to unrelated children; some to both. All these and other factors may combine in a variety of ways and differ from offender to offender. (1982, p. 226)

It is difficult to reconcile these numerous differences between sexual offenders against children, and Groth's typology. It is also difficult to comprehend why men suffering from stress would seek relief through sexual relations with primarily female children, while the more deeply disturbed fixated offenders would primarily target male children. This contention implies that sexually abusing young girls is less disturbed behavior than sexually abusing young boys.

Finally, it is difficult to see how Groth's typology would apply to adolescent offenders. If it is true that regressed offenders' sexual interest in young children only emerges in adulthood, then all adolescent offenders must be regarded as fixated. But can it be true that adolescent sex offenders usually molest boys, premeditate their attacks, act compulsively, and experience no subjective distress?

## Alcohol Consumption

According to Finkelhor, "Abuse of all types is frequently connected with the abuse of alcohol. The statistics are remarkably consistent, showing over half of abuse incidents, either physical or sexual, as being related to the use of alcohol" (1983). Finkelhor suggests that because prior drinking is often difficult to determine, this 50 percent figure is probably an underestimate.

Many studies have pointed to the association of alcohol and incest behavior (Ellis & Brancole, 1956; Lustig et al., 1966; Kaufman et al., 1954; Hersko et al., 1961; Gebhard et al., 1965, pp. 223, 225; Meiselman, 1978; see Katz & Mazur for a more complete listing, 1979, p. 261).

In her discussion of alcohol in relation to father-daughter incest, Karen Meiselman maintains that alcohol very often deadens the father's moral constraint, thus allowing the first act of incest to occur (1978, p. 93). Gebhard et al.'s research on incarcerated sexual offenders reveals that in each of the four categories of offenders, the percentage of offenders who were either drunk or drinking at the time of the offense was always higher when it was children, rather than minors or adults, who were sexually abused (see Table 6.2, in Chapter 6).

Table 6.2 also shows that the more taboo the nature of the offense, the more often alcohol was involved. For example, the following percentages of different kinds of sexual offenders were drinking or drunk:

76 percent of the heterosexual aggressors against children (meaning child rapists);

38 percent of the incest offenders against children;

35 percent of the homosexual offenders against children;

29 percent of the heterosexual offenders against children who did not use violence.

Researchers invariably point out that it is not legitimate to infer from these or other comparable data that alcohol *causes* the abuse. But one wonders what the impact on the prevalence of sexual abuse would be if adults suddenly abstained from consuming alcohol.

## Perpetrators' Self-Perception as Powerless

Several clinicians describe sexual offenders as frequently feeling powerless, and believing that they are not meeting the ideals of masculinity in our society. These men are seen as acting out in part "to compensate for their perceived lack of or loss of power" (Finkelhor, 1983, p. 19; Groth, 1979). To the extent that this is true, this sense of powerlessness may serve to overcome some men's internal inhibitions against acting out sexual desires toward children.

Florence Rush includes a chapter entitled "From the Sensuous Woman to the Sensuous Child: Liberation or Backlash?" in her 1980 book. Like other feminists who have written on this subject, Rush is convinced that the promotion of the notion of the sensuous child is part of a backlash in which some men have turned to children for sex in order to feel more powerful.

Similarly, as already mentioned, Gloria Steinem has argued that some men desire young girls as sexual partners because they can no longer dominate adult women as easily as they could in times past (1977). She and other feminists viewed the growing popularity and proliferation of child pornography (before it was banned in the late 1970s) as a backlash against the effects of the women's liberation movement. The current popularity of Brooke Shields, both when she was prepubescent and now that she is an adolescent, is another example of this phenomenon. It appears that the collective male ego has suffered a setback that has made young girls increasingly desirable to increasing numbers of men.

## Perpetrators' Frustration in Sexual Relationships

Many studies report that marital discord and disturbed family relationships often exist prior to the onset of the incestuous abuse (Katz & Mazur, 1979, p. 258). Herbert Maisch, for example, reported that 88 percent of the families he studied had symptoms of "disorganization" before the incest occurred (1972, pp. 138, 159). Hence, incest is frequently seen as a symptom of a disturbed family (Lustig et al., 1966; Molnar & Cameron, 1975; Hersko et al., 1961; Tormes, 1968; Weinberg, 1955; Lewis & Sarrel, 1969; Cavallin, 1966; Machotka et al., 1967).

A focus on family dysfunction has merit, but can also be misused. This theory allows the responsibility for the offense to be diverted from the father. There are many examples in the literature of wives and daughters being blamed for the sexual abuse. The tendency to blame women was discussed in the section on the causes of rape; incest victims have been even more subject to blame than have victims of rape by strangers.

As Katz and Mazur point out, one of the commonest themes in the literature on incest has been a focus on "the mother's absence, illness, or rejection of sexual relations, making normal conjugal intercourse unavailable to the father" (1979, p. 259; also Weiner, 1964; Lustig et al., 1966; Hersko et al., 1961; Kaufman et al., 1954; Ferracuti, 1972; Finkelhor, 1979; Herman, 1981). Maisch, for example, reported that the marital sexual relationships of 39 percent of incest offenders were unsatisfactory before they sought out their daughters as a replacement (1972, p. 139). However, Katz and Mazur point out that "some fathers who violated the incest taboo had frequent sex relations with their wives," presumably at the same time that they were sexually abusing their daughters (1979, p. 259).

In general, Gebhard et al. found the frequency of sexual relations among sex offenders to be similar to that of other prisoners, or men in the noncriminal control group (1965). And there is some agreement by researchers that at least a subgroup of incestuous fathers are hypersexual (Meiselman, 1978, p. 98; see also Lukianowicz, 1972, p. 307, Shelton, 1975, Weiner, 1962).

In spite of Gebhard et al.'s general conclusion just cited, they went so far as to suggest that the "typical" incestuous offender against children was "preoccupied with sexual matters" (1965, p. 229). This "pathological obsession with sex" expresses itself in

> much time spent in sexual fantasy, in talking too much about sexual matters, in increasing or attempting to increase marital coitus markedly, in seeking increased visual stimuli, in unnecessary nudity bordering on exhibition, and in preoccupation with mouth-genital contact. One often gains the impression that these men, frustrated in many areas of life, seek happiness by sexual overcompensation. (1965, p. 227)

## Role Confusion

Roland Summit and JoAnn Kryso single out two characteristics as common to those who sexually abuse their own children: a lack of impulse control, and a confusion of roles (1978). Herman also emphasizes that many daughters who are sexually abused by their fathers have become the little mother in the family, responsible for younger siblings and domestic chores. Often they are placed in this role because their mothers are absent, sick, alcoholic, or are for some other reason unable to play the traditional maternal role. (More will be said about this aspect of incest families in Chapter 14.) In such circumstances, according to Herman,

None of the fathers adapted to their wives' disabilities by assuming a maternal role in the family. Rather, they reacted to their wives' illnesses as if they themselves were deprived of mothering. As the family providers, they felt they had the right to be nurtured and served at home, if not by their wives, then by their daughters. (1981, p. 79)

Herman maintains that when the daughter is made to play the little mother, it can be a setup for her ending up as the little wife as well. Herman suggests that when young girls are observed acting out the little mother role, it should be recognized as a danger sign that incestuous abuse could be occurring, or might occur in the future (1981).

# 14

# FACTORS REDUCING SOCIAL INHIBITIONS AGAINST CHILD SEXUAL ABUSE

## Male Supremacy and the Power Disparity Between Adults and Children

I resisted, but he said, "You do what you're supposed to do because I'm the parent and you're the child." (Respondent who was molested by her adoptive father when she was 13; the Russell survey)

Instances in which an unusually assertive child was able to discourage an adult's sexual advances do exist. Similarly, in the days of slavery, some exceptional slaves were doubtless able to talk their masters out of beating them, or selling their children, or copulating with their wives, or doing whatever it was that they intended. But just as, in those cases, the final decision rested with the master, the final choice in the matter of sexual relations between adults and children rests with the adult. (Herman, 1981, p. 27)

David Finkelhor points out that abuse tends to gravitate to the relationships with the greatest power differential (1981, p. 3). "This principle," he argues,

is clearest in sexual abuse of children. The most widespread form of reported sexual abuse consists of abusers who are both male and in authority positions within the family victimizing girls in subordinate positions. This is a case of abuse across the axis of both unequal sexual power (males victimizing females) and unequal generational power (the older victimizing the younger). Abuse of boys by males appears to be much less common, and abuse of either boys or girls by female family members extremely rare in comparison. (1981, pp. 3–4)

Finkelhor concludes that more research on the dynamics of power is needed to understand how it facilitates sexual abuse of children as well as other forms of family abuse (1981, p. 5).

Male supremacy—and the resultant power imbalance in the fami-ly—reduces both the internal *and* external inhibitions of the father and other males. In *Father-Daughter Incest,* Judith Herman explains that

> We have found that a frankly feminist perspective offers the best explanation of the existing data. Without an understanding of male supremacy and female oppression, it is impossible to explain why the vast majority of incest perpetrators (uncles, older brothers, stepfathers, and fathers) are male, and why the majority of victims (nieces, younger sisters, and daughters) are female. (1981, p. 3)

In *The Best Kept Secret: Sexual Abuse of Children,* Florence Rush also emphasizes the key role óf male supremacy in the occurrence and prevalence of incestuous abuse, as well as in extrafamilial sexual abuse of children (1980a).

Herman sees another element in her causal theory as being equally important. Male supremacy, she argues, creates the social conditions that favor the development of father-daughter incest. But it is what she calls the sexual division of labor "that creates the psychological conditions that leads to the same result" (1981, p. 62). (This theory was also discussed in the section on "Male Sex-Role Socialization" in Chapter 5.) Herman's theory in a nutshell is as follows:

> Male supremacy invests fathers with immense powers over their children, especially their daughters. The sexual divison of labor, in which women nurture children and men do not, produces fathers who are predisposed to use their powers exploitatively. The rearing of children by subordinate women ensures the reproduction in each generation of the psychology of male supremacy. It produces sexually aggressive men with little capacity to nurture, nurturant women with undeveloped sexual capacities, and children of both sexes who stand in awe of the power of fathers.

> Wherever these conditions obtain, father-daughter incest is likely to be a common occurrence. In any culture, the greater the degree of male supremacy and the more rigid the sexual division of labor, the more frequently we might expect the taboo on father-daughter incest to be violated. Conversely, the more egalitarian the culture, and the more the childrearing is shared by men and women, the less we might expect to find overt incest between father and daughter. The same logic applies to particular families within any one culture. The greater the domination of the father, and the more the caretaking is relegated to the mother, the greater the likelihood of father-daughter incest. (1981, pp. 62–63)

There may be a flaw in Herman's theory: The predatory sexual behavior of many men reared in this culture might not be totally eradicated if fathers were to share the nurturant role with mothers. The change in parental roles advocated by Herman is indeed an essential step toward equalizing the power balance between husbands and wives, and hence has important implications for the prevention of incestuous abuse. But it seems unlikely that the masculinity and virility mystiques would be eradicated by fathers becoming nurturers.

It may be that the more unsupervised access fathers have to their daughters, the more likely they are to sexually abuse them—*unless* the socialization of male sexuality also undergoes considerable simultaneous change. However, if this *is* the case—currently available research provides no way of knowing whether or not it is—Herman's theory is not necessarily invalidated. It *would* mean that there must be other changes concomitant with the change in parental roles.

There is another, more troubling problem with Herman's theory. The fact that mothers have been the primary nurturers has not prevented them from *physically* abusing their children, although they almost never sexually abuse them. Why is this? One possible explanation is that mothers' greater restraint with regard to sexual abuse has more to do with women's sexual socialization than with the sexual division of labor in the family.

## Mother Who Is Absent, Sick, Powerless

Maternal collusion in incest, when it occurs, is a measure of maternal powerlessness. (Herman, 1981, p. 49)

A substantial amount of research has shown an association between child sexual abuse and mothers being "absent, sick, powerless or alienated from their children" (Finkelhor, 1979; Herman, 1981; Kaufman et al., 1954; Maisch, 1972; Raphling et al., 1967). In these families "the power relations are such as to provide little restraint on sexual impulse toward a child" (Finkelhor, 1981, p. 7).

Herman is one of the many theorists who emphasize the role of the mother in the occurrence of incestuous abuse. She maintains that "mothers who are strong, healthy, and competent do not tolerate incest. But mothers who have been rendered unusually powerless within their families, for whatever reason, often tolerate many forms of abuse, including sexual abuse of their children" (1981, p. 47). Herman concludes that occasionally, mothers do collude in incest. However, she argues convincingly that when this does occur, it is a measure of maternal powerlessness (1981, p. 49).

David Finkelhor, in his survey of 796 college students, reported the following findings, all of them consistent with Herman's analysis of this issue:

- 58 percent of the girls who had lived without their mothers some time before the age of 16 had been sexually victimized; this is three times the rate of the sample as a whole (1979, p. 125);
- 35 percent of girls whose mothers were often ill had been sexually victimized in childhood, almost twice the rate of the average girl (1979, p. 124);
- 38 percent of girls whose mothers were not high school graduates were sexually victimized, twice the rate of the sample as a whole (1979, p. 124).

In reviewing all of these findings, Herman concluded that "only a strong alliance with a healthy mother offers a girl a modicum of protection from sexual abuse" (1981, p. 48). Herman aptly summarizes the more common analysis of such findings about the mothers of incest victims that has dominated the field for so many years.

The doctor, the man of letters, and the pornographer, each in his accustomed language, render similar judgements of the incestuous father's mate. By and large, they suggest, she drove him to it. The indictment of the mother includes three counts: first, she failed to perform her marital duties; second, she, not the father, forced the daughter to take her rightful place; and third, she knew about, tolerated, or in some cases actively enjoyed the incest. (1981, p. 42)

It has been easier to blame mothers than to face the fact that daughters are vulnerable to sexual abuse when they do not have strong mothers to protect them from their own fathers and other male relatives. But mothers should not have to protect their children from their children's fathers! And a mother's "failure" to protect her child should not be seen as a causative factor in child sexual abuse. Herman is right to emphasize that "only a basic change in the power relations of mothers and fathers can prevent the sexual exploitation of children" (1981, p. 206). This change is a *necessary*—but not *sufficient*—step toward solving the problem.

## Familial Crowding or Sleeping Together

Overcrowded living conditions have frequently been seen as a cause of incest. It was believed to lead to the breakdown of privacy and consequently to sexual abuse (Weinberg, 1955; Finkelhor, 1979). Kirson Weinberg refuted this theory by showing that the ratio of people per room for his sample of 200 incestuous families in Chicago was no higher than the ratio found in the city as a whole. David Finkelhor also reported that in his survey of 796 college students, crowding was not associated with sexual victimization in the family, or outside of it (1979, p. 127).

However, Finkelhor did find that girls with four or more brothers were twice as vulnerable to sexual victimization (i.e., sexual abuse by an older person) and about 50 percent more vulnerable to incest (1979, p. 128). His interpretation was that these girls have to contend not only with their brothers, but with their brothers' friends as well (1979, p. 128).

## Opportunities to Be Alone Together

A father's unemployment is often seen as a catalyst to sexual abuse. The stress and sense of powerlessness presumably involved for him is one reason; another is that it provides the father with easy access to the child for extended periods of time (Riemer, 1940; Meiselman, 1978, p. 89; Finkelhor, 1981, p. 7).

Over half of the fathers in Kirson Weinberg's Chicago sample were supported by other family members or by public agencies (Meiselman, 1978, p. 89). Lukianowicz reported that 70 percent of his sample of incestuous fathers in Northern Ireland were unemployed during a time of almost full national employment (1972).

Other studies have described incestuous fathers as having good occupational histories (e.g., Cormier, Kennedy, & Sangowicz, 1962; Cavallin, 1966; Weiner, 1962). Karen Meiselman speculates that research showing a relationship between chaotic employment histories and incest may reflect a bias introduced by researchers, who obtained their subjects from social agencies that work with the unemployed (1978, p. 90). Kee MacFarlane also points out that federally funded child abuse programs in affluent upper-income locations have seen no shortage of clientele victimized by sexual abuse (personal communication, 1982). MacFarlane maintains that in general, sexual abuse is more likely to occur in stressed families, and that unemployment is but one factor causing stress.

## Familial Social Isolation

Several researchers have suggested that incest is more likely to occur in families that are socially isolated (Riemer, 1940; Weinberg,

1955; Bagley, 1969). The notion is that sexual and affectional attachments that would normally develop with people outside the family are neither sought nor available, so they occur within the family (Finkelhor, 1979, p. 26). Deviance is freer to emerge in circumstances of social isolation because the usual social controls are absent.

"Such families," Finkelhor argues, "are insulated from the scrutiny of public view, which must enforce the incest taboo in unisolated families, and without available models, incestuous behavior may come to be accepted as normal" (1979, p. 26). Furthermore, social isolation provides the offender with increased opportunities to be alone with the child (Finkelhor, 1981, p. 7).

Kee MacFarlane maintains that social isolation commonly accompanies all forms of child abuse and neglect, including sexual abuse. She believes that lack of community prevents people from knowing where to turn when problems emerge (personal communication, 1982).

### Factors Reducing Potential Victim's Ability to Avoid Child Sexual Abuse

The question of the child's "consent" is irrelevant. Because the child does not have the power to withhold consent, she does not have the power to grant it. (Herman, 1981, p. 27)

Just as women should not be expected to have to protect their children from their husbands, children should not be expected to have to protect themselves. They can not be held responsible for their victimization. Hence Preconditions I, II, and III are far more relevant to an understanding of the causes of child sexual abuse than Precondition IV (factors relating to overcoming resistance by the child).

David Finkelhor rightly emphasizes that

Sexual abuse can occur in such a way that resistance by the child is irrelevant to whether abuse occurs. The molester who makes a surprise assault on an unsuspecting child is committing sexual abuse in some cases before the child can react. (1981, p. 7)

Nevertheless Finkelhor suggests that the following factors may make a child more vulnerable to sexual abuse:

(1) Child is emotionally deprived.
(2) Child is socially isolated.

(3) Child knows the adult.
(4) Child has special fondness for adult.
(5) Child is vulnerable to incentives offered by adult.
(6) Child feels helpless and powerless.
(7) Child is ignorant of what is happening.
(8) Child is sexually repressed and has sexual curiosity.
(9) Coercion (1981, Table I, p. 2).

According to Finkelhor, some children who are

> exposed to a person who has sexual feelings toward them and who has overcome any inhibition to act on those feelings, will still manage to avoid being abused. These children may sense the potentially dangerous situation and get away. They may convey such a front of invulnerability that the potential abuser decides to avoid this child. They may react so strongly and decisively to any overture that the process is short-circuited virtually before it gets started. Some children are more resistant to sexual approach than others. (1981, p. 8)

Nevertheless, Finkelhor concedes that the resistance of many children is overcome by coercion. In such cases, the child is sexually abused whether she resists or not. For example, one respondent in Russell's survey became a victim of attempted rape when she was 10 years old despite her strenuous resistance to her stepfather's attack. This is how she described what happened:

> One night my stepfather came into my bedroom.... He said if I hollered he would smother me to death with his pillow. He started to force his penis into me. He got part of the way in and I hit him in the head with a hammer.

Finkelhor maintains that the only vulnerability factor operating when coercion is used by the perpetrator "is whether certain children, by their demeanor or circumstances, are more likely to deter approaches, even coercive ones, before they occur" (1979, p. 8).

Perpetrators of child sexual abuse may also be able to identify and exploit children who have previously been sexually abused. When children demonstrate sexually victimized behavior, it is often perceived as seductive rather than as a symptom of abuse. MacFarlane reports that approximately 25 percent of the children in one study who were in treatment were revictimized by someone else during the treatment period (personal communication, 1982).

It is not only familiarity with the abusive adult that lowers a child's resistance. Also contributing is a lack of education about the danger of sexual abuse. Many children are educated to be alert to the danger of overly friendly strangers, but few are advised to be wary about adults they know. This incomplete education lowers their resistance, especially when they are not warned specifically that it is sexual abuse about which they need to be concerned.

# PART V

# SEXUAL HARASSMENT

## 15

## SEXUAL HARASSMENT IN THE WORKPLACE

### The Incidence of Sexual Harassment

A study on sexual harassment in the federal workplace was initiated by the Subcommittee on Investigations of the House Committee on Post Office and Civil Service. The Merit Systems Protection Board conducted the study; its final report was published in March 1981. This was the first scientifically rigorous survey of such depth and breadth to be done on sexual harassment. This section will focus on the findings of this study.

Some earlier studies have played an enormously important role in raising awareness about the problem of sexual harassment (for example, *Redbook Magazine,* 1976; Farley, 1978; Backhouse & Cohen, 1978; MacKinnon, 1979). But the methodologies available to these sources on the prevalence of sexual harassment fell far short of that achieved by what will be referred to as the Merit Systems study. This study was based on the completed questionnaires of over 20,000 federal employees selected in a stratified random sample. This high rate of return (particularly for a mail questionnaire) plus the use of a random sample makes it valid to generalize the results to all federal employees.

Although no comparable research in the private sector has yet been conducted, Patricia Mathis, the Director of the Office of Merit Systems Review and Studies, concluded that their finding "that people of all ages, salary levels, education backgrounds and hometowns are potential victims—leads us to the observation that sexual harassment cannot be uniquely associated with Federal employment" (1981, p. v).

Sexual harassment was defined in the Merit Systems study as "deliberate or repeated unsolicited verbal comments, gestures or physical contact of a sexual nature that is considered to be unwelcome by the recipient" (1981, p. 2). The research team limited its investigation to experiences that occurred during the 24-month period between May 1978 and May 1980. A disproportionately stratified random sample[1] was drawn from the Office of Personnel Management's Central Personnel Data File, which consisted of civilian employees in the Executive Branch. The four variables selected to stratify the population were sex, minority status, salary, and organization. Questionnaires were mailed to over 23,000 men and women in May 1980 (1981, p. 2). So, how widespread was sexual harassment found to be in the federal workplace?

*Forty-two percent of all female employees and 15 percent of all male employees reported being sexually harassed at work* (1981, p. 3). It is important to remember that these figures apply only to the two years prior to the survey. Had employees been asked about experiences that had occurred at any time during their years in the labor force, the incidence figures would likely be considerably higher.

The researchers were uncertain about whether the men defined the unwanted behavior they were subjected to in the same way as did the women. They pointed out nevertheless that the percentage of sexual harassment reported by men was much higher than they had expected (1981, p. 5).

The sexual harassment reported by the victims took many forms. According to the Merit Systems study,

> Every form except actual or attempted rape or sexual assault was experienced by a sizeable percentage of both men and women. The more ambiguous forms of sexual harassment—"sexual comments" and "suggestive looks"—were reported most often. These forms were more likely to be repeated.

> However, with the exception of actual or attempted rape or assault, most of the victims reported experiencing all forms of sexual harassment repeatedly. In addition, many reported experiencing more than one form of sexual harassment. We also found that the incidents of sexual harassment were not just passing events—most lasted more than a week, and many lasted longer than 6 months. Thus, not only did the sexual harassment occur repeatedly, it was of relatively long duration as well. (1981, p. 5)

Respondents who had worked outside the federal government were asked to compare the federal government with other workplaces. The opinion of the majority was that sexual harassment was no worse in the federal workplace than in the private sector, or in state or local government (1981, p. 6).

## THE IMPACT AND COST OF SEXUAL HARASSMENT

Regarding the cost of sexual harassment in the federal workplace, the Merit Systems study reported that a

> conservative estimate of the cost to the Federal Government due to sexual harassment over the two-year period was $189 million—a sum equivalent to the total salaries of all 465 agency heads and all 7000 senior Federal executives (members of the Senior Executive Service) for six months. The greatest costs were associated with the loss of individual and workgroup productivity as reported by the victims. These figures are conservative for three reasons:

> Victims were far less likely to report a decline in their productivity than a decline in their physical or emotional well-being. Since physical or emotional well-being may in fact affect productivity, the number of victims who reported a drop in productivity may actually be closer to the larger number who stated that their emotional or physical condition declined. Thus, the numbers used to compute the loss due to individual productivity are probably low.

> We assumed that where reported, individual productivity declined by only 10%.

> We assumed that where reported, work group productivity declined by only 1%. (1981, p. 14)

Most victims reported that their careers and work situations did not change as a result of their experiences of sexual harassment, but a sizable minority of women and men described adverse effects, such as leaving their jobs. Victims of the more severe forms of sexual harassment were more likely to report adverse consequences. These consequences were particularly dramatic for the victims of the most severe sexual harassment (1981, p. 15).

## VICTIMS OF SEXUAL HARASSMENT

The Merit Systems study found that the demographic characteristics of victims that were most strongly associated with the occurrence of sexual harassment were age, marital status, and sexual (male-female) composition of the workgroup. Factors that were more weakly related were education level, race, ethnic background, job classification, nontraditional nature of the job, and sex of the imme-

diate supervisor. Based on these factors, the researchers report that
the typical men and women who are likely to be harassed are

> young,
> not married,
> have a higher education,
> members of a minority, racial or ethnic group (if male),
> in trainee positions (or office/clerical positions, if male),
> in non-traditional positions, for their sex, (e.g., female law enforcement
> officers, male secretaries),
> supervised by someone of the opposite sex,
> in immediate work group composed predominately of the opposite sex.
> (1981, p. 6)

## THE PERPETRATORS OF SEXUAL HARASSMENT

Most of the women respondents in the Merit Systems study
reported that their harassers were male, and most of the men reported
that their harassers were female. However, it was far more common
for men than women to report harassment by someone of their own
sex.

Most harassers of both women and men in this survey acted alone
rather than with another person. Most harassers of women were older
than their victims, whereas men usually reported that their harassers
were younger than they were. Both women and men had been
harassed by married individuals, but men more often reported that
their harassers were divorced or single.

Most victims of harassment reported being harassed by someone of
their own race or ethnic background. However, minority women were
more likely than nonminority women to be harassed by a person of a
different race or ethnicity (1981, pp. 9–10).

The Merit Systems study also found that both women and men
reported being harassed by fellow employees more often than by
supervisors. The authors were surprised by this finding because

> before the study, most sexual harassment was thought to be perpe-
> trated by the more powerful supervisors against their more vulnerable
> employees. However, a sizable number of women also reported being
> harassed by supervisors. Thus, supervisors were found to be personally
> responsible for a number of sexual harassment incidents, although not
> the principal cause of the problem. However, supervisors as part of
> their duties have a responsibility to assure that their subordinates work
> in an environment free from sexual harassment in keeping with Federal
> policy prohibiting sexual harassment in the Federal workplace. (1981,
> p. 10)

Another major finding reported by the Merit Systems study was the frequency with which both women and men reported that their harasser had also bothered others at work. These researchers believe that this fact "somewhat negates the view that sexual harassment is principally a matter of isolated instances of personal sexual attraction." They came to the following conclusion:

> Thus it appears that some individuals are more likely to harass than others and that sexual harassment is not necessarily normal interaction among men and women on the job, or that all men and women engage in it as has been intimated by some. (1981, p. 10)

## The Causes of Sexual Harassment

### FACTORS CREATING A PREDISPOSITION TO HARASS SEXUALLY

Laws relating to child molestation, statutory rape, and incest have long recognized that the use of force is not required to consider a child to have been sexually violated. But neither sexual abuse law nor traditional thought recognizes that adults, too, can be vulnerable to nonforceful sexual violation, particularly by people who have power and authority over them—such as employers, doctors, therapists, ministers, teachers.

Many theories advanced to explain why men rape are equally useful in understanding why some men sexually abuse their coworkers or those subject to their authority. For example, the masculinity and virility mystiques affect male sexual behavior in the workplace as well. Theories discussed in earlier sections of this book will not be repeated here, except those which apply specifically to sexual harassment in the workplace.

### Male Sex-Role Socialization

In an article about sexual harassment on the job, Margaret Mead attributed the problem in part to the socialization of males:

> At home and at school we still bring up boys to respond to the presence of women in outmoded ways—to become men who cannot be trusted alone with a woman, who are angry and frustrated by having to treat a woman as an equal—either as a female with power who must be cajoled or as a female without power who can be coerced. (1978, p. 31)

Mead argued for changing these socialization patterns, as well as for developing a new taboo that would clearly and unequivocally enjoin people not to "make passes at or sleep with the people you work with" (1978, p. 33). Like the incest taboo in the family, Mead urged that "the modern business and the modern profession must also develop an incest-type taboo" (1978, p. 31).

Jill Goodman and other writers have pointed out that sexual coercion on the job is a product of a social history throughout which men have "traditionally enjoyed the prerogative of sexual initiative." This in turn "leaves women vulnerable to sexual coercion" (1978, p. 57). Cultural stereotypes about women's so-called proper role and so-called natural interaction between the sexes encourages men to treat women workers as sexual beings first, and as breadwinners second.

Some researchers have argued that, as with rape, power rather than sex is the key issue in sexual harassment (Rivers, 1978, p. 29). Psychologist Lillian Grayson maintains, "There's no man so passionate he can't control himself in the office. He uses sex to get power. It's a form of hostility, like rape" (cited in Rivers, 1978, p. 29). Grayson believes that the man who persists in clearly unwelcome sexual advances feels that his masculinity is on the line. "He can't accept the fact that he is being rejected, so he must believe something is wrong with *her*. She must be frigid, or a lesbian, and thus deserving of the retaliation he will take on her" (Rivers, 1978, p. 29). These dynamics are common in other social situations, such as dating. But when they occur in the workplace, they frequently have additional consequences, particularly economic ones.

### Sexual Harassment as a Form of Social Control and as a Means of Pursuing Men's Economic Self-Interest

Lin Farley, among the first to expose the problem of sexual harassment in the workplace, defines sexual harassment as "unsolicited non-reciprocal male behavior that asserts a woman's sex role over her function as worker" (1978, pp. 14–15). This includes the following: "staring at, commenting upon, or touching a woman's body; requests for acquiescence in sexual behavior; repeated nonreciprocated propositions for dates; demands for sexual intercourse; and rape" (1978, p. 15). It should be noted that Farley's definition excludes the possibility that men can also be the victims of sexual harassment, and she suggests no other term for the sexual harassment of men. Although fewer men than women are sexually harassed in the workplace, particularly *by* women, the problem cannot be defined out of existence.

Farley argues that sexual harassment is a mechanism used by men to keep women in a subordinate position. Before capitalism, she maintains, when the family abode was also the workplace, the men in the family controlled the work of women and children. "The emergence of capitalism," she argues, "threatened this base of control by instituting a 'free' market in labor" (1978, p. 28).

Job segregation by sex, Farley suggests, is the primary factor used to keep women in an inferior position at work (1978, p. 28). Economist Heidi Hartmann points out a number of ways in which job segregation oppresses women:

> Job segregation ... maintains the superiority of men over women because it enforces lower wages for women in the labor market. Low wages keep women dependent on men because they encourage women to marry. Married women must perform domestic chores for their husbands. Men benefit, then, from both higher wages and the domestic division of labor. This domestic division of labor, in turn, acts to weaken women's position in the labor market. (Farley, 1978, pp. 28–29)

Hartmann argues that men have acted to enforce this job segregation at work through the trade unions, while also insisting on maintaining the traditional division of labor in the home that required women to do the childcare and housework (Farley, 1978). According to Farley, sexual harassment has been another method used by men to perpetuate job segregation. This in turn ensures that female wages stay low; that female unemployment is high; and that female seniority is undermined because so many women have to or choose to quit their jobs. It also increases the divisions among women, which makes it difficult for women to organize to change their situation (1978, p. 208).

Deirdre Silverman explains this latter consequence as follows: "When standards of physical attractiveness are used as hiring and promotion criteria, women are set against one another in competitive and self-destructive ways. None of us is ever young enough, or beautiful enough, to work without insecurity about being replaced by someone more attractive" (1981, p. 91).

According to Farley, working women have, by and large, "succumbed to this male extortion by escaping sexual aggression at the expense of their jobs or by keeping their jobs at the expense of their self-respect. They have forfeited their independence and equality at work either way. Meanwhile, the pervasiveness of the aggression has taken a toll on women's drive and desire to work that is beyond calculation" (1978, p. 208).

Deirdre Silverman also points out that women are frequently reminded that no matter what work they do, the most significant thing about them is that they are women and therefore sex objects.

This diminishes women's identification with their work, and limits their success at it (1981, p. 90).

Most of those who have written about sexual harassment in the workplace subscribe to the social control theory to some degree or another. For example, Margaret Mead asks the rhetorical question: "[A]s long as so many men use sex in so many ways as a weapon to keep down the women with whom they work, how can we develop mature, give-and-take working relationships?" (1978, p. 31). And Jill Goodman writes, "The impact of these encounters, which are often deeply disturbing, helps to perpetuate the status of women as subordinates" (1978, p. 57).

Mary Bularzik is a final example of this theory's proponents: Sexual harassment, she argues,

> is used to control women's access to certain jobs; to limit job success and mobility; and to compensate men for powerlessness in their own lives. It functions on two levels: the group control of women by men, and personal control of individual workers by bosses and co-workers. Violence (such as sexual harassment) is used to support and preserve the institutions which guarantee the dominance of one group over others. (1978, p. 26)

## FACTORS REDUCING INTERNAL INHIBITIONS AGAINST SEXUALLY HARASSING

### Cultural Values that Encourage Men's Desire to Sexually Harass Women on the Job

*View that women's place is in the home.* According to Mary Bularzik: "The license to harass women workers, which many men feel they have, stems from notions that there is a 'woman's place' which women in the labor force have left, thus leaving behind their personal integrity" (1978, p. 26).

Similarly, Margaret Mead points out that "For a long time after women began to work away from home, people made a sharp distinction between women who virtuously lived at home and limited 'work' to voluntary efforts and other women who, lacking the support and protection of a father, brother, husband or son, were constrained to work for money" (1978, p. 31). Mead maintains that in primitive societies too, women who obeyed the accepted rules of behavior were not sexually molested, while women who broke the rules were seen as asking for trouble (1978, p. 31).

In this article Mead appears rather blind to the sexual abuse of women by members of their families, whether or not they break the rules. Nevertheless, her point is valid: Nontraditional women and nonconforming women, including those who work outside the home, have been seen by men as fair game and have therefore been particularly subject to sexual abuse.

*The perceived acceptability of discrimination against women.* Feminist theorist and law professor Catherine MacKinnon developed the argument that sexual harassment in the workplace constitutes unlawful sex discrimination within the meaning of the Equal Protection Clause of the Fourteenth Amendment (1979). In the past two years, some courts have concurred with her analysis.

MacKinnon argues that there are two distinct concepts of discrimination. The first, which she calls the "difference" approach, focuses on whether different treatment of the sexes is "arbitrary" and thus illegal, or "rational" and therefore not unlawful. MacKinnon points out that the "difference" approach has been favored in scholarly thinking and has dominated legal doctrine.

The second is the "inequality" approach, which recognizes that the sexes are socially unequal, and would prohibit all practices that subordinate women to men. Since "sexual harassment is seen to disadvantage women as a gender," it is against the law (1979, p. 6). MacKinnon argues that sexual harassment constitutes sex discrimination according to both of these approaches. Nevertheless, she strongly favors the "inequality" approach, and offers many criticisms of the "differences" approach.

MacKinnon also maintains that sexual harassment has kept women subordinated to men, "by using her employment position to coerce her sexually, while using her sexual position to coerce her economically" (1979, p. 7). Because of the economic power wielded by employers, direct physical force is often not necessary and it is the woman's *consent* which is coerced, rather than a specific sexual act (1979, p. 164). MacKinnon concludes from this that "economic power is to sexual harassment as physical force is to rape" (1979, pp. 217–218).

*Sexual harassment as a form of prostitution.* Deirdre Silverman defines sexual harassment as "the treatment of women workers as sexual objects," and points out that it begins with hiring procedures that judge women applicants for factors other than their job qualifications (1981, p. 84). In her attempt to understand why sexual harassment is so widespread and why women are so powerless to handle it on both practical and emotional levels, Silverman applies the model of prostitution: The fact that women who live without men (particularly those with children or the elderly) often live in poverty is the structural condition that demands that these women trade sexual services for economic benefits (1981, p. 85).

Silverman argues as follows:

> This trade of money for sex is fairly clear in some forms of interaction. Our pattern of dating, courtship, and marriage are examples of this. On dates, men pay, and women are expected to repay with sexual favors. In marriage, men are legally required to provide economic support, while women are required to provide sexual services.... The wife who refuses her husband's sexual approaches may be seen, in legal terms, as violating her marriage contract. (1981, p. 85)

While a minority of states have finally made rape in marriage a crime, it is still common for wives to be seen as the sexual property of their husbands (Russell, 1982).

According to Silverman, there is often an implicit prostitution-exchange in work situations:

> men provide the jobs through hiring and promotion, set salary levels and work conditions, and can terminate employment by firing.... In return for these economic favors, women provide sexual services as well as work skills. These sexual services range from providing an attractive female presence to actual sexual encounters. (1981, p. 89)

Hence, when women are unwilling to provide such sexual services, they are seen as breaking their part of the bargain, which in turn provokes anger and reprisals from men. Women, according to Silverman, often feel guilty and ambivalent about refusing advances because "they know they are breaking an agreement that they have been raised to honor" (1981, p. 89). For example, one woman said, "I felt I couldn't make a scene by telling anyone in authority over him. I felt powerless and, oddly, honor-bound not to publicly embarrass him" (1981, p. 89).

Silverman concludes that sexual harassment has been present but invisible as an issue for so long "because men and women have accepted the idea that men are entitled to take the sexual initiative, especially when they are 'paying,' whether it is at work, on a date, or in marriage" (1981, p. 92).

Persuasive as this thoery may be, Silverman's notion that most women feel obliged to provide sexual services in return for their jobs seems less credible than the analysis of Mary Bularzik. She holds that intimidation and fear of losing employment is what has stifled protest, and has resulted in many women submitting to the advances of their employers and supervisors against their wishes (1978, p. 26).

## FACTORS REDUCING SOCIAL INHIBITIONS
## AGAINST SEXUAL HARASSMENT

The Merit Systems Protection Study described at the beginning of this chapter reported that most victims of sexual harassment in the federal workplace responded by passively ignoring it (1981). The most effective actions, however, were found to be the most assertive, such as requesting or telling the person to stop, or reporting the harassment to a supervisor or other official. The most passive actions—going along with the behavior, or ignoring it—were found to be the least effective.

Despite this finding, the authors of the Merit Systems study emphasize that about half of the women and one-third of the men who reported the behavior to a supervisor or other official found that it made no difference or made things worse. They concluded that "much still needs to be done to make supervisors and other officials accountable for resolving these problems informally" (1981, p. 11).

Even more significant, the Merit Systems study reported that

> We found that *very few victims took formal institutional remedies against the sexual harassment—only 2 to 3%*. The majority who took formal actions reported that their doing so made things better. This would indicate that in contrast to the lack of faith in formal remedies ... the system does work for some. However, a sizable minority (41%) indicated that filing the formal action either had no effect or in fact made things worse. (1981, pp. 11, 14; emphasis added)

The Merit Systems researchers tried to ascertain how aware victims and supervisors were of the formal remedies available for sexual harassment. They asked whether their respondents believed that the following actions were available to those who had been sexually harassed:

> requesting an investigation by the organization
> requesting an investigation by an outside organization
> filing a grievance or adverse action appeal
> filing a discrimination complaint
> filing a complaint through special channels set up for sexual harassment complaints (1981, p. 15).

They concluded the following:

> Although most of these actions are in fact available to most employees, we found that most victims and supervisors were relatively unaware of them. The one remedy about which the respondents were most knowledgable was "filing a discrimination complaint."...

In addition, most Federal workers also think that there is much that management can do to reduce sexual harassment. Management actions involving tougher sanctions and enforcement generally were endorsed most often. However, a majority of victims and supervisors also endorsed actions involving publicizing managements policies on sexual harassment. Women were more likely than men to endorse actions intended to help victims cope with the problem, such as setting up a special counseling service. (1981, p. 15)

The Merit System study indicates that by improving the mechanisms available in the workplace for filing sexual harassment complaints, the social inhibitions against acting out such impulses would be increased. However, it is also important that workers be made aware of these mechanisms, and that effective procedures for enforcing them be developed.

### FACTORS REDUCING THE POTENTIAL VICTIM'S ABILITY TO AVOID SEXUAL HARASSMENT

Jill Goodman believes that sexual harassment is the inevitable result of women's historically economically inferior position. She argues, "Women today earn less than men and the earnings gap continues to widen. The median income for women employed full-time, yearround is less than 60 percent that of men, and earnings are a fair gauge of relative economic power" (1978, p. 57). This inferior economic status, Goodman maintains, renders women much more vulnerable to sexual harassment, particularly from more experienced workers with more secure jobs.

Goodman points out that women are not the managers "who determine personnel policies and decide what kinds of behavior will or will not be tolerated" (1978, p. 57). The power disparity—both at work and in society at large—increases women's vulnerability to sexual harassment at work. It follows from this theory that most effective in diminishing sexual harassment in the workplace would be a thoroughly integrated work force in which women hold positions at all levels in all domains of work, and earn pay equal to men's.

### CONCLUSION

Discussion of sexual harassment within the four factors framework could be greatly expanded. The framework could also be used to organize and evaluate research on sexual harassment of students in educational institutions, sexual abuse of patients by doctors, and of clients by therapists and lawyers. Space limitations make a more tho-rough treatment of sexual harassment in this book impossible.

Nevertheless, enough has been presented on this subject to show the usefulness of analyzing sexual harassment within the same frame-work as rape and child sexual abuse. Many of the same factors are involved in creating predispositions in individuals to sexually exploit others in all three ways (rape, child sexual abuse and sexual harass-ment). Some of the same factors also serve to break down internal and social inhibitions against acting on these predispositions, and make potential victims more vulnerable to sexual exploitation in all its many forms.

## Note

1. As explained in the final report,

A "disproportionately stratified" sample is one in which certain categories of participants are selected to be in the sample in greater numbers than they occur in the general population. These categories of participants are intentionally oversampled to ensure adequate numbers for statistical analysis within each category. The sample is "random" in that, within a given category (or stratum), each member has an equal chance of being selected. A random sample enables the researcher to make predictions about the whole population based upon the sample. All final results in this final report are expressed in "weighted" terms, which means that all numbers and percentages are adjusted to reflect each cate-gory's actual size in the Federal population. (1981, p. 2)

# 16

# CONCLUSION

[F]or those who aspire to an image of free womanhood, incest is as destructive to women as genital mutilation or the binding of feet. (Herman, 1981, p. 125)

This book has focused on two major issues: the magnitude of the problems of rape, child sexual abuse, and sexual harassment in the workplace; and the causation of these three forms of sexual exploitation.

Knowledge of the nature and extent of these problems is crucial in attempting to understand the causes of these crimes, as well as in developing strategies to combat them. If, as most people still believe, only a small percentage of women are ever victimized by rape, child sexual abuse, or sexual harassment, the implications are very different than if a majority of women experience at least one of these forms of sexual assault at some time in their lives.

In a critical review of Susan Brownmiller's analysis of rape, historian Edward Shorter maintained that "the average woman's chances of actually being raped in her life time are still minimal" (1977). The Russell survey draws the opposite conclusion.

Some of the major findings of the Russell random sample survey reported in the body of this book about the magnitude of these crimes will be summarized here. The summary will focus on Russell's findings because her data on the prevalence of both rape/attempted rape and child sexual abuse are the most accurate available at this time.

## PREVALENCE OF RAPE

- 44 percent of the 930 women interviewed had been a victim of rape or attempted rape at some time in their lives.
- When wife rape is excluded from the calculation of prevalence, 41 percent of the women reported at least one experience of rape or attempted rape.
- 50 percent of the women who had ever been a victim of rape or attempted rape reported more than one such experience.

- Only 9.5 percent (N = 66) of the nonmarital rapes and attempted rapes experienced by these women were ever reported to the police.
- Only 2 percent (N = 13) of the nonmarital rapes and attempted rapes resulted in arrests.
- Only 1 percent (N = 6) of the nonmarital rapes and attempted rapes resulted in conviction of the perpetrators.
- The Russell survey found tremendous differences between reported cases of rape and those that go unreported. For example, reported cases were much more likely to involve strangers than men known to the victim. More specifically, the report rate by different types of perpetrators varied from a high of 30 percent for stranger rape, to a low of 1 percent for date rape. Hence, conclusions based on reported rapes cannot be generalized to unreported rapes. Data based on incarcerated rapists are an even more unreliable source of information on rape in general.
- The Russell survey estimated the total number of nommarital rapes and attempted rapes of women 17 years and older in San Francisco in 1978, based on the number of such attacks reported by her sample of 930 in the 12 months prior to the interviews. The incidence figure so obtained was 13 times higher than the total incidence reported by the *Uniform Crime Reports* for females of all ages in 1978.
- When rapes that occurred outside of San Francisco in Russell's survey are included with those that occurred in the city, the incidence figure for rape and attempted rape (35 per 1,000 females) is 24 times higher than the incidence of 1.71 per 1,000 females reported by the *Uniform Crime Reports*.
- The Russell survey estimate of the incidence rate of rape and attempted rape in 1978 (35 per 1,000 females) is just over seven times higher than that reported by the National Crime Survey for San Francisco in 1974. Unlike the *Uniform Crime Reports*, the National Crime Surveys include cases not reported to the police. Hence, their incidence figures should closely match Russell's. The large discrepancy between them suggests that many women are not disclosing their sexual assault experiences to the National Crime Survey interviewers.
- Application of the demographic technique of life-table analysis to Russell's sample data provides a basis for estimating a minimum 46 percent probability that a woman in that city will become the victim of rape or attempted rape at some time in her life.
- The Russell survey offers the first solid basis for determining whether or not the increase in reported rape over the years reflects a real increase in the rape rates. The tragic finding of this survey is an alarming increase in the true rape rate from 1931 to 1976 for women in all age groups except the two youngest ones (under 15 and under 10 years of age). These rates have more than trebled in most instances. For example, for all women under 35 years of age, the rape rate increased from 20.1 percent in 1931 to 63.5 percent in 1976.
- When tracing the rape rates for five different cohorts of women, it is evident that the rates become significantly higher for each younger

cohort. For example, the cumulative proportion of women between 30 and 39 who reported a first experience of rape/attempted rape is 58.7 percent; for women between 18 and 29, it is already 53.2 percent.

- When rape and attempted rape are combined, acquaintance rape emerges as the most prevalent type: 14 percent of the 930 women in Russell's survey were victims of rape or attempted rape by acquaintances, 12 percent were victimized by dates, 11 percent by strangers, 8 percent by husbands or ex-husbands, 6 percent by lovers or ex-lovers, 6 percent by authority figures, 6 percent by friends of the respondents, 3 percent by boyfriends, 3 percent by relatives other than husbands, 2 percent by friends of the family.

- When the category of acquaintance rape/attempted rape is expanded to include rape by the respondents' friends, friends of their families, dates, boyfriends, lovers, ex-lovers, authority figures as well as acquaintances, then 35 percent of Russell's sample of respondents were raped at least once by an acquaintance. This compares with 11 percent by strangers, and 3 percent by relatives (other than husbands or ex-husbands).

- The more comprehensive and realistic view of rape provided by Russell's random sample survey suggests that by several measures, rape is actually overrepresented in the upper middle class. This finding gives an idea of how exceedingly distorted our knowledge of rape is at this point in time, due to the tremendous biases in the samples on which prior studies have been based.

## PREVALENCE OF CHILD SEXUAL ABUSE

- 16 percent of Russell's sample of 930 women reported at least one experience of incestuous abuse before the age of 18 years; 12 percent were so abused before the age of 14.

- 31 percent reported at least one experience of extrafamilial sexual abuse before the age of 18 years; 20 percent reported at least one such experience before the age of 14 years.

- When incestuous and extrafamilial child sexual abuse are combined, 38 percent of Russell's respondents reported at least one experience before the age of 18 years, and 28 percent reported at least one such experience before the age of 14 years.

- Extrapolating from these findings, as the random sample permits, this means that over one-quarter of the population of female children in San Francisco have experienced sexual abuse before the age of 14, and well over one-third have had such an experience by the age of 18 years.

- When the definition of child sexual abuse is broadened to include (1) experiences that didn't involve actual physical contact (for example, an adult exposing his/her genitals in a sexual way), and (2) relatively mild experiences of nongenital sexual touching that were excluded from the definition of extrafamilial child sexual abuse—then 54 percent of Russell's sample of 930 women reported at least one experience of child sexual abuse before the age of 18; and 48 percent were abused before the age of 14.

- Despite fluctuations, incestuous abuse has increased over the years from 8.7 percent of the women at risk in 1916 to 28.1 percent of the women at risk in 1956. In 1961 there was a decline to 19.8 percent of the women at risk. There is no way of knowing whether this decline was a temporary fluctuation or the beginning of a trend.

- There was a slight *decrease* in extrafamilial child sexual abuse during this same period. Of the girls under 14 at risk in 1916, 22.9 percent were sexually abused by nonrelatives compared with 20.3 percent in 1961.

- The rate of father-daughter incest reported in Russell's survey is 4.5 percent—four and one-half times higher than the best previous estimate of 1 percent.

- Stepfathers who were primary parental figures in the first 14 years of their stepdaughters' lives were over seven times more likely to sexually abuse their stepdaughters than were biological fathers who were primary parental figures. Of women raised by a stepfather 17 percent were sexually abused by their stepfathers. This compares to 2.3 percent for biological fathers, and .1 percent for biological, step-, and adoptive mothers.

- No figures on the prevalence of incestuous abuse by relatives other than fathers were available prior to the Russell study. Almost 5 percent of the women in her random sample reported at least one experience with an uncle before reaching the age of 18, 3 percent with a first cousin, 2.2 percent with a brother, .9 percent with a male in-law, .9 percent with a grandfather, .3 percent with a sister, and 1.8 percent with some other male or female relative.

- Only 4 percent of all incest perpetrators, and 4 percent of all perpetrators of extrafamilial child sexual abuse, were female.

- When all cases of incestuous and extrafamilial child sexual abuse are combined, 11 percent of the perpetrators were total strangers, 29 percent were relatives, and 60 percent were known but unrelated to their victims.

- Only 2 percent of all cases of incestuous abuse and 6 percent of all cases of extrafamilial child sexual abuse were ever reported to the police.

- Only 1 percent of all cases of child sexual abuse ever resulted in convictions.

- There is no reason to believe that the sexual abuse of female children in San Francisco, where the study was conducted, is any more prevalent than in other cities of comparable size. The same applies to rape and attempted rape of adult women.

The prevalence rates for child sexual abuse, rape and attempted rape discovered by the Russell survey are unprecedentedly—and shockingly—high. Understandably, some may respond by questioning the accuracy and validity of the methodology employed in the survey. In anticipation of such questions, the methodology of the Russell survey was carefully described and its findings placed in the context of other incidence and prevalence studies.

The impact of sexual exploitation on the lives of the victims has been largely omitted from this book. The exception is a discussion of the connection between those who experienced child sexual abuse and those who later perpetrate sexual offenses as adults. Another significant omission is on the subject of treatment of victims and perpetrators. These topics are both deserving of attention; however, the cause of addressing these and other sexual abuse issues in a thoughtful and efficacious manner is best served by beginning with some knowledge of the problem's magnitude.

This book is the first to document thoroughly and rigorously the fact that rape and child sexual abuse have directly affected the lives of so many women in a major U.S. city. When victims of sexual harassment are considered along with victims of rape and child sexual abuse, it is probable that the lives of *all* women are affected by at least one of these forms of sexual exploitation, either directly or indirectly. Many women who have not themselves been victimized by sexual exploitation are close to someone who was victimized directly. Most if not all women have lived in fear of sexual assault, or have curtailed what they do (travel, night-time work, leisure activities, leaving an abusive relationship) in an effort to avoid it.

When a victim discloses a case of father-daughter incest, for example, there is likely to be far more than one victim involved. Even when the father has not directly molested any of his other children, his behavior affects the entire family, not just the daughter he sexually abused. His wife and the other children can be considered secondary victims.

Further, the effects of such an experience on the abused child are often considerable. A significant relationship appears to exist between incest victimization and drug abuse, prostitution, suicide, mental illness, running away from home (which greatly increases the risk of sexual victimization by other perpetrators), and later experiences of rape, including rape and other physical violence in marriage (for example, see Densen-Gerber & Hutchinson, 1978; James & Meyerding, 1978; Russell, 1982, p. 179). Victims of incest also appear more likely to become the mothers of victimized daughters.

The point here is that traumatic experiences of sexual exploitation often reverberate through the lives of those who are close to the victim in many different ways. So the problem becomes much larger even than the number of girls and women who are directly, personally victimized.

The causes of rape, child sexual abuse and sexual harassment must be understood if these crimes are to be effectively combatted. Hence the second focus of this book. A multidisciplinary and multicausal analysis of sexual assault seems the most rewarding; however, theories that stress the psychopathological causation of sexual assault are seriously undercut by the magnitude of the problem. These findings lend much greater validity to theories that stress social and cultural factors.

The analysis presented in this book suggests that many of these same sociocultural theories are useful in understanding all three types of sexual exploitation. Rape, child sexual abuse, and sexual harassment are not separate and distinct problems; understanding their interrelatedness helps us to understand each of them.

Surprisingly little research exists on the important subject of the relationship between child sexual abuse and other crime. What is available is not definitive. Despite this, a pattern does seem to be discernable. Many adolescent and adult males appear to act out their anger about childhood sexual traumas. Many females, in contrast, seem to respond to childhood sexual abuse by internalizing their anger; later, they become victims of additional abuse more often than the perpetrators of it. These women become prostitutes, drug addicts, and/or other types of victims more often than they become molesters, violent criminals, or husband beaters.

The exceptions to this generalization include males who respond by being self-destructive and females who respond by being destructive toward others. In addition, there are both males and females who were sexually abused as children but are not, as adults, destructive to themselves or to others. The factors that determine the different responses of different individuals to their sexual victimization are not yet known.

The pain and trauma caused by rape and other sexual assault constitutes sufficient reason for our grave concern and concerted efforts to ameliorate the situation. To those who are nonetheless unmoved by this pain, or who feel that attempting to eradicate other crime is more important, the fact that sexual abuse appears to be highly related to other crime may represent a more convincing argument.

A comprehensive analysis of available evidence indicates that rape, child sexual abuse, and sexual harassment are perpetrated primarily by males. Furthermore, an analysis of the four most serious crimes of violence about which the police gather data reveals that nine males are arrested for every one female arrested. This male predominance must be explained not only for rape and other sexual exploitation, but for all other crimes of violence as well.

Interestingly, criminologists Julia and Herman Schwendinger also argue that rape must be viewed within the context of other violent crimes. Because the poor are overrepresented among violent criminals, they conclude that these crimes are based on economic oppression, and that the solution requires economic reforms (1983).

The Schwendingers fail to note a far more significant association than that which exists between crime and poverty: the preponderance of males who perpetrate these crimes. The ratio of poor to nonpoor violent criminals is nowhere near the 9:1 ratio of males to females. Indeed, analysis of the Russell survey data shows that when looking at all kinds of rape, not just stranger rape, upper middle class women are overrepresented as victims; and the ratio of black and Latin rapists to white rapists is more like 3:1 or 4:1 than 9:1. (Because of the correlation between race/ethnicity and social class, black and Latin rapists are likely to include more poor men than the white rapists.)

If 90 percent of the crimes of violence were perpetrated by a particular minority group or social class, that minority group or social class would be viewed as a distinct problem and treated accordingly. But despite the fact that 90 percent of the ruling gender is responsible for such crimes, the fact of this collective responsibility is almost universally ignored. This demonstrates the ability of those in power to define what and who the problem is.

As already mentioned, it is crucial to the well-being and survival of the entire population of the United States that the enormity of the problem of male violence be recognized. The steady increase in violent crimes up until 1981—an increase that the Russell data suggest cannot be explained away by population increases or higher report rates—points to a critical problem in the collective male psyche that is proving lethal to women and to men alike.

Theories to explain the increase in crimes of violence abound, but they invariably ignore the 9:1 ratio of male to female arrests for violent crimes. They fail to explain why violence is predominantly perpetrated by males. Since most attempts to solve the problem of violence are based on faulty theories, they are ineffectual. Until the dangerous consequences of this culture's concept of masculine behavior are recognized and changed, male violence toward women, as well as toward other males, will not be halted.

The Schwendingers are not the only researchers who underplay the predominance of males as perpetrators of sexual and other violent crimes. Many experts in the field of sexual abuse have recently begun to argue that the number of female perpetrators has been greatly underestimated. A thorough analysis of the available data and the arguments in support of this view reveal no basis for it (see Chapter 11). Why, then, is there a move afoot to deny or underplay the fact that males are responsible for most sexual crimes, as well as crimes of violence that are not sexual?

At a certain point in the growing recognition of the problem of battered women, some influential experts began emphasizing what they alleged to be the significant, neglected, and submerged problem of battered husbands (Straus et al., 1980). The emerging interest in the female perpetrator of child sexual abuse may be similarly motivated by a desire to discount the predominance of male perpetrators of violence and sexual abuse. Many people—including many experts—feel more comfortable believing that these are general human problems, rather than primarily male problems. Just as it seemed that more scholars in the field would begin coming to terms with the enormous disparity between male and female sex offenders—and addressing the reasons for the disparity—several researchers and child service workers began instead to question the finding. A more valuable contribution to solving the widespread and destructive problem of child sexual abuse will be made by facing the truth—however unpalatable—than by avoiding it.

The truth that must be faced is that this culture's notion of masculinity—particularly as it is applied to male sexuality—predisposes men to violence, to rape, to sexually harass, and to sexually abuse children. If this culture considered it masculine to be gentle and sensitive, to be responsive to the needs of others, to abhor violence, domination, and exploitation, to want sex only within a meaningful relationship, to be attracted by personality and character rather than by physical appearance, to value deep rather than casual relationships, rape would indeed be a deviant act and, most likely, a much less frequent one (Russell, 1975).

If this culture considered it unmasculine for men to want sexual or romantic relationships with partners who are not their equals—partners who are younger, more innocent, vulnerable, less powerful, deferential, and uncritical—then the prevalence of child sexual abuse would also be likely to decline. It would probably decline even more if fathers shared the task of rearing their children equally with mothers, if males were raised with a more nurturing and responsible attitude toward children, and if the family were an institution in which equality existed between male and female adults as well as male and female children.

A great deal of work must be undertaken to bring about the changes necessary to begin to solve the ubiquitous, painful, and destructive problem of sexual exploitation. The first step is to realize the importance of this. The second step is to do it.

# REFERENCES

Albin, Rochelle (1977). "Psychological studies of rape." *Signs: Journal of Women in Culture and Society, 3,* 2.

Allen, Charlotte Vale (1980). *Daddy's girl.* New York: Wyndham.

The American Bar Association (1981). *Child sexual abuse and the law.* Washington, DC: American Bar Association.

American Humane Association (1978). *National analysis of official child abuse and neglect reporting.* Denver: American Humane Assocation.

Amir, Menachem (1971). *Patterns in forcible rape.* Chicago: University of Chicago Press.

Armstrong, Louise (1978). *Kiss daddy goodnight.* New York: Hawthorn Press.

Backhouse, Constance & Cohen, Leah (1978). *The secret oppression: Sexual harassment of working women.* Toronto: Macmillan of Canada.

Bagley, C. (1969). "Incest behavior and incest taboo." *Social Problems, 16,* 4.

Barry, Susan (1980). "Spousal rape, the uncommon law." *American Bar Association Journal* (September).

Bart, Pauline B. (1981). "A study of women who both were raped and avoided rape." *The Journal of Social Issues, 37,* 4.

Bart, Pauline B. (1975). "Rape doesn't end with a kiss." *Viva* (June).

Bass, Ellen & Thornton, Louise (Eds.). (1983). *I never told anyone: Writings by women survivors of child sexual abuse.* New York: Harper & Row.

Bell, Alan P., & Weinberg, Martin S. (1978). *Homosexualities: A study of diversity among men and women.* New York: Simon & Schuster.

Bender, Lauretta, & Blau, A. (1937). "The reaction of children to sexual relations with adults." *American Journal of Orthopsychiatry, 7.*

Beneke, Timothy (1982). *Men on rape.* New York: St. Martin's.

Benson, Donna J. & Thomson, Gregg E. (1981). "Sexual harassment on a university campus: The confluence of authority relations, sexual interest and gender stratification." *Social Problems, 29,* 3.

Benward, J. & Densen-Gerber, J. (1975). "Incest as a causative factor in antisocial behavior: An exploratory study." *Contemporary Drug Problems, 4* (Fall).

Berliner, Lucy (1977). "Child sexual abuse: What happens next?" *Victomology, 2,* 2.

Beserra, Sarah, Jewel, Nancy & Matthews, Melody (1973). Public Education and Research Committee of California. *Sex code of California: A compendium.* Sausalito, CA: Graphic Arts of Marin.

The Boston Women's Health Collective (1971). *Our bodies, ourselves: A book by and for women.* New York: Simon & Schuster.

Bowman, K.M. & Engle, B. (1954). "Certain aspects of sex psychopath laws." *American Journal of Psychiatry, 14,* 690–97.

Brady, Katherine (1979). *Father's days: A true story of incest.* New York: Seaview Books.

Briddell, D., Rimm, D., Caddy, G., Krawitz, G., Scholis, D., & Wunderlin, R. (1978). "Effects of alcohol and cognitive set on sexual arousal to deviant stimuli." *Journal of Abnormal Psychology, 87.*

Briere, John, Malamuth, Neil, & Ceniti, Joe (1981). *Self-assessed rape proclivity: Attitudinal and sexual correlates.* Paper presented at the American Psychological Association Meetings, Los Angeles, August.

Brownmiller, Susan (1975). *Against our will: Men, women and rape.* New York: Simon & Schuster.

Buffum, Peter C. (1982). "Homosexuality in female institutions." In Anthony M. Scacco, Jr. (Ed.), *Male rape.* New York: AMS Press.

Bularzik, Mary (1978). "Sexual harassment at the workplace: Historical notes." *Radical America, 12,* 4.

Bulkley, Josephine (Ed.). (1981). *Child sexual abuse and the law.* A Report of the American Bar Association National Legal Resource Center for Child Advocacy and Protection. Washington, DC: American Bar Association.

Bureau of Justice Statistics (1980, December). *Criminal victimization in the United States, 1978.* U.S. Department of Justice.

Burgess, Ann W., Groth, A. Nicholas, Holmstron, Lynda L., & Sgroi, Suzanne M. (1978). *Sexual assault of children and adolescents.* Lexington, MA: Lexington Books.

Burgess, Ann W., & Holmstrom, Lynda L. (1974). *Rape: Victims of crisis.* Bowie, MA: Robert J. Brady Co.

Burt, Martha R. (1980). "Cultural myths and supports for rape." *Journal of Personality and Social Psychology, 38,* 2.

Burt, Martha R. (1978). "Attitudes supportive of rape in American culture." House Committee on Science and Technology, Subcommittee on Domestic and International Scientific Planning, Analysis and Cooperation, *Research into Violent Behavior: Sexual Assaults.* Hearing, 95th Congress, 2nd Session, January 10–12. Washington, DC: U.S. Government Printing Office.

Burt, Martha R. & Albin, Rochelle (1981). "Rape myths, rape definitions and probability of conviction." *Journal of Applied Social Psychology, 11,* 3.

Butler, Sandra (1978). *Conspiracy of silence: The trauma of incest.* New Glide Publications.

California Commission on Crime Control and Violence Prevention (1982). *Ounces of prevention: Toward an understanding of the causes of violence.* 1982 Final Report, Sacramento.

California Department of Employment Development (1977). *Annual planning report: San Francisco-Oakland standard metropolitan statistical area—San Francisco city and county, 1977–1978.* Sacramento: California Department of Employment Development.

California Department of Finance (1979). *California statistical abstract, 1979.* Sacramento: California Department of Finance.

Cavallin, H. (1966). "Incestuous fathers: A clinical report." *American Journal of Psychiatry, 122.*

Chappell, Duncan, & Fogarty, Faith (1978). *Forcible rape: A literature review and annotated bibliography.* National Institute of Law Enforcement and Criminal Justice, Law Enforcement Assistance Administration, U.S. Dept. of Justice. Washington, DC: U.S. Government Printing Office.

Chappell, Duncan, Geis, Robley, & Geis, Gilbert (Eds.). (1977). *Forcible rape: The crime, the victim, and the offender.* New York: Columbia University Press.

Chappell, Duncan, Geis, Gilbert, Schafer, Stephen, & Siegel, Larry (1977). "Forcible rape: A comparative study of offenses known to the police in Boston and Los Angeles." In D. Chappell, R. Geis, & G. Greis (Eds.), *Forcible rape: The crime, the victim, and the offender.* New York: Columbia University Press.

Check, James V.P. & Malamuth, Neil M. (1981). "Feminism and rape in the 1980's: Recent research findings." In P. Caplan, C. Larsen, & L. Cammaert (Eds.), *Psychology changing for women.* Montreal: Eden Press Women's Publications.

Clark, Lorenne M.G. & Lewis, Debra J. (1977). *Rape: The price of coercive sexuality.* Toronto: Canadian Women's Educational Press.

Cleaver, Eldridge (1968). *Soul on ice.* New York: McGraw-Hill.

Cline, Victor B. (Ed.) (1974). *Where do you draw the line?* Provo, UT: Brigham Young University Press.

Cohen, M.L. & Boucher, R. (1972). "Misunderstandings about sex criminals." *Sexual Behavior, 2.*

Commission on Obscenity and Pornography (1970). *The report of the Commission on Obscenity and Pornography.* New York: Bantam Books.

Commission on Obscenity and Pornography (1971). *Technical report of the Commission on Obscenity and Pornography. Volumes VII and VIII.* Washington, DC: U.S. Government Printing Office.

Cormier, B., Kennedy, M., & Sangowicz, J. (1962). "Psychodynamics of father-daughter incest." *Canadian Psychiatric Association Journal, 7.*

Court, John H. (1976). "Pornography and sex crimes: A reevaluation in the light of recent trends around the world." *International Journal of Criminology and Penology, 5.*

Crocker, Phyllis & Simon, Anne E. (1981). "Sexual harassment in education." *Capital University Law Review, 10, 3.*

Darwin, Miriam R. (1953). "Personal and family data and analysis." In Karl M. Bowman (Ed.), *California sexual deviation research, part II.* Sacramento: Assembly of the State of California.

Davis, A.J. (1968). "Sexual assaults in the Philadelphia prison system and sheriff's vans." *Trans-Action, 6.*

DeFrancis, Vincent (1969). *Protecting the child victim of sex crimes committed by adults.* Denver, CO: The American Humane Association, Children's Division.

DeJong, A., Hernando, A., & Emmett, G. (1983). "Epidemial varieties in childhood SA." *Child Abuse and Neglect, 7, 2.*

Densen-Gerber, Judianne & Hutchinson, S.F. (1978). "Medical-legal and societal problems involving children—child prostituion, child pornography and drug-related abuse: Recommended legislation." In Selwyn M. Smith (Ed.), *The maltreatment of children.* Baltimore: University Park Press.

de Young, M. (1982). *The sexual victimization of children.* Jefferson, NC: McFarland.

Deutsch, Helene (1944). *The psychology of women.* New York: Grune & Stratton.

Diamond, Irene (1980). "Pornography and repression: A reconsideration of 'who' and 'what.'" In Laura Lederer (Ed.), *Take back the night.* New York: William Morrow.

Donnerstein, Edward (n.d.) *Pornography and violence against women: Experimental studies.* Unpublished paper, Department of Psychology, University of Wisconsin, Madison.

Donnerstein, Edward (1980). "Aggressive erotica and violence against women." *Journal of Personality and Social Psychology, 39, 2.*

Drapkin, Israel, & Viano, Emilio (1973). *Victimology: A new focus, vol. III: Crimes, victims, and justice.* Lexington, MA: D.C. Heath.

Dworkin, Andrea (1979). *Pornography: Men possessing women.* New York: G. P. Putnam's.

Eisenhower, Milton S. (1969). *To establish justice, to insure domestic tranquility.* Final Report of the National Commission on Causes and Prevention of Violence. Washington, DC: U.S. Government Printing Office.

Ellerstein, N. & Canavan, W. (1980). "Sexual abuse of boys." *American Journal for Disease of Children, 134.*

Ellis, Albert, & Brancole, Ralph (1956). *The psychology of sex offenders.* Springfield, IL: Charles C. Thomas.

Ennis, Philip H. (1967). *Criminal victimization in the United States: A report of a national survey.* National Opinion Research Center (N.O.R.C.), Univeristy of Chicago. Washington, DC: U.S. Government Printing Office.

Eysenck, H.J., & Nias, D.K.B. (1978). *Sex, violence, and the media.* New York: Harper & Row.

Farley, Lin (1978). *Sexual shakedown: The sexual harassment of women on the job.* New York: Warner.

Federal Bureau of Investigation. (1930–1983). *Uniform crime reports.* Washington DC: U.S. Government Printing Office.

Feild, Hubert S. & Bienen, Leigh B. (1980). *Jurors and rape.* Lexington, MA: Lexington Books.

Feldman-Summers, Shirley & Palmer, Gayle C. (1980). "Rape as viewed by judges, prosecutors, and police officers." *Criminal Justice and Behavior, 7,* 1.

Ferracuti, F. (1972). "Incest between father and daughter." In H.L.P. Reshick & M.E. Wolfgang (Eds.), *Sexual behaviors.* Boston: Little, Brown.

Feshbach, Seymour & Malamuth, Neil (1978). "Sex and Aggression: Proving the link." *Psychology Today* (November).

Finkelhor, David (in press). *Child sexual abuse: Theory and research.* New York: Free Press.

Finkelhor, David (1982). *Child sexual abuse in a sample of Boston families.* Paper presented at the National Conference on Child Sexual Abuse. Washington, DC. 1982.

Finkelhor, David (1981). "Four preconditions of sexual abuse: A model." (To be published in D. Finkelhor, *Child sexual abuse: Theory and research.* New York: Free Press.)

Finkelhor, David (1979). *Sexually victimized children.* New York: Free Press.

Finkelhor, David & Hotaling, Gerald T. (1983). "Sexual abuse in the National Incidence Study of child abuse and neglect." Unpublished paper, February.

Finkelhor, David & Redfield, D. (1982). *Public definitions of sexual abusiveness toward children.*" Unpublished paper.

Finkelhor, David, Gelles, Richard J., Hotaling, Gerald T., & Straus, Murray A. (Eds.). (1983). *The dark side of families: Current family violence research.* Beverly Hills: Sage Publications.

Frieze, Irene (1983). "Investigating the causes and consequences of marital rape." *Signs: Journal of Women in Culture and Society, 8,* 3.

Fritz, Gregory S., Stoll, Kim, & Wagner, Nathaniel N. (1981). "A comparison of males and females who were sexually molested as children." *Journal of Sex and Marital Therapy, 7,* 1.

Fromuth, M.E. (1983). *Long term psychological impact of childhood sexual abuse.* Doctoral dissertation, Auburn University.

Gager, N. & Schurr, C. (1976). *Sexual assault: Confronting rape in America.* New York: Grossett and Dunlap.

Gagnon, John H. (1965). "Female child victims of sex offenses." *Social Problems, 13.*

Gagnon, John H. (1977). *Human sexualities.* Glenview, IL: Scott, Foresman.

Galvin, Jim & Polk, Kenneth (1983). "Attrition in case processing: Is rape unique?" *Journal of Research in Crime and Delinquency* (January).

Gebhard, Paul H., Gagnon, John H., Pomeroy, Wardell B., & Christenson, Cornelia V. (1965). *Sex offenders: An analysis of types.* New York: Harper & Row.

Geis, Gilbert & Chappell, Duncan (1971). "Forcible rape by multiple offenders." *Abstracts on Criminology and Penology, 11,* (July–August).

Gelles, Richard J. (1977). "Power, sex, and violence: The case of marital rape." *The Family Coordinator, 26* (October).

Giarretto, Henry (1982). *Integrated treatment of child sexual abuse.* Palo Alto, CA: Science and Behavior Books.

Giarusso, Roseann, Johnson, Paula, Goodchilds, Jacqueline, & Zellman, Gail (1979). *Adolescents' cues and signals: Sex and assault.* Paper presented at the Western Psychological Association Meeting, San Diego, April.

Gibbens, T.C.N., Way, C., & Soothill, K.L. (1970). "Behavioral types of rape." *British Journal of Psychiatry, 130.*

Glueck, B.C. (1954). "Psychodynamic patterns in sex offenders." *Psychiatric Quarterly, 28.*

Goldberg, J.A. & Goldberg, R.W. (1940, 1974). *Girls on city streets: A study of 1400 cases of rape.* New York: Foundation Books. (Reprinted by Arno Press, New York.)

Goldstein, Michael J., & Kant, Harold Sanford (1973). *Pornography and sexual deviance: A report of the legal and behavioral institute, Beverly Hills, California.* Berkeley: University of California Press.

Gollin, Albert E. (1980). "Comment on Johnson's 'On the prevalence of rape in the United States.'" *Signs: Journal of Women in Culture and Society, 6,* 2.

Goode, William J. (1969). "Violence between inmates." In D.J. Mulvihill, M. Tumin, & L. Curtis (Eds.), *Crimes of violence* (vol. 13). Washington, DC: U.S. Government Printing Office.

Goodman, Jill Laurie (1978). "Sexual demands on the job." *The Civil Liberties Review, 4,* 6.

Goodwin, J. (1982). *Sexual abuse: Incest victims and their families.* Boston: John Wright.

Gordon, Margaret T., Riger, Stephanie, LeBailly, Robert, and Heath, Linda (1980). "Crime, women, and the quality of urban life." *Signs: Journal of Women in Culture and Society, 5,* 3.

Greer, Germaine (1973). "Seduction is a four-letter word." *Playboy* (January).

Griffin, Susan (1981). *Pornography and silence: Culture's revenge against nature.* New York: Harper & Row.

Griffin, S. (1979). *Rape: The power of consciousness.* San Francisco: Harper & Row.

Griffin S. (1971). "Rape: The all-American crime." *Ramparts* (September).

Griffith, S., Clarke-Andersen, S., Buch, C., & Paperny, D. (1981). *Intrafamilial sexual abuse of male children and adolescents.* Paper presented at the Third International Congress on Child Abuse and Neglect, Amsterdam.

Groth, A. Nicholas (1982). "The incest offender." In Suzanne M. Sgroi (Ed.), *Handbook of clinical intervention in child sexual abuse,* Lexington, MA: Lexington Books.

Groth, A. Nicholas (1979). *Men who rape: The psychology of the offender.* New York: Plenum.

Groth, A. Nicholas & Burgess, Ann W. (1980). "Male rape: Offenders and victims." *American Journal of Psychiatry, 137,* 7.

Groth, A. Nicholas & Gary, Thomas S. (1982). "Heterosexuality, homosexuality, and pedophilia: Sexual offenses against children and adult sexual orientation." In Anthony M. Scacco, Jr. (Ed.), *Male rape: A casebook of sexual aggressions.* New York: AMS Press.

Groth, A. Nicholas & Gary, Thomas S. (1981). "Marital rape." *Medical Aspects of Human Sexuality, 15,* 3.

Guttmacher, M. (1951). *Sex offenses: The problem, causes and prevention.* New York: Norton.

Guttmacher, M. & Weihofen, H. (1952). *Psychiatry and the law.* New York: Norton.

Haines, W. et al. (1948). "Commitment under the criminal sexual psychopath law in Cook County, Illinois." *American Journal of Psychiatry, 105.*

Halleck, Seymour L. (1962). "The physician's role in management of victims of sex offenders." *Journal of the American Medical Association, 180.*

Hanmer, Jalna (1978). "Violence and the social control of women." In G. Littlejohn, B. Smart, J. Wakeford, & N. Yuval-Davis (Eds.), *Power and the state.* London: Croom Helm.

Haskell, M. (1974). *From reverence to rape: The treatment of women in the movies.* Baltimore: Penguin.

Hayman, Charles R., Lanza, Charlene, & Fuentes, Roberto (1969). "Sexual assault on women and girls in the District of Columbia." *Southern Medical Journal, 62.*

Hayman, Charles R., Lanza, Charlene, Fuentes, Roberto, & Algor, Kathe (1972). "Rape in the District of Columbia." *American Journal of Obstetrics and Gynecology, 113,* 1.

Hayman, C.R., Stewart, W.F., Lewis, F.R., & Grant, M. (1968). "Sexual assault on women and children in the District of Columbia." *Public Health Reports, 83,* 12.

Herman, Judith (1981). *Father-daughter incest.* Cambridge, MA: Harvard University Press.

Hersko, M. et al. (1961). "Incest: A three-way process." *Journal of Social Therapy, 7.*

Hilberman, Elaine (1976). *The rape victim.* Washington, DC: American Psychiatric Association.

Hite, Shere (1981). *The Hite report on male sexuality.* New York: Knopf.

Hite, Shere (1976). *The Hite report: A nationwide study of female sexuality.* New York: Dell.

Holmstrom, Lynda L., & Burgess, Ann W. (1978). *The victim of rape.* New York: John Wiley.

Hunt, Morton (1979). "Legal rape." *Family Circle,* (January 9).

Hursch, C.J., & Selkin, J. (1974). *Rape prevention research project.* Annual Report of the Violence Research Unit, Division of Psychiatric Service, Dept. of Health and Hospitals, Denver. (mimeo)

J. (1971). *The sensuous woman.* New York: Dell.

Jaffe, Arthur C., Dynneson, Lucille, Bensel, Robert Ten (1975). "Sexual abuse: An epidemiological study." *American Journal of Diseases of Children, 129.* 1975.

James, Jennifer & Meyerding, Jane (1977). "Early sexual experience as a factor in prostitution." *Archives of Sexual Behavior, 7,* 1.

Johnson, Allan G. (1980). "On the prevalence of rape in the United States." *Signs: Journal of Women in Culture and Society, 6,* 1.

Jones, Landon Y. (1980). *Great expectations: America and the baby boom generation.* New York: Coward, McCann & Geoghegan.

Justice, Blair & Justice, Rita (1979). *The broken taboo: Sex in the family.* New York: Human Sciences Press.

Kalamu ya Salaam (1980). *Our women keep our skies from falling.* New Orleans, Louisiana: Nkombo.

Kanin, Eugene J. (1971). "Sexually aggressive college males." *The Journal of College Student Personnel, 12* (March).

Kanin, Eugene J. (1970). "Sex aggression among college men." *Medical Aspects of Human Sexuality, 4* (September).

Kanin, Eugene J. (1957). "Male aggression in dating-courtship relations." *The American Journal of Sociology, 63.*

Kanin, Eugene J. & Kirkpatrick, C. (1957). "Male sex aggression on a university campus." *American Sociological Review, 22.*

Kanin, Eugene J. & Parcell, S.R. (1977). "Sexual aggression: A second look at the offended female." *Archives of Sexual Behavior, 6,* 1.

Karpman, B. (1951). "The sexual psychopath." *Journal of Criminal Law and Criminology, 42.*

Katz, Sedelle & Mazur, MaryAnn (1979). *Understanding the rape victim: A synthesis of research findings.* New York: John Wiley.

Katzenbach, Nicholas de B. (1967). *The challenge of crime in a free society.* A Report by the President's Commission on Law Enforcement and the Administration of Justice. Washington, DC: U.S. Government Printing Office.

Kaufman, Irving, Peck, Alice L., & Lagiuri, Consuelo K. (1954). "The family constellation and overt incestuous relations between father and daughter." *American Journal of Orthopsychiatry, 24,* 2.

Kinsey, Alfred C., Pomeroy, Wardell, Martin, Clyde, & Gebhard, Paul (1953). *Sexual behavior in the human female.* Philadelphia: W.B. Saunders.

Kinsey, Alfred C., Pomeroy, Wardell, & Martin, Clyde E. (1948). *Sexual behavior in the human male.* Philadelphia: W.B. Saunders.

Kirkpatrick, Clifford & Kanin, Eugene (1957). "Male sex aggression on a university campus." *American Sociological Review, 22.*

Kocen, Lynne & Bulkley, Josephine (1981). "Analysis of criminal child sex offense statutes." In the American Bar Association, *Child sexual abuse and the law.* Washington, DC.

Koss, Mary P., Leonard, Kenneth E., Beezley, Dana A., & Oros, Cheryl J. (1981a). "An empirical investigation of the social control and psychopathological models of rape." Unpublished paper.

Koss, Mary P., Leonard, Kenneth E., Beezley, Dana A., & Oros, Cheryl J. (1981b). *Personality and attitudinal characteristics of sexually aggressive men.* Paper presented at the American Psychological Association, Los Angeles.

Landis, J.T. (1956). "Experience of 500 children with adult's sexual relations." *Psychiatric Quarterly, 30.*

Law Enforcement Assistance Administration (1977). *Criminal victimization surveys in San Francisco: A National Crime Survey report.* Washington, DC: U.S. Government Printing Office.

Law Enforcement Assistance Administration (1974). *Crimes and victims: A report on the Dayton-San Jose pilot survey of victimization.* National Criminal Justice Information and Statistics Service.

Law Enforcement Assistance Administration (1972). "San Jose methods test of known crime victims." *Statistics Technical Report No. 1. National Institute of Law Enforcement and Criminal Justice, Statistics Division.* Publication STA-1. Washington, DC: LEAA-NILECJ.

Lederer, Laura (Ed.). (1980). *Take back the night: Women on pornography.* New York: William Morrow.

LeGrand, Camille E. (1973). "Rape and rape law: Sexism in society and law." *California Law Review, 61* (May).

LeVine, Robert (1959). "Gussi sex offenses." *American Anthropologist, 16.*

Lewis, Melvin & Sarrel, Philip M. (1969). "Some psychological aspects of seduction, incest, and rape in childhood." *Journal of American Academy of Child Psychiatry, 8.*

Lipton, G.L. & Roth, E.I. (1969). "Rape: A complex management problem in the pediatric emergency room." *The Journal of Pediatrics, 75,* 5.

Littner, N. (1973). "The psychology of the sex offender: Causes, treatment, prognosis." *Police Law Quarterly, 3,* 2.

Lockwood, D. (1980). *Prison sexual violence.* New York: Elsevier.

Longino, Helen E. (1980). "Pornography, oppression, and freedom: A closer look." In Laura Lederer (Ed.), *Take back the night: Women on pornography.* New York: William Morrow.

Lukianowicz, N. (1972). "Paternal incest." *British Journal of Psychiatry, 120.*

Lustig, N., Dresser, J.W., Spellman, S. W., & Murray, T.B. (1966). "Incest." *Archives of General Psychiatry, 14,* 31.

MacDonald, John M. (1971). *Rape offenders and their victims.* Springfield, IL: Charles C. Thomas.

MacFarlane, Kee (1978). "Sexual abuse of children." In J.R. Chapman & M. Gates (Eds.), *The victimization of women.* Beverly Hills, CA: Sage.

MacFarlane, Kee, & Korbin, J.E. (1983). "Confronting the incest secret long after the fact: A family study of multiple victimization with strategies for intervention." *Child Abuse and Neglect: The international Journal, 7,* 2.

Machotka, P., Pittman, F.S., & Flomenhaft, K. (1967). "Incest as a family affair." *Family Process, 6.*

MacKinnon, Catharine A. (1979). *Sexual harassment of working women: A case of sex discrimination.* New Haven, CT: Yale University Press.

Mailer, Norman (1962). Interview in *The Realist* (December).

Maisch, H. (1972). *Incest.* New York: Stein & Day.

Malamuth, Neil M. (1981a). "Rape fantasies as a function of exposure to violent sexual stimuli." *Archives of Sexual Behavior, 10,* 1.

Malamuth, Neil M. (1981b). "Rape proclivity among men." *Journal of Social Issues, 37,* 4.

Malamuth, Neil M. (1980). "Effects of violent-sexual mass media stimuli." *Aggressive Behavior, 6.*

Malamuth, Neil M. & Check, J.V.P. (1981). "The effects of mass media exposure on acceptance of violence against women: A field experiment." *Journal of Research in Personality, 15,* 4.

Malamuth, Neil M. & Spinner, Barry (1980). "A longitudinal content analysis of sexual violence in the best-selling erotic magazines." *The Journal of Sex Research, 16,* 3.

Malamuth, Neil M., Haber, Scott, & Feshbach, Seymour (1980). "Testing hypotheses regarding rape: Exposure to sexual violence, sex differences, and the 'normality' of rapists." *Journal of Research in Personality, 14,* 1.

Marolla, Joseph A. & Scully, Diana H. (1979). "Rape and psychiatric vocabularies of motive." In Edith Gomberg & Violet Franks (Eds.), *Gender and disordered behavior.* New York: Brunner/Mazel.

Massey, J.B., Garcia, C.R., & Emich, J. P. (1971). "Management of sexually assaulted females." *Obstetrics and Gynecology, 38,* 1.

Masters, R.E.L. (1963). *Patterns of incest.* New York: Julian Press.

Masters, William H., & Johnson, Virginia E. (1976). "The aftermath of rape." *Redbook, 147* (November).

Masters, William H. & Sarrel, Philip (1982). "The men raped by women." *San Francisco Chronicle* (March 15).

McCahill, Thomas W., Meyer, Linda C., & Fischman, Arthur M. (1979). *The aftermath of rape*. Lexington, MA: D.C. Heath.

McCauldron, R.J. (1967). "Rape." *Canadian Journal of Correction, 9,* 1.

McCormack, Thelma (1978). "Machismo in media research: A critical review of research on violence and pornography." *Social Problems* (June).

McDermott, M. Joan (1979). *Rape victimization in 26 American cities.* Washington, DC: U.S. Dept. of Justice, Law Enforcement Assistance Administration.

McGuire, L.S. & Stern, M. (1976). "Survey of incidence and physician's attitudes toward sexual assault." *Public Health Reports, 91,* 2.

McNaron, Toni, & Morgan, Yarrow (Eds.). (1982). *Voices in the night: Women speaking about incest*. Minneapolis: Cleis Press.

Mead, Margaret (1978). "A proposal: We need taboos on sex at work." *Redbook* (April).

Mead, Margaret (1968). "Incest." In *International Encyclopedia of the Social Sciences*. New York: Macmillan and Free Press.

Mead, Margaret (1935). *Sex and temperament in three primitive societies.* New York: Dell.

Medea, Andra & Thompson, Kathleen (1974). *Against rape.* New York: Farrar, Straus & Giroux.

Meier, Elizabeth G. (1948). "Girls involved in sex offenses." In Gladys Meyer (Ed.), *Studies of children.* King Crown Press.

Meiselman, Karin C. (1978). *Incest.* San Francisco: Jossey-Bass.

Merit Systems Protection Board (1981). *Sexual harassment in the federal workplace: Is it a problem?* Office of Merit Systems Review and Studies, Washington DC: U.S. Government Printing Office.

Millett, K. (1970). *Sexual politics.* New York: Doubleday.

Mohr, J.W., Turner, R.E., & Jerry, M.B. (1964). *Pedophilia and exhibitionism.* Toronto: University of Toronto.

Molnar, G. & Cameron, P. (1975). "Incest syndromes: Observations in a general hospital psychiatric unit." *Canadian Psychiatric Association Journal, 20,* 5.

Morgan, Robin (1977). "Theory and practice: Pornography and rape." In *Going too far.* New York: Random House.

Mosher, Donald L. (1971). "Sex callousness toward women." *Technical report of the Commission on Obscenity and Pornography* (vol. 8). Washington, DC: U.S. Government Printing Office.

Mrazek, Patricia Beezley, & Kempe, C. Henry (Eds.). (1981). *Sexually abused children and their families.* New York: Pergamon.

Mulvihill, Donald, Tumin, Melvin, & Curtis, Lynn (1969). *Crimes of violence.* A staff report submitted to the National Commission on the Causes and Prevention of Violence, vols. 11–13. Washington, DC: U.S. Government Printing Office.

National Advisory Commission (1968). *Report on civil disorders.* Washington, DC: U.S. Government Printing Office.

National Center on Child Abuse and Neglect (NCCAN) (1981). *Study findings: National study of the incidence and severity of child abuse and neglect.* U.S. Department of Health and Human Services.

National Commission on the Causes and Prevention of Violence (1969). *Final report of the National Commission on the Causes and Prevention of Violence.* Washington, DC: U.S. Government Printing Office.

National Crime Panel Surveys (1975a). *Criminal victimization surveys in 13 American cities.* Washington, DC: U.S. Department of Justice, LEAA.

National Crime Surveys (1975b). *Criminal victimization surveys in the nation's five largest cities.* Washington, DC: U.S. Department of Justice, LEAA.

National Crime Surveys (1974). *Crime in eight American cities.* Advance Report. Washington DC: U.S. Department of Justice, LEAA.

Nobile, Philip (1977). "Incest: The last taboo." *Penthouse* (December).

Pagelow, Mildred Daley (1981). *Woman-battering: Victims and their experiences.* Beverly Hills: Sage.

Palm, R., & Abrahamsen, D. (1954). "A Rorschach study of the wives of sex offenders." *Journal of Nervous and Mental Disease, 119.*

Person, Ethel S. (1980). "Sexuality as the mainstay of identity: Psychoanalytic perspectives." *Signs: Journal of Women in Culture and Society, 5,* 4.

Peters, Joseph J., Meyer, L.C., & Carroll, N.E. (1976). *The Philadelphia assault victim study.* Final Report from the National Institute of Mental Health. R01MH 21304.

Peters, Joseph J. (1976). "Children who are victims of sexual assault and the psychology of offenders." *American Journal of Psychotherapy* (July).

Peters, Joseph (1975). *Social psychiatric study of victims reporting rape.* A study presented at the American Psychiatric Association 128th Annual Meeting, May 7, Anaheim, California.

Peters, Joseph J. (1973). "Child rape: Defusing a psychological time bomb." *Hospital Physician* (February).

Petrucelli, Alan W. (1982). "Reverse rape." US (November 23).

Phelan, Patricia (1981). *The process of incest: A cultural analysis.* Unpublished doctoral dissertation, Stanford University.

Plummer, K. (1981). "Pedophilia, constructing a sociological baseline." In Mark Cook & Kevin Howells (Eds.), *Adult sexual interest in children.* London: Academic Press.

Pomeroy, Wardell B. (1976). "A new look at incest." *Forum* (November).

Queen's Bench Foundation (1976). *Sexual abuse of children.* San Francisco: Queen's Bench Foundation.

Queen's Bench Foundation (1975). *Rape victimization study: Final report.* San Francisco: Queen's Bench Foundation.

Rachman, S. & Hodgson, R.J. (1968). "Experimentally-induced 'sexual fetishism': Replication and development." *Psychological Record, 18.*

Rada, Richard T. (Ed.) (1978). *Clinical aspects of the rapist.* New York: Grune & Stratton.

Rada, Richard T. (1975). "Alcohol and rape." *Medical Aspects of Human Sexuality, 9,* 3.

Radzinowicz, L. (1957). *Sexual offences.* London: Macmillan.

Ramey, James (1979). "Dealing with the last taboo." *SIECUS Report, 7* (May).

Raphling, D.L., Carpenter, B. L., & Davis, A. (1967). "Incest." *Archives of General Psychiatry, 16,* 4.

*Redbook Magazine* (1976). "Questionnaire: How do you handle ... sex on the job?" *Redbook* (January).

Reinhardt, J., & Fisher, E. (1949). "The sexual psychopath and the law." *Journal of Criminal Law and Criminology, 39.*

Riemer, S. (1940). "A research note on incest." *American Journal of Sociology, 45.*

Rivers, Caryl (1978). "Sexual harassment: The executive's alternative to rape." *Mother Jones, 3,* 5.

Rosenfeld, Albert (1981) "When women rape men." *Omni* (December).

Rossman, Parker (1976). *Sexual experiences between men and boys.* New York: Association Press.

Rush, Florence (1980a). *The best kept secret: Sexual abuse of children.* Englewood Cliffs, NJ: Prentice-Hall.

Rush, Florence (1980b). *Child pornography.* Paper presented at Conference on Pornography: A Feminist Perspective. Pittsburgh, May 17.

Russell, Diana E.H. (1984). "The prevalence and seriousness of incestuous abuse: Stepfathers vs. biological fathers." *Child Abuse and Neglect: The International Journal, 8.*

Russell, Diana E.H. (1983a). "The incidence and prevalence of intrafamilial and extrafamilial sexual abuse of female children." *Child Abuse and Neglect: The International Journal, 7, 2.*

Russell, Diana E. H. (1983b). "The prevalence and incidence of forcible rape and attempted rape of females." *Victimology: An International Journal, 7,* 1–4.

Russell, Diana E.H. (1982). *Rape in marriage.* New York: Macmillan.

Russell, Diana E.H. (1980). "Pornography and violence: What does the new research say?" In Laura Lederer (Ed.), *Take back the night: Women on pornography.* New York: William Morrow.

Russell, Diana E.H. (1975). *The politics of rape.* New York: Stein & Day.

Russell, Diana E. H., & Howell, Nancy (1983). "The prevalence of rape in the United States revisited." *Signs: Journal of Women in Culture and Society, 8, 4.*

Russell, Diana E. H. & Van de Ven, Nicole (Eds.). (1976). *Crimes against women.* Millbrae, CA: Les Femmes.

Sanday, Peggy Reeves (1979). "The socio-cultural context of rape: A cross-cultural analysis." Final Report for Grant #R01 MH28978, National Institute of Mental Health, Department of Health, Education and Welfare.

Scacco, Anthony M., Jr. (Ed.). (1982). *Male rape: A casebook of sexual aggressions.* New York: AMS Press.

Scacco, Anthony M., Jr. (1975). *Rape in prison.* Springfield, IL: Charles C. Thomas.

Schiff, Arthur F. (1973). "A statistical evaluation of rape." *Forensic Science, 2* (August).

Schiff, Arthur F. (1971). "Rape in other countries." *Medicine, Science and the Law, 11,* 3.

Schiff, Arthur F. (1969). "Statistical features of rape." *Journal of Forensic Sciences, 14,* 1.

Schram, Donna D. (1978). "Forcible rape: Final project report." Washington, DC: National Institute of Law Enforcement and Criminal Justice, Law Enforcement Assistance Administration, U.S. Department of Justice.

Schultz, LeRoy G. & DeSavage, J. (1975). "Rape and rape attitudes on a college campus." In L.G. Schultz (Ed.), *Rape victimology.* Springfield, IL: Charles C. Thomas.

Schultz, LeRoy G. (Ed.). (1975). *Rape victimology.* Springfield, IL: Charles C. Thomas.

Schwendinger, Julia R. & Schwendinger, Herman (1983). *Rape and Inequality.* Beverly Hills: Sage.

Scully, Diana, & Marolla, Joseph (1983). "Incarcerated rapists: Exploring a sociological model." Final Report for Department of Health and Human Services, NIMH.

Seghorn, Theoharis K. & Boucher, Richard J. (1980). "Sexual abuse in childhood as a factor in adult sexually dangerous criminal offenses." In Jean-Marc Samson (Ed.), *Childhood and sexuality: Proceedings of the international symposium.* Montreal: Editions Etudes Vivantes.

Sgroi, Suzanne M. (1982). *Handbook of clinical intervention in child sexual abuse.* Lexington, MA: Lexington Books.

Shelton, W.R. (1975). "Study of incest." *International Journal of Offender Therapy and Comparative Criminology, 19, 2.*

Short, J.F., Jr., & Nye, F.I. (1958). "Extent of unrecorded juvenile delinquency: Tentative conclusions." *Journal of Criminal Law, Criminology and Police Science, 49.*

Shorter, Edward (1977). "On writing the history of rape." *Signs: Journal of Women in Culture and Society, 3,* 2.

Silverman, Deidre (1981). "Sexual harassment: The working women's dilemma." *Building feminist theory: Essays from quest.* New York: Longman.

Smith, Don D. (1976). *Sexual aggression in american pornography: The stereotype of rape.* Paper presented at the Annual Meetings of the American Sociological Association, August.

Smithyman, Samuel David (1978). *The undetected rapist.* Doctoral dissertation, Claremont Graduate School.

Sneak Previews (1980). #304, October 23. Produced by PBS-TV, Chicago. (Unpublished transcript.)

Steinem, Gloria (1977). "Pornography—not sex but the obscene use of power." *Ms.* (August).

Stoltenberg, John (1977). "Toward gender justice." In Jon Snodgrass (Ed.), *For men against sexism: A book of readings.* Albion, CA: Times Change Press.

Strauss, Murray, Gelles, Richard & Steinmetz, Suzanne (1980). *Behind closed doors: Violence in the American family.* Garden City, N Y : Doubleday.

Summit, Roland, & Kryso, JoAnn (1978). "Sexual abuse of children: A clinical spectrum." *American Journal of Orthopsychiatry, 48,* 2.

Svalastoga, K. (1962). "Rape and social structures." *Pacific Sociological Review, 5.*

Symons, Donald (1979). *The evolution of human sexuality.* Oxford, England: Oxford University Press.

Tormes, Yvonne M. (1968). *Child victims of incest.* The American Humane Association, Children's Division.

Tucker, Donald (1982). "A punk's song: View from the inside." In Anthony M. Scacco, Jr. (Ed.), *Male rape: A casebook of sexual aggressions.* New York: AMS Press.

U.S. Bureau of the Census (1970, 1980). *Characteristics of the population* (vol. 1.) Washington DC: U.S. Government Printing Office.

Viano, Emilio C. (Ed.). (1976). *Victims and society,* Washington, DC: Visage Press.

Von Hentig, Hans (1948). *The criminal and his victim.* New Haven, CT: Yale University Press.

Weinberg, S. Kirson (1955, 1976). *Incest behavior.* Secaucus, NJ: Citadel Press.

Weiner, Irving B. (1964). "On incest: A survey." *Excerpta Criminol, 4,* 137.

Weiner, Irving B. (1962). "Father-daughter incest: A clinical study." *Psychiatric Quarterly, 36.*

Weis, K. & Borges, S.S. (1973). "Victimology and rape: The case of the legitimate victim." *Issues in Criminology, 8,* 2.

Weiss, C. & Friar, D. (1975). *Terror in prisons: Homosexual rape and why society condones it.* New York: Bobbs-Merrill.

West, Dorothy (1982). "I was afraid to shut my eyes." In Anthony M. Scacco, Jr. (Ed.), *Male rape.* New York: AMS Press.

West, D.J., Roy, C. & Nichols, F. L. (1978). *Understanding sexual attacks.* London: Heinemann.

Wolfgang, M.E. & Ferracuti, Franco (1967). *The subculture of violence.* London: Tavistock.

Wolfgang, Marvin E. (1957). "Victim precipitated criminal homicide." *Journal of Criminal Law, Criminology, and Police Science, 48,* 1.

Wulkan, Donna & Bulkley, Josephine (1981). "Analysis of incest statues." In the American Bar Association, *Child sexual abuse and the law.* Washington, DC: American Bar Association.

# AUTHOR INDEX

# SUBJECT INDEX

# ABOUT THE AUTHOR

DIANA E. H. RUSSELL, is a Professor of Sociology at Mills College (Oakland, CA), where she has taught since 1969. Dr. Russell was Principal Investigator of a study funded by the National Institute of Mental Health on rape and other sexual assault. Subsequently she became the Principal Investigator of a study on incestuous abuse funded by the National Center on Child Abuse and Neglect.

She is author of *The Politics of Rape* (Stein & Day, 1975), author and coeditor of *Crimes Against Women: The Proceedings of the International Tribunal* (Les Femmes, 1976), coeditor with three others of *Against Sadomasochism: A Radical Feminist Analysis* (Frog in the Well, 1982), and author of *Rape in Marriage* (Macmillan, 1982).

Dr. Russell was one of the main organizers of the International Tribunal on Crimes Against Women in 1976, and one of the founders of Women Against Violence in Pornography and Media in 1977. She has lectured widely across the country on the topics of rape, child sexual abuse, pornography, and other forms of violence against women.

Dr. Russell is currently working on a book entitled *The Incestuous Abuse of Females.*

## OTHER BOOKS BY THE AUTHOR

*Rebellion, Revolution, and Armed Force* (Academic Press, 1974)

*The Politics of Rape: The Victim's Perspective* (Stein & Day, 1975)

*Crimes Against Women: The Proceedings of the International Tribunal.* Coauthored and coedited with Nicole Van de Ven (Les Femmes, 1976; 2nd edition, Frog in the Well, 1984)

*Rape in Marriage* (Macmillan, 1982)

*Against Sadomasochism: A Radical Feminist Analysis.* Coedited with Robin Linden, Darlene Pagano, Susan Leigh Star (Frog in the Well, 1982)